ALSO BY
PHILIP KAPLAN

ONE LAST LOOK
(with Rex Alan Smith)

THEIR FINEST HOUR
(UK title: THE FEW),
(with Richard Collier)

LITTLE FRIENDS

LITTLE FRIENDS

THE FIGHTER PILOT
EXPERIENCE IN
WORLD WAR II
ENGLAND

PHILIP KAPLAN
ANDY SAUNDERS

RANDOM HOUSE   NEW YORK

FOR NEAL, MARGARET, CLAIRE AND JOE

Grateful acknowledgement is made to the following for permission to reprint previously published material:

THE BODLEY HEAD: Excerpt from "Operation Calling" by David Bourne. Published by The Bodley Head. Reprinted by permission.

ESTATE OF NORMA MILLAY ELLIS: "First Fig" by Edna St. Vincent Millay from *Collected Poems*, published by Harper and Row. Copyright 1922, 1950 by Edna St. Vincent Millay. Reprinted by permission of Elizabeth Barnett, literary executor.

FABER AND FABER, LTD.: Excerpts from "War" by Nigel Weir and "The Local" by W. Kemp from *Verses of a Fighter Pilot* by Nigel Weir and W. Kemp; excerpts from *Spitfire Pilot* by D. M. Crook; excerpts from "To Any Member of My Generation" from *Personal Sonnets* by George Barker. Reprinted by permission of Faber and Faber, Ltd.

FARRAR, STRAUS & GIROUX, INC., and FABER AND FABER, LTD.: "A War" from *The Complete Poems of Randall Jarrell*. Copyright 1951, © 1979 by Mrs. Randall Jarrell. Rights throughout the British Commonwealth are controlled by Faber and Faber, Ltd. Reprinted by permission of Farrar, Straus & Giroux, Inc., and Faber and Faber, Ltd.

DAVID HIGHAM ASSOCIATES: Twelve lines from "Aeroplanes" from *Poems* by Herbert Read, published by Faber and Faber, Ltd. Reprinted by permission of David Higham Associates.

PAMELA HOLMES: Excerpts from "War Baby" by Pamela Holmes. Copyright © Pamela Holmes. Reprinted by permission.

METHUEN AND CO., LTD.: Excerpts from "The White Cliffs of Dover" by Alice Duer Miller. Reprinted by permission of Methuen and Co., Ltd., as publishers.

RANDOM CENTURY GROUP: Excerpts from "20th Century Requiem" from *Arena* by Patricia Saunders, published in 1948 by Hutchinson; excerpts from "Oxford in Wartime" from *New Poems* by Mary Wilson, published by Hutchinson, a division of the Random Century Group. Reprinted by permission of the Random Century Group.

RANDOM HOUSE, INC.: Excerpts from *The Look of Eagles* by John T. Godfrey. Copyright © 1958 by Random House, Inc. Reprinted by permission of Random House, Inc.

RANDOM HOUSE, INC., and FABER AND FABER, LTD.: Excerpt from "Yes We Are Going to Suffer, Now" by W. H. Auden from *Collect Poems* by W. H. Auden, edited by Edward Mendelson. Copyright 1945 by W. H. Auden. Rights throughout the British Commonwealth are controlled by Faber and Faber, Ltd. Reprinted by permission of Random House, Inc., and Faber and Faber, Ltd.

SALAMANDER OASIS TRUST: Excerpts from "Still No Letter" by John Wedge and excerpts from "Polish Airman" by Stuart Hoskin, published in *Poems of the Second World War: The Oasis Selection* (Dent). Reprinted by permission of The Salamander Oasis Trust, London.

Library of Congress Cataloging-in-Publication Data

Kaplan, Philip.
    Little friends/by Philip Kaplan and Andy Saunders.
        p.   cm.
    Includes bibliographical references and index.
    ISBN 0-394-58434-1
    1. World War, 1939–1945—Aerial operations, American/British. 2. Fighter planes. 3. United States Army Air Forces, 8th and 9th—History. 4. Royal Air Force, British—History. 5. United States Army Air Forces—Military life. 6. Royal Air Force, British—Military life. 7. World War, 1939–1945—Personal narratives, American and British. I. Saunders, Andy. II. Title.
UG1242.F5K37   1991
358.4′383—dc20   90-27133

Manufactured in Japan
98765432

First Edition

CONTENTS

FIGHTER PILOT 6
OVER HERE 8
FLYING THE MISSION 20
THE IRON 34
TAKING CARE OF BUSINESS 64
GROUND-BOUND 76
ON THE NOSE 86
ON BECOMING AN EAGLE 94
SPECIAL OPERATIONS 106
THE VILLAGERS 118
LITTLE FRIENDS: THE BEGINNING 128
THOSE GIRLS 140
VERY SPECIAL DELIVERY 154
OTHER FRIENDS 166
A GERMAN ESCORT PILOT 174
AT LIBERTY 186
PILOTS 196
THE A-2 208
LITTLE FRIENDS: SUCCESS AT LAST 212
GOING BACK 232
BIBLIOGRAPHY 246
SELECTED FIGHTER INFORMATION SUMMARY 248
INDEX 255

FIGHTER PILOT

During World War II he had total control of a 400 mph fighter and eight machine guns—with no radar, no auto-pilot, and no electronics.

At the touch of a button he could unleash 13 pounds of shot in 3 seconds. He had a total of 14 seconds ammunition. He needed to be less than 250 yards from the enemy to be effective.

He and his foe could maneuver in three dimensions at varying speeds and with an infinite number of angles relative to each other. His job was to solve the sighting equation without becoming a target himself.

His aircraft carried 90 gallons of fuel between his chest and the engine.

He often flew over 35,000 feet with no cockpit heating or pressurisation. He endured up to six times the force of gravity with no "g"-suit.

He had no crash helmet or protective clothing other than ineffective flying boots and gloves.

He had about three seconds in which to identify his foe, and slightly longer to abandon the aircraft if hit. He had no ejector seat.

He was also a navigator, radio operator, photographer, air-to-ground attacker, rocketeer and dive-bomber.

Often, as in my case, he was only nineteen years old. He was considered too young and irresponsible to vote, but not too young to die.

His pay was the modern equivalent of just under sixty new pence per day in 1940.

Should he have been stupid enough to be shot down and taken prisoner, a third of that sum was deducted at source by a grateful country and never returned.

However, every hour of every day was an unforgettable and marvelous experience shared with some of the finest characters who ever lived.

—Paddy Barthropp, 1990, a fighter pilot of the Royal Air Force in World War II

You love a lot of things if you live around them. But there isn't any woman and there isn't any horse, not any before nor any after, that is as lovely as a great airplane. And men who love them are faithful to them even though they leave them for others. Man has one virginity to lose in fighters, and if it is a lovely airplane he loses it to, there is where his heart will forever be.

—Ernest Hemingway

OVER HERE

I want to see you shoot the way you shout.

—Theodore Roosevelt

All day like an automaton/She fits the shells into the gauge, Hour after hour, to earn her wage/To keep her and her little son:/All day, hour after hour, she stands/Handling cold death with calloused hands. She dare not think, she dare not feel/What happens to the shells that she/Handles and checks so carefully,/Or what, within each case of steel/Is packed as, hour by hour she stands/Handling cold death with calloused hands.

from "Shells"
by Wilfrid Gibson

EVERYTHING ABOUT BRITAIN was strange to the newly arrived Yank. The countryside was greener than anything he had ever seen back home. The weather was lousy and so was the food. The houses looked ancient. The money made no sense to him. The people drove on the wrong side of the street. And when they spoke to him, he couldn't always understand what they said. As Oscar Wilde had put it: "We really have everything in common with America these days except, of course, the language." And there were the shortages, the blackout, the bomb damage, the barrage balloons, the long lines of shoppers, the crowded trains, the sight of so many men and women in so many different uniforms . . . and the haggard but unbeaten civilians.

The American fighter pilot, however, had made a relatively smooth transition to the UK assignment. First, there had been a trickle of U.S. volunteers into the RAF during the first year of war in Europe, then a flood of aviators for the Eagle Squadrons preceded the great deluge of airmen arriving late in 1942 to serve with the 8th and 9th U.S. Army Air Forces in Britain. With the same mission, and sometimes the same airfields and equipment, the fighter pilots of the USAAF and the RAF were thrown together—living, flying, fighting and dying alongside each other.

The 31st Fighter Group was the first American fighter unit to be sent to Europe. Its official diarist commented that "operationally we worked direct with the British, which in England was highly efficient—about as good as could ever be attained." It was, for the 31st, a close partnership strengthened by the use of

British aircraft on British bases. The 307th Fighter Squadron at Biggin Hill, the 308th at Kenley and the 309th at Westhampnett, all part of the 31st FG, flew the Spitfire operationally, and the Dieppe raid on August 19, 1942, was their first task of action. There, Second Lieutenant Samuel F. Junkin of the 309th shot down a Focke Wulf FW 190 and became the first USAAF pilot to claim a kill in the European air war. For the first time, pilots of the 8th Air Force had flown in combat side

by side with RAF fighter pilots. Later that day, the American 308th was led into action over the Dieppe beachhead by RAF Squadron Leader Pete Wickham, temporarily detached from No. 111 Squadron. The Americans later awarded him the Silver Star for "outstanding aerial technique, operational skill and great determination and courage." His brief leadership role with the 308th was not the end of his involvement with the U.S. Army Air Force. From July to October 1944, he was assigned to

a U.S. fighter group, in which he again served with distinction. But his earliest experiences alongside American fighter pilots had been at North Weald, where he led 111 Squadron on the same station with 350 (Belgian) Squadron and 71 (Eagle) Squadron. Another RAF 111 Squadron pilot at North Weald, George Heighington, had good reason to remember the American fliers with appreciation. On June 2, 1942, the North Weald wing was detailed for a sweep of the Cap Gris Nez area, but

Live as long as you may,/the first twenty years/are the longest half of your life.

—Southey

The walk to headquarters, occasionally asking directions, was enlightening. There was a base hospital, the Red Cross club for enlisted men, tennis courts, volley-ball courts, armament building, movie house, PX, photography shop, enlisted men's barracks, and, finally, headquarters. The streets and sidewalks were paved and the grass was carefully cut. In back of all this, three huge hangars loomed, and everything was painted with the characteristic camouflage. Fifteen-hundred officers and men lived on this base, all slaves to the forty-eight P47s sitting around the field. This was Debden.

from *The Look of Eagles*
by John T. Godfrey

far left: Pilots of the 9th AF grab a quick meal at a mess kitchen in the Normandy area in August 1944. top: 4th Fighter Group personnel awaiting a meal at Debden. center: USAAF cooks at work on an American fighter station in England. left: A well-stocked post exchange on a WWII U.S. base in the UK.

above: Robert Hofton in 1940 and 1990. above right: Remains of the RAF eagle he painted on a barn wall at Fowlmere while stationed there with 19 Squadron. The eagle resulted when former commercial artist Hofton was asked to decorate the barn for a squadron party just before Christmas 1940. below: P-47 Thunderbolts are loaded aboard an England-bound cargo ship at an American east coast port.

A Nissen hut at Goxhill,
home to the 78th Fighter
Group, 8th AF, in 1942.

recent losses had reduced the number of available aircraft. To make up for the shortfall, 111 Squadron borrowed a Spitfire from 350 Squadron and assigned it to Heighington.

"It had been a last-minute arrangement and I only went to collect the aircraft as we were due to taxi out for take-off, so had little or no time to set it up for my own use. During the flight out I set the seat for my own height, adjusted the rudder pedals and set the throttle quadrant the way I wanted it. Then, as soon as we got over France, we were jumped by a whole hell of a lot of ME 109s and I switched on my gunsight ready to do battle. Nothing! It just didn't light up. Now this was not a good time to discover you had a malfunction in your gunsight, but I did my best. This turned out to be quite inadequate and I was immediately shot to pieces. As my logbook records: 'Cannon shells in wing and fuselage. Port cannon shot away. Starboard magazine exploded blowing away wing plates. Plates blown from port wing and tail unit. Engine misfiring.' I was virtually dead in the air, just sitting at thirty thousand feet over Dunkirk and at the mercy of the next Luftwaffe pilot to spot me. Then, salvation. Another Spitfire arrived and escorted me back to England in a gentle dive, my engine eventually dying on me before I made a successful dead-stick landing at Manston—severely shaken and lucky to be alive.

The pilot who saved me never identified himself, but after I made a lot of inquiries he turned out to be a member of one of the Eagle Squadrons, Number 133. I'd like to know exactly who he was so I could write him my much-belated thanks. That Yank saved my life."

In addition to Spitfires, Hurricanes were flown by American pilots in the Eagle Squadrons. Carroll "Red" McColpin, a former Eagle pilot, much preferred them, to the extent that when he was transferred to a Spitfire unit he felt he had been downgraded. "The Hurricane was a beautiful-flying airplane. If you kept your eyes open nobody could shoot you down in one of those. As long as you could see them they couldn't get you. And it could out-maneuver a Spitfire. Easily. But it was slower on altitude capabilities and with a slower dive. A good old bird it was, with a hell of a lot of firepower. Rugged too. I liked the four sets of controls to your elevators, rudders and stuff. That meant you could get shot up on one side and still have control. I liked it a lot."

The American Mustang, conversely, was used extensively by the RAF. It ultimately proved to be the outstanding fighter of the war. The RAF was quick to recognize the plane's potential and, by VE Day, it was operating at least 320 Mustangs. The aircraft was a type that had proved its worth in a variety of roles. RAF pilots flying Mustangs escorted their bombers, which were harrying German shipping off the Norwegian coast in mid-1944. Sometimes, though, this cover was not provided by the RAF. On August 8, 1944, the famed 4th Fighter Group, USAAF, flew cover

17

She's the girl that makes the thing/That drills the hole, that holds the spring/That drives the rod, that turns the knob/That works the thingummybob/It's a ticklish sort of job Making a thing for a thingummybob/Especially when you don't know what it's for./And it's the girl that makes the thing That holds the oil that oils the ring/That makes the thingummybob that's going to win the war . . .

—Anonymous

HOLDING the LINE!

for these RAF bombers off Norway. With the British Mustangs away in southern England to counter the V-1 flying-bomb threat, the American pilots of the 4th took on the job. Although this round-trip was less than eight hundred miles, it was at low level across the North Sea all the way. In addition to the hazard of sea spray, survival time, if a pilot went into water that cold, was measured in minutes. One of the participating RAF bomber pilots recalled his feelings for his American escorts: "They were splendidly and magnificently heroic."

Mostly, British and American fighter pilots got along well, but there was friction at times. The Yanks were accused of being "overpaid, oversexed, overfed and over here." The Americans countered that the Brits were "underpaid, undersexed, underfed and under Eisenhower." And they grumbled about the food. One fighter pilot swore that " . . . the British subsisted on some of the most appalling food known to man or beast. Have you ever tried biting on a kipper for breakfast? Worse still, have you had those things they call brussels sprouts? If I ever have to crash my plane I'll make sure I do it on a brussels sprout field."

Living conditions varied greatly in both the American and British air forces. Established prewar bases like Debden, North Weald, Digby, Martlesham Heath and Tangmere had permanent brick accommodations, centrally heated and comfortably furnished. But those unfortunate enough to be assigned to one of the hundreds of muddy bases built during wartime could expect squalid shacks,

leaky tin Nissen huts or drafty Maycrete buildings. It was a constant struggle to keep warm and dry, with potbellied stoves giving off as much smoke as they did heat. Worse,

some pilots found themselves under canvas, especially at the "advanced landing grounds" near England's south coast around D-Day.

One 31st Fighter Group pilot sums it up: "Here we were, Johnny-come-latelys to these Limeys who had taken it on the chin for so long. France . . . Dunkirk . . . the Battle of Britain . . . then the Blitz. They'd been there and they had done it. They sure had the edge on us when it came to experience and we knew it. Respected it. What did we have to offer? That's how some of us felt in the beginning . . . inadequate. But never once did these RAF types act superior to us freshmen. They welcomed us as equals . . . and that was the key to our getting along, so far as we in the thirty-first were concerned. At this stage in the air war we knew we weren't equals to our battle-hardened pals . . . but we sure were determined to be! At first they might have had their doubts, but as true English gentlemen they hid them well. Their attitude, and our approach, made for a wonderful partnership. Sure, we were different. The way we did things, even the way we spoke. But the record of the fighter pilots of the eighth and ninth Air Forces speaks for itself, and the RAF guys had blazed a trail for us to follow. We did so with pride and we did it well. The truth is, we couldn't have done it without each other."

FOR SALE: UNIQUE BARGAIN. SECOND-HAND, FIRST-RATE, ALMOST INCREDIBLE AUSTIN 7, FAMILY SALOON. EXCELLENT CONDITION; GUARANTEED FULLY AEROBATIC, UNTAXED, UNSERVICEABLE. IT'S THE TOPS! PRICE £1 OR NEAR OFFER. POSITIVELY LAST DAY. P/O F.D.S. SCOTT-MALDEN. LATE 611 SQUADRON. SIC TRANSIT . . .

—Notice on mess notice board, RAF Digby, Lincolnshire, 1941

above left: A favored hangout of 19 Squadron pilots from Fowlmere, The Chequers, 1940. above: The Chequers, 1990. left: An RAF Spitfire pilot at ease on his airfield.

WALTER J. KONANTZ flew Mustangs with the 338th Fighter Squadron, 55th Fighter Group, at Wormingford. What follows is his description of a typical mission day.

0500 hours: The door bursts open in our twelve-man Nissen hut, and the CQ flips on the lights and wakes everybody up. A few of the pilots aren't flying today and they can go back to sleep. Those who are flying get dressed and go to the central latrine to brush their teeth and shave.

0530 hours: A big GI truck picks us up and takes us to the mess hall, where we have the usual breakfast of powdered eggs, greasy bacon, burned toast and black coffee. The mess hall is close enough to the briefing room that we all walk over there as each finishes his last cup of coffee.

0615 hours: We find our designated seats in the briefing room. A flight leader sits in the front row with his wing man (number two) immediately behind him. The number-three man (element leader) sits behind number-two, and directly behind him sits the number-four man (tail-end Charley). The briefing officer can then tell at a glance if anyone is missing and in what position in the formation they are flying. The big map on the wall behind the briefing officer has a red string from our base to the rendezvous point, then to the bombers' target. Zigs and zags in the string show the turning points to help us avoid known flak concentrations. The target for today is Berlin, which is a five-and-a-half-hour

FLYING THE MISSION

The Fourth Fighter Group is going to be the top fighter group in the Eighth Air Force. We are here to fight. To those who don't believe me I would suggest transferring to another group. I'm going to fly the arse off each one of you. Those who keep up with me, good; those who don't, I don't want them anyway.

Lt.Col. Donald J. M. Blakeslee
on taking command of the 4th FG,
January 1, 1944

In fair weather prepare for foul.

—Thomas Fuller

Members of the Debden-based 4th Fighter Group pay attention to a mission briefing in October 1943.

21

mission for us, and over eight hours for the bombers. We are given our engine start times, take-off times, bomber-rendezvous time and target time. Flak locations are covered, expected enemy opposition is discussed, and the weather for launch, en route, target area and recovery time is briefed. All pilots hack their GI wristwatches to the exact time and the briefing is concluded. We then check out our parachutes, zip on the anti-G suit, put on a heavy jacket, don the Mae West life vest; heavy gloves and fur-lined boots complete the suiting-up. The cockpit heater in the P-51 only works when the outside air temperature is warm enough that you don't need it anyway. On the way out of the briefing room, they have several boxes of candy bars for "in-flight lunches" and I grab a couple of bars. We gather outside the briefing room, where we are picked up by several GI trucks and hauled to the various dispersal areas where our planes are parked. On arrival at my parking area, my crew chief takes my parachute and places it in the cockpit. I ask him if all the fuel tanks, including the two pressed-paper 110-gallon external tanks, are topped off. He assures me they are full and, trusting him implicitly, I don't bother to check them. He is now standing on the wing helping me buckle into the 'chute and seat harness. He climbs down and stands by the nose of the plane with a fire extinguisher at his side to monitor the engine start.

0730 hours: Some of the planes are starting up and beginning to move, but my start-engine time (written on the back of my hand)

When a man wants to murder a tiger/he calls it sport:/when the tiger wants to murder him he calls it ferocity.

from *Maxims for Revolutionists*
by George Bernard Shaw

left: The crumbling control tower at Goxhill near Hull. above: A sail from the dinghy pack of an American fighter pilot. The pack was recovered from a crash site in England.

is still ten minutes away.

To "go on a bounce" is what we called attacking an enemy plane. If, for instance, Red Section saw a Jerry, Numbers One and Two men would attack first. Numbers Three and Four men would hesitate and then follow down to prevent any other plane from attacking the first two. Blue Section, which would be another four planes, would hover overhead to protect Red Three and Four. If four planes were to be attacked, Red Section would go down first, the Blue Section would follow, and White Section would hover overhead for protection along with Green Section. Now one squadron is participating in the attack of four planes. If larger groups of planes were to be attacked, one squadron of sixteen planes would go down at a bounce, the remaining two squadrons would act similarly to flights or sections and give support. This was the plan of fighting for the entire Eighth Air Force. It was all sound and practical on paper, but in the heat of combat, individual fights were, of course, a common occurrence.

from *The Look of Eagles*
by John T. Godfrey

0740 hours: It is time to start my engine. I flip the master switch on, hold the spring-loaded primer switch a few seconds, turn on the ignition switches and hold the starter switch. The prop blades turn a couple of revolutions and the Merlin engine catches with a few pops and bangs, then roars to life with some puffs of black smoke. I let it warm up a couple of minutes, signal the crew chief to pull the wheel chocks, and taxi to the line of planes waiting at the hardstand exit to get on the taxiway. I have also written on the back of my hand the identification code letters of the airplane I am to follow and, when he passes by on the taxiway, I pull out behind him. There is a long string of idling P-51s on the taxiway leading to the take-off end of the runway. There are forty-eight fighters flying this mission, three squadrons of four flights, each flight consisting of four planes. There are also two spares cranked up who will fly to the German border in case they are needed to fill in for an air abort. If they are not needed, they will return to home base. While waiting in the take-off line, I recheck all my engine instruments, crank in five degrees of right rudder trim (the engine torque is terrific at low speeds and high power), lower the flaps ten degrees for the heavy take-off weight and check my fuel selector valve on left main.

0800 hours: I taxi onto the runway behind two or three airplanes waiting to take off. I am leading Acorn Blue flight today, so I line up on the left side of the runway and my wing man lines up on the right side. Up ahead is a pilot standing by the left side of the runway with an orange-and-white checkered flag. He flags off each pair of airplanes when he sees that the preceding pair has cleared the ground. The pair ahead of us is on the take-off roll, so I move up even with the flag man, hold the brakes and rev up to about 25 percent power. The flag man waves the flag over his head in a circular motion to rev up, then drops it to signal brake release. As soon as we start moving, I slowly advance power to sixty-seven inches of manifold pressure and three thousand RPM. My wing man does the same and we take off together in close formation. As soon as we clear the ground, I signal for landing gear up and, when reaching 140 MPH, I signal for flaps up. I can still see two planes ahead of me; the others have disappeared into the one-thousand-foot overcast. I watch the two planes ahead enter the overcast, note their heading, then set my climb course a few degrees to the right of theirs so my wing man and I will not be running into their prop wash while on instruments. The overcast is only five thousand feet thick and we break out in bright sunlight at six thousand feet. Most of the other P-51s are in sight now and we begin closing up with the others into the briefed formation.

0830 hours: All forty-eight Mustangs are in formation, with the two spares following the last flight of four. We are now climbing through to eighteen thousand feet over the North Sea. I switch the fuel selector to the eighty-five-gallon aft fuselage tank to burn it down to forty gallons to ease the tail-heavy condition before switching to the external drop tanks. My wing man, Acorn Blue Two, is about two hundred feet to my right and fifty feet back. My element leader, Acorn Blue Three, is about two hundred feet to my left and fifty feet back. His wing man, Acorn Blue Four, is another two hundred feet out and fifty feet in back of Blue Three. This spreadout battle formation allows the pilots to look around for enemy aircraft without the total concentration required in close-formation flying.

0900 hours: We approach the long stream of east-bound bombers. It is so long that we cannot see the lead B-17s nor the tail end of the stream. We are nearing our rendezvous time and point. Acorn Red Two was elected (as are all of the greenest pilots on their first few missions) to leave our formation, slide up to the side of the bombers and slowly rock his wings while never pointing his nose at them so as not to be mistaken for an ME 109. His job is to get close enough to the bombers to read the symbols on the vertical tail surfaces to see if they are the ones we are assigned to escort. When our bombers are found and identified, our squadron leader puts two flights on either side and two or three thousand feet higher than the B-17s. Our other two squadrons do the same things with their box of bombers farther up the line. I have switched the fuel selector to the left external tank. I will try to run each external tank fifteen minutes before switching to the other one to keep them evenly balanced.

25

above: 4th Fighter Group
P-51 Mustangs over
England, September 1944.

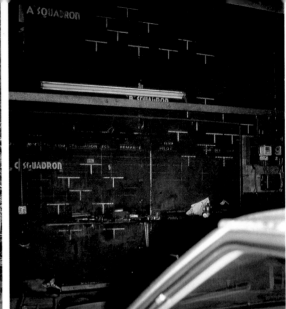

0935 hours: We are crossing the border into Germany now, still climbing through twenty-nine thousand feet and all the planes, bombers and fighters alike, are leaving long vapor trails through the sky. These are caused by the moisture in the engine exhaust freezing instantly when it is ejected into the thirty-degrees-below-zero outside air. I switch to the right drop tank as my plane is getting slightly right wing–heavy.

1000 hours: Some fighters farther up the stream report sighting some FW 190s, but we don't see any.

1030 hours: Our bombers are turning onto their final bomb run, heading toward Berlin, and have not yet been under attack by German fighters. As the bombers head in on their bomb run, we back off some distance from them as we see no need for us to share the murderous flak barrage they are getting. The sky around them is black with 88mm flak bursts. I see one B-17 receive a direct hit that explodes his bombs in a massive ball of black smoke and flames. The only recognizable pieces are his four engines falling from the fireball. A minute later, another B-17 slants out of his formation with his left engines and wing on fire. Many B-17s are straggling behind with one or two engines shut down. The weather over Berlin is clear and we can see the flashes of the exploding bombs all over the center of the city. Two more smoke-trailing B-17s leave their formation and head down. I catch a quick glimpse of some of the Fortress crews bailing out, but have no time to count

them to see if they all got out.

1135 hours: We move back over our home-bound bombers and escort them to the Holland border. Since we did not have to drop our external tanks early in anticipation of a dogfight, we have enough fuel to do a little strafing on the way home. I exhausted my drop tanks a short time ago and dropped them from twenty-five thousand feet over an unknown German town, hoping they might do some damage. Acorn Blue flight goes down to five thousand feet, searching for something to strafe. We soon find a freight train puffing along and in a short time it is riddled wreckage, the engine is spurting steam in all directions.

1150 hours: Acorn Blue flight is headed home but we stay at five thousand feet still looking for more targets of opportunity. I spot three ME 109s cruising along at our altitude on a crossing path some distance ahead of us. We swing in behind them and go to full power in a stern chase. They see us now and they go to full power, evidenced by the thin streams of black smoke coming from their exhaust stacks. We slowly close on them and, when in range, I open fire on the leader. He is carrying a single external tank under his belly and my armor-piercing incendiary bullets set it afire. He drops the flaming tank and dives toward the ground as the other two 109s break in opposite directions. I press on with the leader and, after some more hits, he bellies in at 250 MPH in a snowcovered field, sliding to a stop in a grove of trees. As I pass over the wreckage,

Clear skies, brilliant sunshine were the devilish beguilement of the heavens during those midsummer days. Day after day, week after week, the fierce turmoil raged high up in that blue dome, while the very elements stood aside and watched. A break in the weather, if only for a day, could alone have given us a respite from the full ardours of a battle in which we were so sadly outnumbered in men and machines. Even clouding of the sun would have helped. Climbing into a brilliance which the enemy wisely exploited as a tactical advantage, was a hazardous and often nerve-racking business, for it meant that escorting German fighters were able to see us long before we saw them.

from *The Way of a Pilot*
by Barry Sutton

Little Walden hosted the 361st Fighter Group in late 1944. above left: Remnants of pierced-steel planking runway material. above right: A well-preserved operations-room state board. The building was in use as a repair garage in 1990. left: One of Little Walden's few remaining Nissen huts in 1990.

All quit their sphere
and rush into the skies.

from *Essay on Man*
by Pope

the pilot is climbing out and waving at me.
Acorn Blue Three gets one of the other ME
109s and Acorn Blue Four gets the last one.

1220 hours: Our fuel supply forces us

A cannon-armed Spitfire
photographed on a RAF
fighter station in December
1942. right: The front of a
P-38 Pilot's Check List.

homeward and we climb to fifteen thousand feet to be safe from light ground fire in Nazi-occupied Holland. As we approach the North Sea, we see two B-17s limping along on three engines and escort them across the water.

1300 hours: We are nearing England now and wave good bye to the two crippled bombers. I take off my oxygen mask and light a cigarette, then I eat my two "inflight lunch" candy bars. This is my first opportunity to take off the oxygen mask on the mission.

1330 hours: Acorn Blue flight is in a tight echelon-right formation a mile out from the runway at 250 MPH and thirty feet off the ground. When we come to the runway, we reduce power, fan upward in a tight lefthand climbing turn, then lower the flaps and landing gear. Each pilot fans upward a second later than the man in front of him so that all four planes are evenly spaced for individual landings. None of us has more than fifteen gallons of fuel left, but the weather is clear and we could have landed at any number of closer RAF or U.S. bases had our fuel supply been really tight. We have to forego our "victory rolls" over the runway, though, due to our low fuel state.

1340 hours: As I taxi into my circular hardstand, my crew chief notices the tape missing from my gun muzzles and leaps up on the wing. He wants to know what I had shot at. He has another swastika painted on the plane before nightfall. A few minutes after I arrive at the hardstand, a GI truck pulls up

OFFICIAL AAF PILOT'S CHECK LIST

P-38H Airplanes	V-1710-89 and 91 Engines
P-38J Airplanes	V-1710-89 and 91 Engines
P-38L-1 Airplanes	V-1710-111 and 113 Engines
F-5B, F-5C, F-5E Airplanes	V-1710-89 and 91 Engines
F-5F Airplanes	V-1710-111 and 113 Engines

For detailed instructions see Pilot's Handbook AN 01-75-1 in data case.

BEFORE STARTING ENGINE

1. Check Form 1.
2. Check Form F—Weight and Balance Clearance (AN 01-1B-40).
3. With ignition OFF, pull engines through by hand.
4. Close canopy and make sure it is locked.
5. Controls free and proper movement. Control lock secure.
6. Rudder and aileron tabs 0 deg, elevator tab 3 deg back.
7. Tank selector valves, RESERVE ON.
8. Cross feed switch, OFF.
9. Electric fuel pumps, ON. Check for 15 to 16 psi pressure and turn pumps OFF.
10. Turn bomb selector switches ON, and arm switch to SAFE.
11. Throttles, 1/10 OPEN.
12. Propeller control, INC RPM (full forward).
13. Propeller selector switches, AUTO CONSTANT SPEED.
14. Mixture, IDLE CUT-OFF.
15. Carburetor air filter as required.
16. Propeller circuit breakers, ON.
17. Propeller feathering switches, NORMAL.
18. Set clock and altimeter.
19. Oxygen pressure, 400 to 450 psi.
20. Armament master switch, OFF.
21. Aileron boost control, ON, if installed.
22. Prime the left engine two to four strokes.
23. Battery switch OFF, if battery cart is used; ON, if battery cart is not used.
24. Left ignition, BOTH.
25. Generator switch, ON.
26. Left fuel booster pump, ON.
27. Inertia starter switch to LH (left hand) until inertia starter reaches max rpm.
28. Left fuel booster pump, ON.
29. Engage switch to LH (left hand) still holding starter switch in LH.
30. As soon as the engine definitely fires, place mixture control in AUTO RICH. Return to IDLE CUT-OFF if engine stops.
31. Stop the engine if oil pressure does not register within 30 seconds after starting.
32. Start the right hand engine in the same manner.
33. Lock the primer pump down.
34. Battery switch ON, before disconnecting battery cart.
35. Inverter switch, ON. (Compass switch on later models.)
36. Coolant flap override switches, OFF.
37. Intercooler flaps, OPEN, if installed.
38. PUSH to test turbo warning lights, if installed.
39. Check fuel quantity.

DURING WARM-UP

1. Warm-up at not over 1400 rpm until oil pressure is steady below 75 psi.
2. Extend and retract flaps to check hydraulic system.
3. Normal fuel pressure (16 to 18 psi). Check for normal fuel pressure with electric fuel pump OFF.
4. When oil temperature has reached 40°C, or shows an increase of at least 10°C, and coolant temperature reaches 85°C, increase rpm to 2300.
   a. Check propeller control levers. Move levers DEC RPM then INC RPM, full forward.
   b. Check propeller selector switches DEC RPM, then INC RPM, then return to AUTO CONSTANT SPEED. Note: Propeller warning lights should burn when switches are not set to AUTO CONSTANT SPEED on P-38H airplanes only.

15 May 1945
Supersedes pilot's check lists of previous dates.

Down hard on the behind/The parachute; you are blind/With your oxygen snout/But click, click, click, click, you feel/And the harness is fixed./Round the wing/And "Out of the cockpit, you,"/Clamber the rung/And the wing as if a wasp had stung/You, hop and jump into the cockpit,/Split second to spike/The Sutton harness holes,/One, two, three, four,/Thrust with your/Hand to the throttle open . . ./"Operations" called and spoken.

from "Operations Calling"
by David Bourne

I've tried for many an hour and minute/To think of this world without me in it./I can't imagine a new-born day/Without me here . . . somehow . . . some way./I can not think of the autumn's flare/Without me here . . . alive . . . aware./I can't imagine a dawn in spring/Without my heart awakening.

from "Somehow"
—Anonymous

A portion of the old main runway at Goxhill, 1990.

and we climb in the back with several other pilots and head for mission debriefing. The flight surgeon is standing at the door of the debriefing room, pouring us each a shot of "mission whiskey." We get this before debriefing, I suppose, to relax us and make us more talkative. The intelligence officer debriefs each flight (four pilots at a time), and any member can interrupt and add to what others say. We are queried on what we saw, where we saw it, what time we saw it, and where it was headed. We are asked how many bombers we saw go down, enemy aircraft sighted, how many, etc. Three of us have to fill out separate encounter reports on the three ME 109s we have claimed as destroyed. From the debriefing room we walk a short distance to our squadron-operations building to check the mission board to see who is scheduled to fly again tomorrow. We also run the previous day's gun-camera film, which is all spliced together on one reel.

1500 hours: GI trucks begin running pilots back to the barracks where most will sack out until suppertime.

1730 hours: Shuttle trucks come by about every ten minutes for the next hour to take us to the mess hall. This meal is usually better than the monotonous breakfast. We occasionally have steak or other meat. After the evening meal, many go to the nearby Officers' Club for a few drinks and merrymaking, but I hop a truck back to the barracks with a sack of steak scraps for Lassie, my Scottie dog who lives in the barracks with me. I have a bottle of

30

scotch in my footlocker and those barracks mates who are here don't miss too much by not going to the Officers' Club.

2130 hours: The dog has been fed and those pilots flying tomorrow put their drinking cups away and think about going to bed.

2140 hours: The base loudspeaker system announces; "This station is under Red Alert. Seek shelter." The message is repeated a couple of times. This is the signal for us to load our GI .45 pistols and run outside. Our base is right in line with London, so the V-1 buzz bombs launched from HE 111 aircraft over the North Sea pass over us en route. We stand on top of the bomb shelter, pistols in hand, waiting for a buzz bomb to go over. They are usually only a few hundred feet high and can easily be seen at night by the plume of fire from the ram-jet engine. The distinctive noise is also a help in locating them. If one comes over, pistol shots from several bomb shelters can be heard. No one has ever hit one as far as we know. One comes over at about 2 A.M. but no one gets up to seek shelter or to shoot at it. The rumble gets louder, then the engine quits. It is so close we can hear it whistling as it glides. Too late now to seek shelter. I just pull the covers up over my head and wait. Soon there is a thunderous blast that blows open the barracks doors. It has exploded less than a mile away. We close the barracks doors and everyone tries to get back to sleep. There are only three more hours until wake-up time.

0500 hours: The barracks door bursts open, the CQ flips on the lights and . . .

far left: John Godfrey (leaning against wall of Alberto Vargas pin-up girls) and other 4th Fighter Group members relaxing at Debden. above: Walter and Harold Konantz, brothers who both flew with the Wormingford-based 55th Fighter Group. Walter is holding "Lassie," his Scottie. left: USAAF pilots preparing for a fighter mission.

33

THE IRON

THEY WERE THE TOOLS for the job. Like the pilots who flew them, the fighter aircraft of World War II represented high performance and deadly intent. Splendid names like Mustang and Spitfire, Thunderbolt and Hurricane, Typhoon and Lightning imply the speed, power and agility of these warplanes. They were state-of-the-art machines designed for a short but efficient life as hunter-killers.

No combat plane is perfect in all respects. Knowing an aircraft's limitations is as fundamental to combat survivability as is knowing its capabilities. The most serious limitation of the P-47 Thunderbolt was its comparatively slow rate of climb. It was, however, a remarkably rugged airplane, armed with a wing-mounted battery of eight .50 caliber Browning machine guns. Underwing rockets and bombs could add to its firepower for the ground-attack role. It was the biggest single-seat, single-engined Allied fighter of the war, and its shape soon earned it the nickname Jug. With its bulbous front and tapering fuselage it certainly resembled a milk jug.

If the Thunderbolt didn't climb very well, it could surely dive. Its pilots attributed this characteristic to what they called the milk-bottle effect. Gravity and the massive Pratt & Whitney Twin Wasp 2800 engine driving a huge four-blade propeller made its dive impressive by any standard. Its great size, though, made the first impression on pilots new to the P-47. "Gee," said one Spitfire veteran as he looked into a Thunderbolt cockpit for the first time, "you could walk around in there!"

The Thunderbolt was more than just big. It was an ace maker. In it many 8th and 9th Air Force pilots achieved that status. It was the airplane with which the high-achieving 4th and 56th Fighter Groups first became famous. Once the early engine and radio problems common to the aircraft were overcome, the Thunderbolt became an oustanding fighter—appreciated by its pilots and respected by the Luftwaffe. In the early 1990s a magnificently restored P-47 is still flown regularly by Stephen Grey of The Fighter Collection, Duxford, England.

"Settle into the cockpit and space plus comfort prevail. Start the 2800 engine and it begins to feel like a 'class act.' Taxi to the hold and it feels like a beautifully damped Mack truck. At run-up it purrs rather than barks.

"Put the hammer down for take-off and there is no kick in the back or dart for the weeds. It runs straight and true—if sedately.

"Put the wheels in the wings and it turns into a crisp-handling fighter, with beautiful ailerons, oustanding controls, great visibility and a sensation of pedigree.

"True, it does not climb with the best of them, but stuff the nose toward the greenery and the air-speed indicator will wind to the stop and stay there faster than other prop fighters that I have flown. Circuit work, landing and ground handling are docile and beautifully mannered.

"Fortunately, or regrettably, I have not had to fight in the Jug. However, from a little 'arm wrestling' with others behind the hangar

Oh, Hedy Lamarr is a beautiful gal/And Madeline Carroll is too;/But you'll find, if you query, a different theory/Amongst any bomber crew./For the loveliest thing of which one could sing/This side of the Heavenly Gates/Is no blonde or brunette of the Hollywood set,/But an escort of P-38s . . .

from "Kohn's War" by Frederic Arnold

A dragonfly/in a flecked grey sky.

Its silvered planes break the wide and still/harmony of space.

Around it shells/flash their fumes/burgeoning to blooms/smoke-lilies that float/along the sky.

Among them darts/a dragonfly.

"Aeroplanes" by Herbert Read

left: An American war worker at Lockheed's Burbank P-38 facility.

right: Shining example of
P-47D production at the
Republic Farmingdale
(Long Island) plant.

I know that the Jug could fight incredibly
well, if differently. If I were able to transpose
myself back to the forties and had a choice, I
feel my survival instincts would tell me to
choose the Jug but my competitive instincts
would tell me only to fight on my terms with a
lot of airspace underneath me.

"The sheer rugged, technical quality of
the airplane is its charm, the handling a joy.
When I climb out and walk away, I always
find myself looking back at the 47 with affection . . . what a character."

The Typhoon was the RAF's Thunder-
bolt. Though not quite so big, it was still very
large and could deliver equally heavy punishment. But it never achieved the same degree of
success. Only one Typhoon from the 3,317
built survives, and this is a nonairworthy example in the RAF Museum at Hendon near
London. Above fifteen thousand feet the Typhoon's performance could not match that of
the Spitfire, the aircraft it was intended to
replace. There were problems with its Napier
Sabre engine and, more seriously, there were
airframe structural failures. But the "Tiffie"
is remembered fondly by many who flew it.
One was Jimmy Kyle, once a twenty-year-old
pilot with 197 Squadron.

"I first flew the Typhoon Mark 1A, with
the car door–type hood, on December 20,
1942, nine months after it had entered service
with the Royal Air Force. The pilot sat high in
this big fighter. I stepped in and settled on the
hard dinghy base attached to the parachute,
which fitted into the bucket seat of the cockpit. I strapped in, clipped on the face mask,
plugged in the RT and switched on the oxy-

gen. With its long nose, three prominent propeller blades, thick anhedral/dihedral wing, wide undercarriage and four evenly-spaced cannons, the Typhoon conveyed an impression of power and brute strength.

"When settled and feeling at ease, I started the engine with a bang. It could be temperamental. The twenty-four-cylinder Napier Sabre was provided with a Coffman starter used in conjunction with a Kigas primer. The amount of priming required depended on the engine temperature and it was imperative to get the combination right for the engine to start without delay. When the starter switch was thrown the engine would spring to life with a loud explosion, causing clouds of acrid exhaust smoke to stream from either side of the cowling. The smoke quickly thinned and disappeared as the engine warmed up with an even roar.

"I spent a few minutes checking temperatures and pressures. Noting all was well, re-tightening the primer, I waved 'chocks away' to the ground crew, released the brakes, rolled forward, checking that the brakes operated, and taxied slowly out for take-off.

"Tense and excited, cautiously edging forward, I waited for take-off clearance and swung the nose into the wind and lined the plane up onto the runway . . . positioning it dead center, completing the cockpit checks and revving the engine to clear it. I held hard on the brakes, then slowly released them and gradually opened the throttle to maximum take-off power.

"As the stick was pushed forward and the tail unit lifted, there was an unpleasant ten-

The fifes cry death and the sharp winds call. Set your face to the rock; go on, go out/Into the bad lands of battle, into the cloud-wall/Of the future, my friends, and leave your fear.

from "Advice for a Journey"
by Sidney Keyes

above left: RAF Spitfire crossing the English coast. above center: A book of military aircraft for children. left: *No Guts—No Glory!*, the Republic P-47 Thunderbolt of The Fighter Collection, Duxford Airfield, in 1990. above: Shoulder patch of the 9th U.S. Army Air Force.

dency for the aircraft to swing to starboard. This inherent swing could lead to eventual loss of control if application of the port rudder wasn't anticipated. Being aware of this inbuilt idiosyncrasy I gently fed in a fraction of port rudder slightly before the tail unit was fully up, to prevent the swing.

"The engine surged to a roar as the Typhoon hurtled down the runway. I checked all instruments, eased the control column back and was airborne. Climbing out I was surprised at the ease of the take-off. Selecting 'wheels up' and the small amount of flap I used to offset undercarriage strain on the bumpy runway, I noted the green lights go on and then out, indicating undercarriage up, and settled the aircraft in the climb at the recommended speed of about 300 MPH. The feeling of power and speed was marvelous. I quickly found myself at a high altitude and leveling out. I then put the aircraft and myself to our respective limits.

"I completed a sequence of aerobatics, stalls, slow rolls, loops, upward rolls, incipient spins and some barrel rolls on the way down. All the maneuvers were easy to perform but I sustained high G loads that I had not experienced before. The thrust of Gs pushed my sagging jaw and chin down to my chest, and the centrifugal forces drove my blood from my brain into my boots, my vision graying and my legs feeling like lead. By easing the controls, I could in seconds return to the normal if and when it became too hard to bear.

"On returning to the circuit and slowing to a landing configuration, I carried out a normal continuous curved approach with wheels down and locked. Then, with full flap selected, I turned onto short final—a normal fighter approach, only this one being a little faster than most other aircraft at the time. The ground rushed up quickly. The approach speed in the turn was between 120 and 130 MPH, gradually reducing to 95, and further still when rounding out for touchdown at 75 MPH.

"I landed safely and, quickly completing the after-landing checks without stopping, taxied back to the dispersal, exhilarated and pleased with the thirty-minute flight. Stepping from the cockpit I jumped to the ground among eager faces awaiting my arrival. All were anxiously awaiting their turn to fly the Typhoon.

" 'How did it go?' they asked. 'Marvelous,' I said, explaining every detail of the trip to those around me. I then signed the authorization book, 'DCO. Duty Carried Out.' "

Jimmy Kyle survived his tour on Typhoons and the Typhoons survived their early mechanical and structural problems. An increased frequency of low-altitude German attacks on British coastal towns allowed the Typhoon to establish itself as a premier low-level interceptor. It would later excel as the Allies' key ground-attack aircraft for the RAF's 2nd Tactical Air Force.

Of all the fighter aircraft of World War II, the P-51 Mustang was simply the best of the Allied examples. This exceptional airplane employed an American airframe and a British engine to achieve its remarkable success. Initially developed using an Allison engine, it was designated Mustang I when first received

Necessity is often the spur to genius.

—Balzac

. . . once the teething period was over, the Typhoon was magnificent. It was a big hefty aeroplane but it had the power it needed. It was very fast, and so heavy and "clean" that it went downhill like a rocket in reverse, and took a long time to slow up. It handled beautifully— very like its older brother, the Hurricane—and the noise of its Sabre engine in full song down the runway was glorious.

—Hugh Bergel, OBE, formerly Officer Commanding, No.9 Ferry Pool, ATA

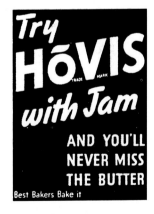

left: The cockpit, control column and instrument panel of a Hawker Typhoon.

by the RAF. A Rolls-Royce test pilot, Ronnie Harker, flew the Mustang I at Duxford in a brief test flight and was impressed. He recognized the potential of the airplane, noting in his report: "The aircraft should prove itself a formidable low and mid altitude fighter . . . with a powerful and good engine like the Merlin 61 its performance should be outstanding." Harker knew that he was on to something very special in the Mustang— something with great potential. The U.S. Army Air Corps was, however, initially reluctant to abandon its reliance on air-cooled engines in favor of the liquid-cooled Merlin for one of its fighters. But it would have no cause to regret the change, as the Mustang was to become the most formidable fighter in its inventory.

The plane was developed through the Mustang III variant for the RAF; its production as the P-51B accelerated as the United States entered the war. But it was the later P-51D version that has been generally acknowledged as the ultimate fighter aircraft of World War II. Visibility for the pilot was excellent from the bubble-type canopy, a revolutionary concept in the early 1940s. But it was *range*, already exceptional and then extended through the addition of drop tanks, that transformed the P-51 into the great airplane it became.

Mustang pilot Robin Olds recalls: "Here was a fighter. High or low. Straight down or in a shuddering Lufberry, you knew no one could match you. The gyro sight was deadly accurate, the firepower devasting. Gun-camera results were like Hollywood, a far cry from

He who has great power should use it lightly.

—Seneca

the blurred, jumpy imagery produced by the gun camera in the P-38, where some knothead had mounted the camera right under a 20mm cannon.

"As for actual combat performance, the P-51 was good at everything, more than matching German machines in what they could do. In all, it was a fighter pilot's dream. Just ask any pilot who ever strapped a Mustang to his bottom and set out across the North Sea to do battle with the wily Hun."

Certainly, among the greatest contributions of the USAAF to victory in Europe was the part played by its fighters in achieving and maintaining air superiority. The Mustang had a leading role in that effort and caused one Luftwaffe fighter pilot who was defending the Reich in 1945 to comment: "In 1940 Galland was asking for a squadron of Spitfires. Right now I'd sell my soul to the devil for just one Mustang."

For most who flew R. J. Mitchell's wonderful Spitfire, it is their first flight in the type that remains their most enduring memory.

John Nesbitt-Dufort: "I strongly suspect that most pilots experienced the same slight feeling of awe as I did when gazing out for the first time over the apparent yards of engine that separated me from the propeller. Brakes on, petrol on, rad shutters open, fine pitch, switches off. I gave her three full dopes on the priming pump, nodded to the airman on the trolley ack and he held his thumb up. 'All Clear!' Opening the throttle a shade I threw the booster-coil switch and then ignition, and pressed the starter button. After about two revolutions there was a puff of black smoke as

she caught with a roar. I immediately throttled back and switched off the booster coil. The trolley ack was disconnected and after a brief warming-up I ran up, checked mags and pitch and then waved away both the chocks and the windswept character who had draped himself over the tail. I saved time by carrying out my preflight checks as I taxied, weaving wildly, to the downwind side of the airfield. Coarse weaving was an absolute necessity as the Spit was completely blind dead ahead with the tail down. Stopping the regulation forty-five degrees out of wind I had a final check around the cockpit. Taking a deep breath I gently pushed the handled throttle fully open. There was an immediate and pronounced tendency to swing to the left but this was easily checked by coarse use of opposite rudder, and with a centralized control column the tail appeared to come up on its own.

"Now for the ticklish part: Changing hands I selected 'up' and with my now free right hand, pumped up the undercarriage avoiding, I hoped successfully, the novice's tendency to pump the control column at the same time. After closing the canopy I adjusted boost and revs climbing at 160 MPH. This was the fastest airplane that I had ever flown and I was duly impressed; throttling back to cruising boost and revs I felt all the controls in turn, elevators very light, ailerons and rudder not quite so light but all sensitive and very positive. All the controls stiffened up appreciably, but in no way unpleasantly, as the speed built up. Medium and steep turns in either direction and then daringly a roll—she went round as though she had been on rails! The little

The makers had stipulated that the emergency boost must not be used for more than five consecutive minutes, but now the occasion seemed to warrant this risk. I throttled back, pushed the red half-lever fully forward and then opened up the main throttle again. Immediately the aircraft seemed to leap forward with a jolt, hitting me in the back as it did so, and the engine started to vibrate—black smoke pouring out of each exhaust port. The engine vibration transmitted itself to the entire aircraft and I began to appreciate the maker's instructions. The strain on the engine must have been phenomenal. I opened my radiator to its fullest extent to try to cool it a bit, for the Glycol temperature was rising rapidly and threatening to pass the danger mark.

from *Clouds of Fear* by Roger Hall, DFC

above left: Early RAF Mustangs being run up at their UK base. left: The flight line at the Mines Field (Los Angeles) North American Aviation facility, which produced P-51 Mustangs, T-6 Texans (Harvards) and B-25 Mitchell bombers.

airplane handled beautifully, her flying characteristics what one might expect from such delightful lines.

"Time to come in again. I located myself quite a distance from the airfield and closed the throttle to test for a stall with the gear and flaps up. Even with the nose held fairly high the speed took a long time to fall off, then after a definite shudder the nose dropped smartly but cleanly at just under eighty-four MPH. Ye Gods! I thought, that's a bit quick. For some silly unknown reason I didn't test for stall with gear and flaps down, which would have reassured me, but instead headed to join in the circuit with about twenty pupils in Oxfords and Harvards making frantic darts at the ground with varying degrees of success.

"In those days air traffic was not controlled from the tower—it was just a case of everyone for himself and devil take the hindmost. I reduced speed, pumped down the undercarriage and slid back the cockpit canopy. Then by dint of a rather splitarse final turn in at about 130 MPH I insinuated myself in between two indignant Harvards and after snapping down the flaps came whistling in at 100 MPH over the hedge. Far too fast! I floated, pump-handling furiously across two-thirds of the field to eventually sit down firmly at just over 72 MPH to finish my run only twenty yards from the boundary. I was sweating profusely and more than somewhat ashamed of my performance; still, with not a little pride I made the first entry of the magic words 'Spitfire Mk I No. N3174' in my log book."

Flying the Spitfire in combat was a different matter entirely, and those who flew both Hurricanes and Spitfires into battle often swear allegiance to one type or the other, an argument further complicated by later developments of both types. While the Hurricane advanced from eight machine guns to twelve, and from twelve machine guns to four cannon, its basic airframe remained largely unchanged. The Spitfire, however, was developed far beyond the original Mitchell concept at Supermarine Aviation. Extended wingtips, clipped wingtips, high-back fuselages, bubble canopies, advanced Merlin and Griffon engines . . . all were implemented as wartime advances of this most versatile of RAF fighters.

New Zealander Alan Deere flew many Spitfire marks into combat through the entire course of the war. He has no doubt about its superiority over the Messerschmitt ME 109. "The Spitfire was a better aircraft than the 109. Not in all respects, but overall a better aircraft. Anything the 109 could do we could do better . . . except a dive. They could run away from us then but in a turn or sustained climb we could match them. Top speed or cruise was much the same, but the Spitfire just had the edge."

In the interminable wrangle over the relative merits of Spitfire versus Hurricane, only the viewpoints of pilots who flew them are normally considered. Eric Marsden, 145 (Hurricane) Squadron fitter, has an interesting perspective. "If we'd had nothing but Spits we'd have lost the fight in 1940. The turnaround time on the ground was so poor that Jerry couldn't have failed to get us. The Spit I and II took twenty-six minutes to turn

left: A Mustang of the 363rd Fighter Squadron, 357th Fighter Group (Leiston) over English farmlands in 1944. above: The shoulder patch worn by 8th Air Force personnel.

From the point of view of sheer piloting pleasure the Hurricane was not quite in the same class as the Spitfire (nor was any other aeroplane), but it soon became an old and trusted friend, and was regarded with affection.

—Hugh Bergel, OBE, formerly Officer Commanding, No.9 Ferry Pool, ATA

Even though the Spitfire got the lion's share of publicity, the Hurricane won the Battle of Britain. It destroyed more planes than all other defenses, on the ground and in the air, added together. It gave the world time to win World War II.

—John W. R. Taylor, Editor, *Jane's All the World's Aircraft*

right: RAF pilots muscle a Spitfire of their squadron from a maintenance facility in December 1942.

around, compared to a Hurri's nine minutes . . . that is, complete service—re-arm, refuel and replenish oxygen—from down to up again."

In 1990, the RAF and the pilots who regularly fly the preserved Hurricanes and Spitfires of the Battle of Britain Memorial Flight from Coningsby believe that both aircraft types are equally precious, both an equal privilege to fly. In the cockpit of one of the Memorial Flight's Spitfires, Squadron Leader Paul Day makes a rapid, professional evaluation of its layout. It is a point of view unclouded by sentimentality. Looking over the controls, dials and switches, Day is quite sure about what he likes and dislikes. "The undercarriage lever . . . where that is positioned is really undesirable. On the pilot's right it means a change of hand from the control column to operate. Not a good idea."

Slapping the curved side pieces of the front canopy, he points out that they too, are cause for concern. "The glass is contoured and not of good optical quality. That plays all sorts of tricks from a cockpit where visibility should be of paramount importance, but turns out to be a real problem. For instance, up front that whacking great engine obscures most of the sky. At five hundred feet for example, you are blind for three miles ahead of you. Then, what is going on beneath those wings? Miles of airspace obscured by them. Looking behind . . . well, that's a real labor of love. There is a teeny makeup mirror for rearward vision but that's of little practical value. As for the instrument panel . . . not badly laid out, but all the engine instruments are grouped to

48

above: The grave of Spitfire designer R. J. Mitchell near Eastleigh. below: .303 caliber ammunition similar to that used by many of the RAF fighter aircraft of WWII. right: The cockpit panel and spade-grip control column of a Vickers-Supermarine Spitfire in the Battle of Britain Memorial Flight, Coningsby, Lincolnshire.

the right. They aren't terribly eye-catching. In a tight spot all sorts of things could be going on there which you might not notice. The system for arming and firing, though, is simple, effective and good."

Summing up, and despite his dislikes, Day felt that "Mitchell had got it right." Given the technology of the late 1930s, it is surely a fair view . . . especially when set against Day's evaluation of the Messerschmitt ME 109. It was, after all, how the Spitfire shaped up against the 109 that counted. Lowering himself into the Messerschmitt cockpit, Day's opinion of the little fighter was quickly formed. As he closed the heavily-framed hood, he described it as "like a modified Kaiser's helmet."

"Well, good grief! It's terrible. Not for the squeamishly claustrophobic. There is twenty-five percent less working room in here and up front the vision is even worse. All you can see is Krupp of Essen. Looking behind is a hundred percent worse than in a Spit."

Squadron Leader Day has never flown the Messerschmitt, but in delivering his verdict he is absolutely certain: "I wouldn't choose to go to war in one given that the opposition had Spitfires."

Nick Berryman was a Hurricane man. Although he never flew one operationally, it is an airplane he remembers vividly as this entry from his log book shows:

Friday, October 16, 1942. Flew Master for twenty minutes, then pushed off in a Hurri. Very careful indeed. Twenty minutes for cockpit check which I carried out

about five times. Eventually ready to go. Got off OK, but unable to find undercart lever. Terrible moments expecting to spin in any minute. Aircraft bucking about all over the place. Climbed to one thousand feet, then selecting "wheels down" found myself at seventeen hundred feet. Forgot radio procedure completely and unable to remember call sign. Suddenly, a crosswind coming in to land. All became calm and she came in as gentle and easy as a bird. Now, at long last, a Hurricane has flown me."

"Not exactly a macho way of describing one's first flight in a fighter aircraft, but that is exactly how it was. Over a beer in the bar that night I probably said, 'Hurricanes? A piece of cake.' "

On reflection, Nick was able to understand what had gone wrong on that first flight: the bucking caused by the odd location of the undercarriage lever and the procedure for operating it—left hand from throttle to control column, right hand from control column to undercarriage lever. "Previously, I had never held a control column in my left hand apart from the odd occasion when I needed to scratch my right ear."

Like so many Hurricane pilots, Nick learned to love and respect the airplane. "Give it half a chance and it would do its best to safeguard the pilot. There was little or no swing on take-off and in flight it was comfortable. Apart from the undercarriage, all the tits and knobs were in the right places. It was delightfully steady in all attitudes and steep

I think that these moments just before the clash are the most gloriously exciting moments of life. You sit there behind a great engine that seems as vibrant and alive as you are yourself, your thumb waits expectantly on the trigger, and your eyes watch the gun sight through which in a few seconds an enemy will be flying in a veritable hail of fire. And all round you, in front and behind, there are your friends too, all eager and excited, all thundering down together into the attack! The memory of such moments is burnt into my mind forever.

—F/L D.M. Crook, DFC

Many things difficult to design/prove easy to performance.

—Samuel Johnson

right: One of the first RAF Spitfires to fly a ground-attack sweep into Germany. This aircraft is taxiing from its dispersal point on April 26, 1944. Operating in a Nazi-occupied sector between Aachen and Cologne, Spitfires shot up German fighters and gliders, railway wagons and locomotives in a series of highly successful sweeps.

turns were a joy. So, too, were aerobatics, which I could carry out more accurately on Hurricanes than Spits, which I tended to over-aileron. I'm told that fifteen degrees of flap milked down in a dogfight situation would leave your tail-chasing adversary wondering why he could not stay with you. Landing was no problem. One bounce it would absorb without a murmur. Two bounces it would remind you to be careful and I never saw anyone bounce three times. If you did that, it would take over and drop in fairly straight on its wide legs. Without doubt, the Hurricane helped me to a state of proficiency I would never have achieved on any other fighter. It was a winner all the way. And yes, the airplane was probably more capable than many of the pilots who flew it."

Geoffrey Page shares Berryman's opinion of the Hurricane. Page flew it in combat. "In the Hurricane we knew that the ME 109 could out-dive us, but not out-turn us. With that knowledge one obviously used the turning maneuver rather than trying to beat the man at the game in which he was clearly superior. With a 109 sitting behind you, you'd stay in a really tight turn and after a few turns the position would be reversed and you'd be on his tail. In short, I'd say that the Hurricane was a magnificent airplane to go to war in."

It was the twin-engined, fork-tailed P-38 Lightning that was, perhaps, the most revolutionary Allied fighter of the war. However, while the plane was novel in concept and appearance, the Lightning's performance in the European air war was less than brilliant. Brought to Britain for long-range bomber-

It took both the Spitfire and the Hurricane to win the Battle of Britain. The Hurricane inflicted more damage on the enemy than the Spitfire. Neither could have achieved it [victory] on its own. Both complemented each other very well.

—Jeffrey Quill. Spitfire test pilot

above and right: An early engine test of the Canadian-built Hawker Hurricane restored by The Fighter Collection, Duxford Airfield, Cambridgeshire, 1990.

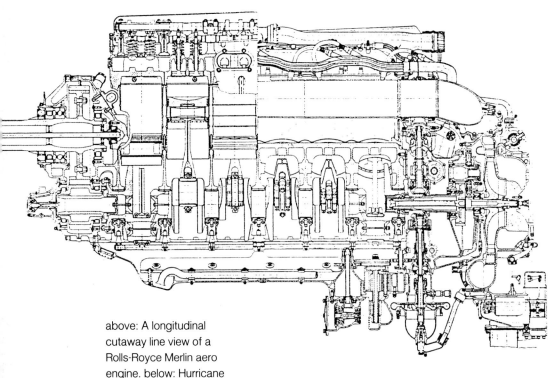

above: A longitudinal cutaway line view of a Rolls-Royce Merlin aero engine. below: Hurricane pilot Nick Berryman in 1942.

escort work in the autumn of 1943, it had the advantage of range over the P-47 Thunderbolt: It could take the 'big friends' deeper into enemy territory. Many pilots who flew the Lightning on operations from England have mixed feelings about it. Royal Frey, former curator of the USAF Museum, Wright-Patterson AFB, Ohio, flew the P-38 with the 20th Fighter Group from Kings Cliffe and Wittering. "With its tricycle gear, counterrotating props, muffled engine exhausts through the turbos and fairly heavy weight, the P-38 was a sheer delight on take-off. You would take the runway, line up, brake to a full stop and advance the throttles to at least forty-four-inches of manifold pressure, to where the turbos would cut in. The nose would gradually drop as the increasing pull of the props forced the

nose strut to compress, and the whole plane would shake and vibrate. A quick glance at the instrument panel and off the brakes. Up popped the nose and you bounded forward like a racehorse from the starting gate.

"As you gathered speed down the runway, the heavy weight of the plane deadened any bumps and you felt as if you were in a Cadillac. The turbo exhausts made the engines sound extremely muffled, as in a high-powered pleasure boat—no loud cracking or roar so usual in those days of reciprocating engines. No torque to swing the nose and beautiful visibility down the runway from the level attitude of the tricycle gear. At seventy MPH you gently eased back on the control yoke, and at ninety-five to a hundred MPH the plane lifted softly into the air. What complete comfort for a combat plane.

"With its inherent stability the P-38 was extremely easy to fly and once trimmed for straight and level flight, it was a hands-off airplane. If you put it into an unusual attitude (within reasonable limits) and then got off the controls, it would slowly waddle and oscillate around in the air and eventually return to straight and level flight. This was because its center of lift was above its center of gravity, i.e., most of the mass of the airplane was slung under a wing having a large amount of dihedral. Other fighters of the era tended to drop off on one wing or the other.

"The Lightning was an excellent gun platform, although it was more difficult than in a P-47 or P-51 to get strikes on a target because the four .50 caliber guns and one 20mm cannon were grouped so closely to-

New Lockheed P-38 Lightnings being cleaned and assembled at an American air depot in England in April 1944.

above: A Sydney Camm memorial (Camm designed the Hurricane and other Hawker aircraft), and the site of the Hawker drawing offices (from 1931 to 1934) at Kingston-upon-Thames near London.

gether in the nose. However, if we got any strikes at all, we had a much better chance of getting a victory—those five weapons put out such a heavy column of projectiles that they bored a large hole through anything they hit.

"The P-38 also had the famous Fowler flap, which, at half-extended position, greatly decreased turn radius at altitude, with very little additional drag. Incorporated into the P-38 for combat, this feature was given the name 'maneuver flaps', and with it I actually turned with late-model Spitfires during 'rat races' over England, and turned inside FW 190s in action over Europe.

"Although the Lightning could turn very tightly once it got into a bank, getting it into the bank was another matter. Late K and L series Lightnings had aileron boost, but this feature came too late for those of us who took on the Luftwaffe deep inside Germany in late 1943 and early 1944. Because of the weight of the plane and the poor leverage of a control wheel compared to that of a control stick, the

Lightning's roll rate approximated that of a pregnant whale. If we ever got behind a single-engine fighter in a tight turn, all the other pilot had to do was flip into an opposite turn and dive; by the time we had banked and turned after him, he was practically out of sight.

"In addition to an agonizingly slow roll rate, the P-38s I flew in combat had two other very limiting features—restricted dive and [extremely low] cockpit temperature. It was suicide to put the P-38 into a near-vertical dive at high altitude; all we P-38 pilots knew it, and I believe all the Luftwaffe pilots knew it, for they usually used the vertical dive to escape from us. You could 'split S' and do other vertical-type maneuvers at high altitude, and as long as you continued to pull the nose through the vertical, you always held your airspeed within limits. But let the nose stay in the vertical position for more than a few seconds and the nose would actually 'tuck under' beyond the vertical position, and it

As I walked down by Lewis Lane/To buy a roasting duck/There passed a broken Hurricane Dismembered on a truck.

Her wings lay folded at her side,/A blackened, tattered pall,/And gaping bullet-holes supplied/the context of her fall.

from "Passing of a Hurricane" by "Ariel"

center left: The Hawker experimental department at Kingston, where the prototype Hurricane was assembled in 1935. below left: K5083, the prototype Hurricane, at Brooklands Aerodrome in October 1935. below: Nick Berryman, 1990.

below: A P-38 Lightning assembly line on a ''Family Day'' open house at Burbank, July 31, 1944. right: New and heavily armed P-38s on the Burbank flight line.

would be impossible to recover from its dive. The only salvation was to pop the canopy, release your seat belt and hope you would clear the plane as you were sucked from the cockpit. The 20th Group lost two P-38s in vertical dives over England before we went operational, but both pilots bailed out successfully.

"The other limiting feature, cockpit temperature, would be more correctly identified as paralyzing. Cockpit heat from the en-

below: A P-38 Lightning assembly line on a ''Family Day'' open house at Burbank, July 31, 1944. right: New and heavily armed P-38s on the Burbank flight line.

60

Call it Lightning ⚡
— SAY THE PILOTS

Nobody had time to name this Lockheed fighter plane when it was born. They just called it by a number, P-38.

Then the pilots sent it climbing over eight miles straight toward the stratosphere, up where even the highest-flying bombers couldn't go. They brought it screaming down out of the clouds like forked vengeance. They jammed down the throttle and it flew faster than any fighter ever flew before. They pressed the trigger-button and saw how *concentrated* fire-power from its cannon and machine guns could rip apart anything on wings—and there was only one name for it: *Lightning*.

So that's its name, a name it's earned from British and American pilots alike, a name to watch: Lockheed *Lightning*. Lockheed Aircraft Corporation… Vega Aircraft Corporation… Burbank, Calif.

To be prepared for war is one of the most effectual means of preserving peace.

—Washington

right: The control yoke and instrument panel of a Lockheed P-38 Lightning at the Museum of Flying, Santa Monica, 1990.

gine manifolds was nonexistent. When you were at thirty thousand feet on bomber escort and the air temperature was –55° F outside the cockpit, it was –55° F inside the cockpit. After thirty minutes or so at such a temperature, a pilot became so numb that he was too miserable to be of any real value; to make matters worse, he did not particularly care. Only his head and neck, exposed to the direct rays of the sun, retained any warmth.

"Not only did the numbness seriously decrease a pilot's efficiency, the bulky clothing he wore further restricted his efforts. For example, I wore double-thickness silk gloves, then heavy chamois gloves and topped these with heavy leather gauntlets (all British issue). Inside all these layers were fingers almost frozen stiff and completely without feeling. Flipping a single electrical switch required deep concentration, skill and luck, and the P-38 cockpit was loaded with electrical switches. How we envied the P-47 and P-51 pilots with a heat-producing engine in front of them to maintain a decent cockpit temperature.

"Admittedly, the P-38 was outperformed by the P-47 and P-51 in the skies over Europe, but many of its difficulties were the result of unnecssary design deficiencies and the slow pace of both the AAF and Lockheed in correcting them. One can only ponder about how much more rapidly the troubles would have been remedied if the slide-rule types had been flying the plane in combat against the Luftwaffe. But I will always remember the P-38 with the greatest fondness. Even with all her idiosyncrasies, she was a real dream to fly."

62

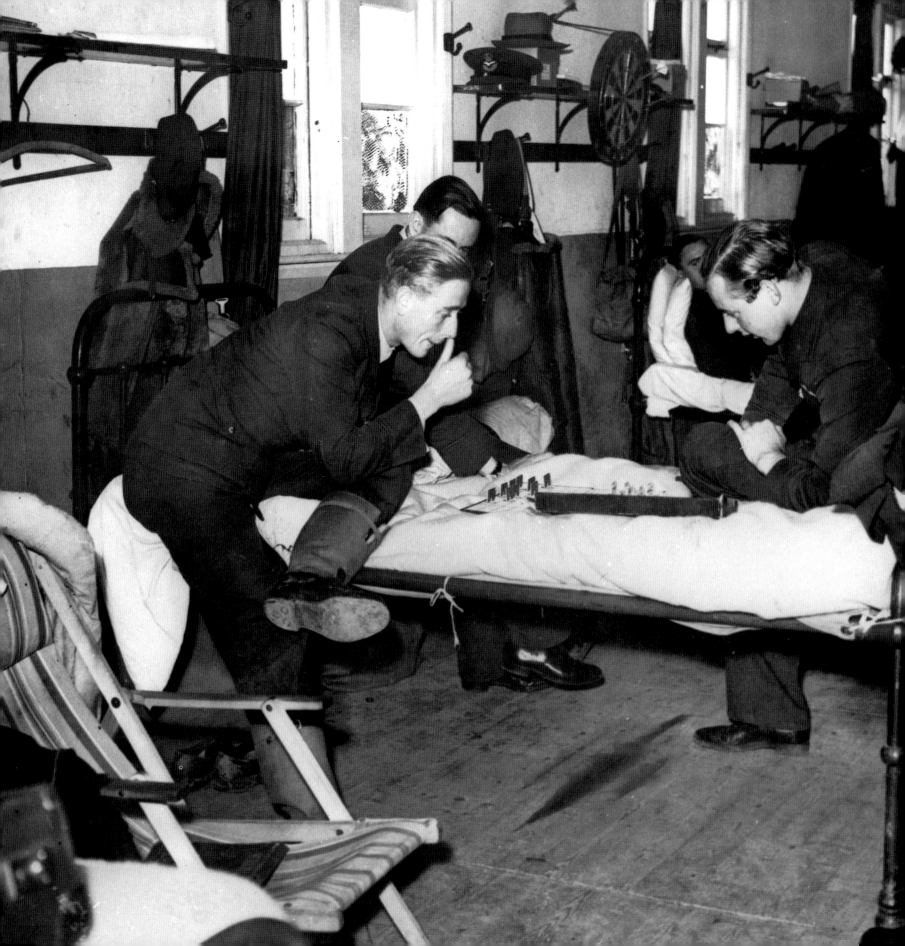

THERE HAD ALREADY BEEN the Battle of France and the air fighting over Dunkirk. But with the Battle of Britain came the most significant and sustained aerial conflict thus far in the war, and both witnesses and participants were left with profound impressions.

Pilot Officer Roger Hall was a twenty-three-year-old Spitfire pilot with No. 152 Squadron flying from Warmwell in Dorset. He describes a typical day's operations during September of 1940.

"The telephone, that prosaic little household instrument, would become your absolute master and its monotonous ring would harbinger moments of drama to come. The word 'scramble' became the code for emergency take-off at the approach of enemy aircraft, which were known as bandits. An unidentified aircraft was known as a bogey. At this time, most unidentified aircraft coming from the south were German and the majority of take-offs were scrambles."

"Pull your fingers out, Mandrake. What the bloody hell are you playing at? Get off the air, I can see them, you boys should learn to keep awake, stupid clots. Control had certainly slipped up badly here. We should have been scrambled long before the bombers had got anywhere near the English coast."

"Hallo Maida Leader—Mandrake calling—what are your angels now?—over."

"Hallo Mandrake—Maida Leader answering angels two-seven—Maida Leader over."

"We were now just starting to make vapor trails and white plumes were streaming away from each of our machines, the vapor

TAKING CARE OF BUSINESS

When the bloom is off the garden,/and I'm fighting in the sky, when the lawns and flower beds harden, and when weak birds starve and die,/and death-roll will grow longer,/eyes will be moist and red;/and the more I kill, the longer shall I miss friends who are dead.

"War"
by F/O Nigel Weir,
DFC

I do not like the way the cards are shuffled, But yet I like the game and want to play.

from "Whist"
by Eugene F. Ware

left: Pilot Officer R.G.A. Barclay (lighting pipe) and other 249 Sq. pilots in quarters at North Weald. The pilots are playing a game of L'Attaque.

from Chumley's aircraft passing over the top of my head in thick, opaque funnels. Vapor trails observed from the air seemed to give the aircraft and those flying them a sort of dignity, serene and splendid. We reached angels three-zero and the CO called up control to advise them. They told us to orbit our position and await further instructions. We began to circle now, on the turn to the south, I could see more vapor trails out to sea and a good deal higher than our own, coming toward us. The CO had seen them too. He called control, giving them the 'Tally-ho,' and told Maida squadron to start weaving behind and keep a good lookout for those 109s above us.

"Looking into the sun through my fingers, I could just make out the 109s starting to dive. Instinctively my right hand left the control column and operated the transmitter as I shouted, 'Look out, Maida aircraft—109s coming down now at six o'clock above.' I switched over to 'receive' again and Cocky at once led A Flight into a tight turn to port. I stopped weaving, to slide up close behind Chumley and follow. We practically formed a little circle, so tight was the turn, and I could almost feel the nose of Cocky's machine coming up behind my tail and felt more secure because of it. The 109s had certainly picked us out for special treatment for about eight or nine of them flashed down into the middle of our circle, going straight through it and firing like blue murder as they passed. I wondered if anyone had been hit. It seemed only a few minutes since we had first been attacked by the 109s, but I had still to fire at something. The bombers had turned south, or should I

say, the main body of them had. Quite a number had been shot down by the looks of it and Hurricanes continued to press the rest. I was going toward them, weaving violently as I went, when I saw something that was to change my whole outlook. There was a Hurricane approaching the bombers from the port rear by itself and firing at one of them. The rear gunner was replying with what must have been very accurate fire for suddenly the Hurricane became a mass of flames and the blow could only have been inflicted by the gunner, for there were no enemy fighters in the immediate vicinity.

"I watched the Hurricane turn over on its back and fall away. The pilot himself was on fire as he fell from the machine. As the Hurricane went into a shallow dive, he released his parachute but, as it opened, its shrouds caught fire. The pilot, who had now succeeded in extinguishing the flames on himself, was desperately trying to climb up the shroud lines before they burned through. I witnessed this scene with a hypnotic sort of detachment, not feeling myself able to leave as I circled above. I was thankful to see the flames go out and the parachute behave in a normal manner. I felt a great relief well up inside me, but it was to prove short-lived.

"Two 109s appeared below me coming from the north and traveling very fast toward the south as though they were intent upon getting home safely to France. I disregarded the pilot hanging from the parachute and diverted my attention to the 109s, which appeared to be climbing slowly. I felt I should get my first confirmed aircraft now and turned on

66

ROYAL AIR FORCE STATION
WARMWELL
FORMERLY WOODSFORD
1937 — 1946
A MEMORIAL DEDICATED
TO THOSE MEN AND WOMEN WHO
WHILST SERVING WITH THE ROYAL
AIR FORCE, UNITED STATES ARMY
AIR FORCE, MILITARY AND ALLIED
FORCES AT R.A.F. WARMWELL
MADE THE SUPREME SACRIFICE
IN DEFENCE OF FREEDOM.
LEST WE FORGET. IITH JUNE 1989

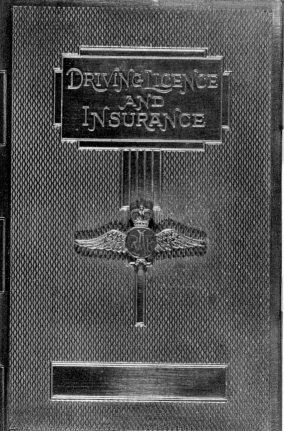

center above: The Warmwell Memorial. above right: Former 152 Sq. Spitfire pilot Roger Hall, 1990. center below: A silver-plated RAF driving license and auto insurance holder. right: A fifty-year-old RAF cap badge.

"Dispersal," the operational centre of the squadron, was a wooden hut with a telephone and an orderly constantly attending it. This was the telephone that gave us instructions to scramble. There were also twelve beds, ordinary iron beds with mattresses and blankets, arranged on the two sides of the hut. The pilots rested on them when they were at readiness, or even slept on them for the remainder of the night after a pub crawl. To come straight down to dispersal on arrival back from a pub crawl and get into bed was to ensure that one was there for readiness at dawn. If the weather were unsuitable for flying, or, as we knew it, "unoperational," well then one was able to sleep on undisturbed. Dispersal was so called because outside it the aircraft were dispersed as an obvious precaution against bombing. They were arranged in a haphazard way to minimise this possibility, although it

was as much a token dispersal as anything. They had to be accessible, and it is doubtful if any machine would have escaped a deliberate strafing or even a well placed stick of bombs had an enemy force surprised us.

from *Clouds of Fear* by Roger Hall, DFC

Alone in the silence of the hour before dawn/I speak my sorrow. For now of the living/None is left, none to learn, To know of things hidden in my soul's heart.

—Anonymous

above: 152 Sq. Sergeant Pilot Denis Robinson, Warmwell, 1940. right: Sgt. Pilot Robinson's Spitfire shortly after his harrowing crash landing near Wareham on August 8, 1940.

my back to dive on them. When I was in the dive I laid my sights well in front of the forward 109 with lots of deflection, for I was coming down upon them vertically. The leading 109 was firing and I looked to see what he was firing at but could see no other aircraft near him. Then I saw it all in a fraction of a second, but a fraction that seemed an eternity. He was firing at the pilot at the end of the parachute and he couldn't possibly miss.

"I saw the tracers and the cannon shells pierce the center of his body, which folded before the impact like a jackknife closing, like a blade of grass that bends toward the blade of the advancing scythe. I was too far away to interfere and now was too late to be of any assistance. If to see red is usually a metaphorical expression, it became a reality to me at that moment, for the red I could see was that of the pilot's blood as it gushed from all the quarters of his body. I expected to see the lower part of his body fall away to reveal the entrails dangling in midair but by some miracle his body held together. His hands, but a second before clinging to the safety of the shroud lines, were now relaxed and hung limp at his sides. His whole body was limp also, like a man just hanged, the head resting across one shoulder, bloody, scarlet with blood, the hot, rich blood of youth that had coursed through his veins for perhaps not more than nineteen or twenty years. It had now completely covered and dyed red an English face that looked down on but no longer saw its native soil.

"I now noticed black smoke coming away from Chumley's machine and I thought at first his engine was on fire. The smoke was

sweeping past my own aircraft and instinctively I looked to see what was behind us, but there was nothing. 'Christ, I'm on fire!' was all that came from Chumley as he realized his predicament. He was apparently throttling his engine back, for I could see the blades of his prop slow down and finally stop altogether. I felt a sensation of horror for an instant, expecting to see his machine burst into flames at any moment, and drew back some distance behind him. I seemed unable to say anything to him on the RT, thinking that nothing I could say would be of any use.

"Chumley pulled his aircraft round in a shallow turn to starboard, slowing down considerably as he went, his propeller quite still. I expected to see him bail out and hoped he would. The smoke seemed to get a little less severe, so his engine must have been cooling off. 'I'm going to make for Tangmere, Roger,' I heard him say, and saw him dive his machine out of the turn and in the direction of Tangmere, which was some way to the east of Southampton Water. 'Are you OK?' I asked. 'Oil pipe's gone for a Burton,' he told me. I said I would stick around until he got down lower and he said, 'OK, I'll be all right.'

"When we had got down to five thousand feet the smoke from Chumley's machine had all but stopped and he was now above the aerodrome at Tangmere, maneuvering into position for a forced landing. I stayed at five thousand feet and watched him land, which he did with wheels down, and get out of the aircraft. I could see a lot of smoke coming from the forward part of the aircraft, but the crash tenders and fire engines were already spraying

Optimism: A cheerful frame of mind that enables/a tea kettle to sing though in hot water up to its nose.

—Anonymous

foam all over it. I started to climb up again toward the northwest to see if I could find the others. I felt a bit shaken but I seemed to be getting inured to this sort of thing and felt fairly well blooded. When I reached fifteen thousand feet again I checked my fuel, flew back to base and landed. I did not feel like talking and went to bed; but I was restless and sleep came slowly.

"There existed no counterpart to our mode of life in any other sphere of human experience on earth. None could gauge or even hope to intrude into our thoughts who had not lived similarly. Our mental wavelength was unique."

Roger Hall's operational flying experiences exacted a heavy personal price. As a result of the prolonged mental stresses of combat, he lost his flying category in 1942 and became another "casualty" of the air war.

Sergeant Denis Robinson also flew Spitfires with 152 Squadron and, like Roger Hall, his Battle of Britain experiences have left him in continuing wonder at his own survival. The following occurred on August 8, 1940:

"The facts are not particularly gratifying for either myself or Pilot Officer Beaumont, who ended up being shot down with me that day. We were returning from a patrol in which we had intercepted the enemy and had used up all our ammunition. We were going back to Warmwell to refuel and re-arm. There were three of us flying in vic formation with Beaumont on the left of the flight leader and myself on the right. We were getting ready for the approach to Warmwell and flying in very tight formation. When I say tight, I mean tight—

left: Frank Wootton's painting, "Spitfires in the Rain," 609 (West Riding) Squadron, the first Spitfire squadron to score 100 victories. below: Denis Robinson, 1990.

probably less than a foot from the leader's wingtips. Therefore, Beaumont and I had our eyes and concentration firmly fixed on the leader's aircraft. We were preparing to give Warmwell a bit of a show on arrival. Unfortunately, a couple of ME 109s had ideas for a different kind of show. They spotted us and carried out an attack on our unprotected rear, which we had offered them on a plate. We ought to have known better, and did. We knew that it was vital to keep a good lookout at all times, but were lulled into a false sense of security and had relaxed our vigilance briefly. After all, we had had our scrap . . . were nearly safely home and, anyway, we had no ammo.

"The first thing I knew was the thud of bullets hitting my aircraft and a long line of tracer bullets from the attacker streaming out ahead of my Spitfire. I slammed the stick forward as far as it would go. For a brief second my Spitfire stood on its nose and I was looking straight down at Mother Earth, ten thousand feet below. Thank God my Sutton harness was good and tight. I could feel the straps biting into my flesh as I entered the vertical with airspeed building up alarmingly. I felt fear mounting. Sweating, mouth dry and near panic. No ammo and an attacker right on my tail. All this happened in seconds, but now the airspeed was nearly off the clock. I simply had to pull out and start looking for the enemy. That's what I did, turning and climbing at the same time. As I opened the throttle fully to assist the climb, I noticed little wisps of white smoke coming from the nose of my fighter. God, no! Fire! Suddenly, the engine stopped. Apparently a bullet in the glycol tank had

dispersed all the coolant and even the faithful Merlin could not stand that for long at full power. So that explained the white smoke. Blessed relief. The dread of being burned to death was one of the worst fears. It drew heavily on any reserves of courage one had. You can imagine that by now, my eyes were searching . . . wildly, frantically looking for my adversary—but, as often happens in air combat, not a single plane was to be seen in the sky around me. The release of tension as I realized my good fortune is something that cannot be described. You only know what it feels like to be given back your life if you have been through that experience. The monumental problems that still confronted me, sitting in the cockpit of a battle-damaged Spitfire with an inoperative engine, seemed almost trivial in comparison with my situation of a few seconds before. This experience had a profound effect on me and remains with me to this day. Nothing ever assumed quite the same degree of importance again.

"The end of the episode was something of an anticlimax. I still had plenty of altitude and time to think. I prepared to bail out and began going through the procedure in my mind. Release the Sutton harness, make sure all connections to flying helmet are free, slide the canopy back, roll the aircraft until inverted, push the stick forward and out you go. Then start counting—how many? My memory went blank. Was it three or ten? God! There is a vast difference between the two, I thought. Well, as long as the interval is sufficient to get clear of the aircraft before pulling the D-ring it should be OK. During this soliloquy I'd got the Spit into a steady glide. It was flying reasonably well and responding to the controls almost normally. I surveyed the damage from the cockpit. Not much, apart from a few bullet holes here and there—particularly in the starboard wing. It seemed a shame to abandon the old bus to certain destruction. After all, she'd served me well and didn't we need aircraft almost as much as pilots? Besides, I was by no means convinced that the bail-out procedure I had rehearsed was not without considerable risk. I could get caught up in the cockpit paraphernalia . . . I might be struck by the tailplane . . . or what if the parachute didn't open? No. I convinced myself it was too dangerous. I would stay with her and force-land in a suitable field. By now most of the fields looked pretty small, so I decided it would be

wheels-up. I picked a field that looked suitable, slid back the canopy and commenced an approach. At about two hundred feet the boundary loomed up. Full flap and a flare-out near the ground achieved a creditable touchdown. So far so good. I was quite pleased with myself as the Spit slithered across the grass. Then suddenly, I felt her going up onto her nose and, I thought, over onto her back. With an almighty crash the canopy slammed shut over my head and the cockpit filled with dust, completely blinding me. The aircraft seemed to be upside-down and I was trapped. That awful fear of burning returned at full strength. I grabbed the canopy with all my might and threw it backward. To my utter amazement it shot back easily, and the excessive adrenaline-boosted force I had used nearly tore my arms

All done and over—
That day long ago—
The white cliffs of
Dover—/Little did I
know.

from "The White Cliffs
of Dover"
by Alice Duer Miller

left: P/O R.G.A. Barclay of
249 Squadron, RAF. below:
The Air-Sea Rescue
Squadron of the RAF
saved the lives of hundreds
of downed pilots and
airmen in WWII. Here a
rescued pilot is being
hauled from his dinghy,
aboard a Walrus
amphibian.

above: Charles Neville Overton, who was a pilot officer in 609 Squadron, RAF. above right: The Horse and Jockey was a regular stop for RAF fighter pilots at nearby Wellingore and Digby. right: A pillbox on Chesil Beach, Dorset, near Warmwell. far right: An intricate, mazelike trench shelter in a wood at the former RAF fighter station Hawkinge, near Dover.

from their sockets. Now I could see that the aircraft had finished up vertically on its nose, in a ditch I hadn't seen from the air.

"My actions now became somewhat comic. It was obvious that I could easily jump clear and I commenced to do so without much hesitation. To my utter horror, I couldn't move. Suddenly, I realized I was struggling against the Sutton harness, still buckled firmly in place. An instant pull released the pin. I was free. As I stood up to jump my head was jerked violently backwards. This time it was my flying helmet still attached to the radio and oxygen sockets in the cockpit. Removing this final impediment I jumped to the ground, leaving my helmet in the cockpit. To my surprise, the Spitfire didn't burn. I stood back and took in the scene as locals arrived to convey me off to a pub in nearby Wareham and fill me with whisky. I had a slight bullet graze on my left hand but was otherwise unhurt and felt strangely elated. Next day I was back on ops again."

Robinson's survival was probably attributable to two factors. First, his instant reaction of stick hard forward into a vertical dive and the resultant smoke from his engine may have convinced the ME 109 pilot that he had been successful in his attack, or perhaps Robinson had caused the attacker to overshoot his target. Second, ME 109s operating over the Dorset coast far from their French bases were short of fuel and couldn't hang around at length in a dogfight or chase situation. For Denis Robinson, telling his story is a cathartic experience. "In a difficult-to-describe way, it is as though I'm speaking for the chaps who did not make it. Their final story would have been infinitely more readable then mine, but telling my tale has helped me to deal with my survival syndrome. One constantly asks: 'Why did I survive . . . why did others not?' "

Let us, then, be up and doing,/With a heart for any fate;/Still achieving, still pursuing,/Learn to labor and to wait.

from "A Psalm of Life" by Longfellow

75

GROUND-BOUND

STAFF SERGEANT MERLE OLMSTED was an aircraft mechanic serving with the 362nd Fighter Squadron, 357th Fighter Group, at Leiston near the Suffolk coast. He rose to assistant crew chief and later to crew chief, responsible for a P-51D Mustang fighter.

"Aircraft Maintenance—in those days it was called the Engineering Section—consisted of the flight-line crews, usually three men: two mechanics (the crew chief and assistant crew chief) and an armorer. For every four aircraft there was a flight chief to coordinate requirements and activities. Then there were two hangar crews, each operating on twelve-hour shifts. They did things that could not be done out on the line, such as engine changes. Assigned to the hangar crews were an electrician and a propeller man. Each squadron also had its assigned painter and carpenter. For heavy maintenance, we had the 469th Service Squadron on base. They were not a part of the fighter group, but were certainly part of the 'family.'

"We were always busy, routinely so. There was some boredom broken by occasional excitement. The schedule of the flight-line crews depended on the briefing times for the pilots. The mechanics were awakened each morning by the CQ, who turned on the lights and always said something like: 'Briefing at 0730, maximum effort, maximum range.' We usually, but not always, went to breakfast first. Often, one of the two of us would go directly to the aircraft and start the preflight while the other one went to breakfast first. That way one of us would be at the airplane all the time. On arriving there, all aircraft covers

would be removed and a walkaround inspection made to see if any leaks had developed overnight. Drop tanks, which had been fitted the night before, were fueled. The propeller was pulled through four to six blades. The battery cart was hooked up and the engine was started for a brief run-up to high power, to check mag drop, pressure and temperatures. The fuel selector was switched to the left and right tanks to draw fuel into the lines, which would make the engine cut out a few times until the lines were full . . . which was why this little operation had to be done on the ground. With these essential preparations complete, there remained other work to be done before the pilots came to their planes.

"The tanks would be topped off to replace the few gallons used in the run-up. About then, the armorer would arrive to charge the guns. When his preflight was completed, there was just enough time for last-minute details like polishing the windshield and canopy. Smears or specks on the Plexiglas caused distractions and distortions, and sometimes recriminations from the pilots. Worse, such seemingly minor flaws might lead to a pilot not coming home. The ground crews did their best to maintain the aircraft perfectly for their pilots.

"The pilot would arrive and I would help him strap in and hook up. Then it was start-up time, the chocks were pulled, the Mustang taxied out to its assigned position for take-off. Then, they were gone. My buddies and I would watch them go with a sense of relief and not a little envy.

"Now it was time to sit around and sweat

Sometimes you waited and they didn't come back. Sometimes your plane came back and you saw others waiting and theirs didn't come back. Fortunately, although the planes didn't come back, quite often the pilots did. In fact, one time . . . it was at Elm Park underground station, and two of our pilots came up out of the station with their parachutes tucked under their arms. They'd come back from their sorties by underground.

—Dave Davies,
AC1 Engine Fitter
232 (Natal) Squadron,
Hornchurch

For want of a nail the shoe was lost;/for want of a shoe the horse was lost;/and for want of a horse the rider was lost;/being overtaken and slain by the enemy . . .

from *Poor Richard's Almanac*
by Benjamin Franklin

Good luck is a lazy man's estimate/of a worker's success.

—Anonymous

left: USAAF ground crewmen carefully load .50 caliber linked ammunition into the wing of their fighter.

above: In 1989, Merle Olmsted, formerly an aircraft mechanic and crew chief in the 357th Fighter Group at Leiston . . . and Hubert "Hub" Zemke, former commanding officer of the 56th fighter Group, "Zemke's Wolfpack," at Halesworth. right: A P-47 Thunderbolt is prepared for action by its ground crew in WWII England. far right: The Air Ministry tool kit of an RAF aircraft mechanic, 1940–45.

it out. Free time for the ground crews. Since the planes were usually gone during the noon hour, we would go to midday chow. I remember that the food was not really bad, considering the circumstances, but being a picky eater I passed up the meals I didn't like. If the mission being flown was an especially rough one the waiting ground crews might not be too hungry. When I didn't care for the chow I would go over to the small PX on base and make do with a candy bar. An officer presided over that PX and, as he appeared to have very little to do, I decided that the next time around I would like to be a PX officer. Then it was time to get back to the flight line so I walked, biked or caught a ride out for the final wait.

"The way the aircraft looked as they returned told the ground crews a lot. Were they in the same formation as at departure, or were they straggling in? Where was *Joan* and what was wrong with *Rolla V*? Was that *Floogie II* doing a victory roll? Soon they were all back— at least all those who were coming back.

"As the Mustangs rolled into the dispersals the gun muzzles were observed to see if the red tape covers had been shot away, indicating combat. A final blip of throttle brought each fighter swinging around to a stop on the hardstand. The propeller would mill to a stop, the canopy back and harness undone, greetings were shouted between pilot and ground crewmen. 'Did you get anything?' 'What happened to *Joan*?' 'Any defects, sir?' As the pilot climbed from his cockpit and went off to debriefing, the ground crew was already at work . . . covers off the guns . . . postflight checks

WIRELESS /MEC TOOL BOX USED BY
CPL W RAY 1940-1945. ALL ITEMS
ARE GENUINE AND MARKED A.M 1939

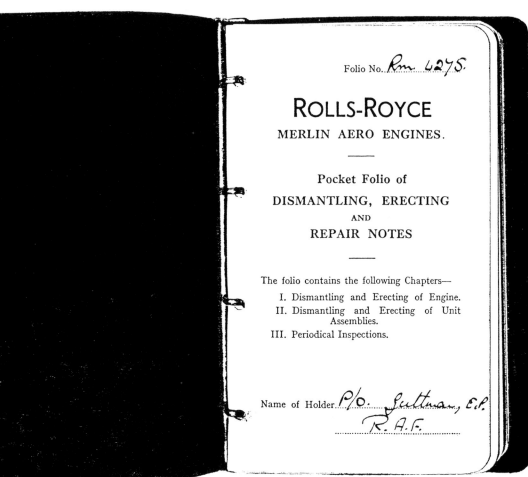

Folio No. *Rm. 4275.*

ROLLS-ROYCE

MERLIN AERO ENGINES.

———

Pocket Folio of

DISMANTLING, ERECTING

AND

REPAIR NOTES

———

The folio contains the following Chapters—

  I. Dismantling and Erecting of Engine.
 II. Dismantling and Erecting of Unit
     Assemblies.
III. Periodical Inspections.

Name of Holder *P/O. Guttman, E.P.*
                      R. A. F.

. . . new drop tanks fitted . . . oil washed from the crankcase breather. Popping and cracking as the hot engine cooled, our plane sat on its concrete pan and we replaced the covers on the canopy and pitot tube, secured the control locks in place and, finally, went off to evening chow. Then back to our living quarters. Maybe there would be a chance to get away from the base for a few hours. Tomorrow would be just the same as today. The food, the cold, the mud and, really, a lot of satisfaction in the jobs we were doing. That experience was one of the high points of my life."

Eighteen-year-old Eric Marsden was posted to 145 Squadron at Kenley as a Fitter II E just before the Battle of Britain. "When I got there I found out they had gone! Someone thought that 145 had gone to Croydon, but when I got there the afterguard was all that was left. No. 145 had moved on to Filton, but we were to go down to Tangmere the next day where the squadron was to be based."

In view of the frantic and confused military situation of the period, the bureaucracy that had left Eric chasing 145 around southern England may be excused. The squadron was soon to be whipped into an efficient unit. Ultimately, that efficiency would mean a squadron of serviceable Hurricanes with confident and combat-ready pilots. Certainly the glamour and recognition would go to the pilots, the CO and flight commanders, but serviceability and the pilot's confidence and feeling of security about the aircraft would be seen to by the ground crews. Just as the pilots were molded into a battle "team" by the squadron and flight commanders, the ground crews were led and inspired by effective leaders. The officer-in-charge was the engineering officer, but each of the squadron's flights, A and B, had its NCO-in-charge. Eric was in B Flight.

"The NCO-in-charge was known as Chiefy, even to his face, once one was accepted. Irreverently, this particular one was known as Jesus from his cherubic face and halo of golden curls, albeit thinning from advanced age. He was in his thirties.

"On the early Hurricanes the compressed-air system was maintained in flight by a BTH compressor. We had to check the oil level through a spring-loaded plunger and the only way of getting the castor oil in was with the flight's one and only syringe. It could take quite a time to go to the store, find that the syringe was out and then track it down along the flight line. Then there were the cowlings. The top engine cowlings, and the extra-thick cowl over the fuselage tank, could be absolute pigs to replace. Fitting them was an art involving heavy blows with the flat of the hand in just the right places, and most were individual to particular kites. Sometimes cowling up after a daily inspection could take longer than the inspection itself. Daily inspections were the routine checks that each airplane was subjected to to keep it in tip-top order, with each prescribed check meticulously entered in the aircraft's logbook. RAF Form 700 had to be signed and countersigned. I was 'engines' but I had a rigger as a partner for the DIs. We each

above left: 357th Fighter Group mechanics at Leiston unpacking new 108-gallon pressed-paper long-range droppable fighter fuel tanks. left: A Rolls-Royce factory handbook for the Merlin aero engine. below: USAAF ground crewmen awaiting the return of their fighter group from a mission into occupied Europe.

They also serve who only stand and wait.

—Milton

had our own specified jobs according to our trade schedules. Check all fastenings, pipe joints, etc. Check and topup oil, fuel, coolant, oxygen. Such routine, however, was not without its problems. Every Hurricane built was equipped with a special Hawker tool, a combined tank-cap key/screwdriver to fit the fasteners of the removable cowlings, panels and fairings. Unfortunately, everyone down the delivery chain, from manufacturer to squadron, was convinced they had to have one. That meant that we who really needed to have one didn't. We had to make do. But lack of proper equipment to do the job was not confined to just specialized tools. We couldn't get soft cloth or Perspex polish for the Perspex and glass of the cockpits and had to use our own Bluebell or Brasso and whatever rags we could scrounge up. One day, our flight commander came back in a towering rage. Instead of getting down from his kite he ordered the rigger and myself up onto the wing. 'Look at that,' he said, pointing to the tiniest speck in the righthand lower corner of the windscreen. 'I've had the entire flight chasing that damned speck all over France.' He tore us off a proper strip, but when Chiefy explained the shortages he vanished in the direction of Main Stores. Presumably he expressed his opinions in a similar fashion because after that there were no more shortages of these materials.

"Actually, the ground crews practically worshiped their pilots. By July and August of 1940 our pilots were getting distinctly 'frayed around the edges' and I know that one or two considered themselves 'write-offs.' It didn't affect their flying or their attitude to fight-

left: A wooden ammunition box (cannon rounds) from WWII England. top: Armorers of the 4th Fighter Group, Debden, ready their 336th Fighter Squadron P-51C Mustang for its next mission. above: A surviving painted reminder to 357th FG aircraft mechanics at Leiston, 1990.

ing—it was just that they no longer had any hope of survival for themselves. It was a grievous time for us on the ground. We could do little to help. We couldn't take their places— though most of us would have given anything for the chance—and it probably wouldn't be incorrect to say that our respect and liking for our pilots almost became a kind of love at this time. We had to watch them—indeed, help them—take off to go and die in ones and twos. To make matters worse the fitters, riggers, armorers and aircraft hands of 145 could often hear their pilots in action, fighting and dying. A loudspeaker above the crewroom door al-

lowed us to hear the radio chatter between our pilots in the air, sometimes a facility of dubious value. Hearing someone you like in dire trouble can be quite unfunny."

For the ground types like Eric, there was no socializing with the pilots. The pilots were mostly officers. The ground crews, who toiled under the hot sun, in freezing cold and rain, with bloodied fingers and soiled clothes, were a breed apart. They were "other ranks" or NCOs, and RAF protocol and King's Regulations forbade fraternization between them and the officers. Nevertheless, a friendliness that stopped just short of familiarity transcended the taboos of officialdom. "We ground crew had a good relationship with our pilots. Not of the 'Hi Mac' variety as with our U.S. friends later in the war . . . but they did take the trouble to know us by name and we could—and did—talk with them about the war, the squadron affairs and the daily round." Thumbing his nose at authority, and crossing the officer–other ranks divide, Pilot Officer Roy Marchand, a Hurricane pilot with 73 Squadron, recalled his feeling for his own "nuts-and-bolts" team in a letter home that he concluded with: "Must close now. I want to go and stand my fitter and rigger a beer or two. Boy, they deserve it."

The privilege of rank and flying was not all that separated the pilots from the "erks." There was also the pay. If the pilot's pay was poor, then that given to the lesser mortals on the ground must be classed as miserly. Eric recalls: "As Leading Aircraftman/Flight Mechanic, I think I was then on three shillings and sixpence per day. That's what it was in 1939 as an RAF (Volunteer Reserve) Fitter II E Under Training. Some time after the war started we were told that we had been remustered as Flight Mechanics (Under Training) at two shillings per day and we would have to repay the difference from September 2 in deductions! This meant that for some time we only got one shilling and sixpence per week— the service minimum upon which it was reckoned that we could clean our shoes and buttons. It made you glad to be a volunteer and not a conscript. . . . " At that time, the most junior rank of pilot officer in the General Duties (Flying) branch of the RAF (VR) could

expect to pocket the princely sum of eleven shillings per day.

At the height of that summer 145 Squadron was operating from Westhampnett, a small grass airfield just down the road from Tangmere (which controlled Westhampnett administratively). It was here that Eric grew to know his pilots. "There was Flight Lieutenant Adrian Boyd, the B Flight commander, 'Boydy' to one and all. For me he has always been one of the great pilots of the war—as much for his ability to lead and train men, as for his ability as a fighter pilot. If his 'scores' were not up with the top aces this was undoubtedly through his habit of crediting 'kills' to beginner pilots. Another was Pilot Officer Nigel Weir. He was very keen to get a German Mae West. They were considered far superior to the RAF-issue ones and highly prized. Nigel Weir was so anxious to get his that he landed in a field alongside a German kite he had shot down. He must have startled the farmer's wife by borrowing a bucket in which to carry the prize home between his legs on the floor of the Hurricane. It was somewhat bloody and he had it soaking in water, but he wore it with considerable pride once it was cleaned up. Another favorite among the ground crews of 145 was a Pole, Flight Lieutenant Pankratz. Whenever he was asked how many Jerries he had shot down in a fight, he would say: 'I'm not interested in how many I have shot down—only in how many are left.' "

Eric Marsden and Merle Olmsted will not forget their pilots. Nor will their pilots forget those who were ground-bound.

Ten Little Fighter boys taking off in Line/ One was in coarse pitch, then there were nine/ Nine little fighter boys climbing "through the gate"/One's petrol wasn't on, then there were eight/Eight little fighter boys scrambling up to heaven/One weaver didn't and then there were seven/Seven little fighter boys up to all the tricks/One had a hangover then there were six/Six little fighter boys milling over Hythe/One's pressure wasn't up and then there were five/ Five little fighter boys over France's shore/ One flew reciprocal and then there were four/ Four little fighter boys joining in the spree/ One's sight wasn't on and then there were three/Three little fighter boys high up in the blue/One's rubber pipe was loose then there were two/Two little fighter boys homing out of sun/Flew straight and level and then there was one/One little fighter boy happy to be home/Beat up dispersal and then there were none/Ten little Spitfires nothing have achieved/A.O.C. at Group is very very peeved/"Fifty thousand Smackers thrown down the drains/'Cause ten silly baskets didn't use their brains"

left: The enlisted men's club on a USAAF fighter station in England.

ON THE NOSE

IN THE LONG HISTORY of warfare man has decorated his weaponry, the primary purpose being to identify and distinguish friend from foe. In addition to national insignia and unit markings, the aircraft of World War II bore colorful designs motivated by individual pride, superstition and the desire to personalize them.

RAF fighter pilots, reflecting their Air Ministry's staid and conservative policy, tended to be restrained in decorating their aircraft.

If you wish in this world to advance/Your merits you're bound to enhance;/You must stir it and stump it,/And blow your own trumpet,/Or, trust me, you haven't a chance.

from *Ruddigore* by W. S. Gilbert

It was a wonderful feeling seeing my own VF-P all painted up in the morning light. I'd given Larry two pounds for the painter to do a good job. Written in letters four inches high in front of the cockpit was *Reggie's Reply*, and on the cowling there was a picture of Lucky (my dog) looking out of a horseshoe.

from *The Look of Eagles* by John T. Godfrey

far left: Original artwork for the design applied to the aircraft of then-Squadron Leader Douglas Bader, 242 (Canadian) Squadron. left: A fighting eagle representation on The Fighter Collection's Hurricane, Duxford Airfield, 1990.

right: A "presentation" Spitfire. center: The P-38 Lightning of Capt. Mark Shipman. below: The P-51 Mustang of Lt. Ralph K. Hofer, 4th Fighter Group, Debden.

Gentlemen of the Jury: The one, absolute, unselfish friend that man can have in this selfish world, the one that never deserts him, the one that never proves ungrateful/or treacherous, is his dog.

"Eulogy on the Dog" by Senator George Graham Vest

HENDON PEGASUS

Texas Ranger

Salem Represen

U.S. ARMY P-51B-15-NA
SERIAL NO. AAF 42-106924

SUITABLE FOR AROMATIC FUEL

"Ferocious Frankie," the P-51D of 361st FG pilot Wallace E. Hopkins, at Bottisham.

There were, however, a few exceptions. Flying Officer Richard Stevens of 151 Squadron emblazoned the entire engine cowling of his Hurricane with a magnificent dragon and eagle. Many of 43 Squadron's Hurricanes wore the striking and colorful "fighting cock" emblem of the squadron on their cowlings. Somewhat more conventional were the designs applied to "presentation" or "gift" airplanes purchased by public subscription. These machines often carried the crest of the sponsoring community. *Hendon Pegasus* was one such Spitfire, donated through the Hendon Spitfire Fund. The most famous of RAF fighter art was probably that applied to the Hurricanes of Douglas Bader's 242 Squadron during 1940. Depicting a flying boot kicking an Adolf Hitler caricature in the buttocks, it was an unusually bold design for the time.

The Germans often painted their fighters with bright yellow, red, white or green unit-identification marks and favored the use of shields and crests in heraldic styles. The Messerschmitts flown through much of the war (and in Spain before it) by the well-known fighter leader Adolf Galland were decorated with a likeness of Mickey Mouse. Galland has confided in recent years that the cartoon character, which happened to have been created around the time of the Spanish Civil War, was one that he especially admired.

In explosions of candy stripes and checkerboards, the U.S. Army Air Force marked its fighters to indicate fighter groups, with an additional color to show the squadron within the group. This was usually denoted by a single dominant color on the rudder fin. The

far left: An example of German nose art now preserved in the Tangmere Military Aviation Museum.
center left: A colorful representation of the 43 Squadron "fighting cock."
left: A personalized 603 (City of Edinburgh) Squadron Spitfire.

The boast of heraldry, the pomp of pow'r, And all that beauty, all that wealth e'er gave, Awaits alike th' inevitable hour./The paths of glory lead but to the grave.

from "Elegy Written in a Country Churchyard" by Thomas Gray

The Eagle Squadron emblem on The Fighter Collection (Duxford Airfield) Hurricane that has been painted to represent an aircraft flown by Pilot Officer Andrew Mamedoff, 609, 71 and 133 Squadrons.

SO WHAT THE HELL

"Miss BOX

Every man has three
characters—/that
which he exhibits,/that
which he has,/and that
which he thinks he has.

—Alphonse Karr

The DEACON

356th Fighter Group at Martlesham Heath carried red spinners with a red-and-blue diamond pattern on the cowlings of its Mustangs; the 359th at East Wretham had emerald-green spinners with a matching cowling band, and the 78th at Duxford showed a black-and-white checkerboard pattern on its cowlings. Together with the large star-and-bar national insignia, it made for one of the most colorful air forces ever assembled. There was a suggestion of the medieval jousting knight about the look. The pilots were the knights, the airplanes their chargers and the colors their decorated helmets and shields.

Individual, pilot-originated markings were another matter and became a unique art form. The most popular place for such decoration was on the nose of the aircraft, or sometimes beneath the cockpit rail. It was often a sexy pinup girl, and some airplanes were named for the pilot's wife, a sweetheart or daughter. And there were nicknames such as *Miss Behavin'*, *Mama's Boy*, *Hun Hunter*, *Passion Wagon*, *Nooky Booky* and *Morphine Sue*.

Kill markings were used by all the air forces to display their scores of enemy aircraft claimed. They often took the form of their opponent's national symbol or colors such as the row of swastikas below Robert Stanford-Tuck's cockpit canopy, the line of Iron Crosses on Don Gentile's fuselage or the RAF roundels designed as victory tabs on Werner Mölders' rudder. Whatever form it took, however, the decoration of fighter planes in World War II reflected the personalities of the men who flew them.

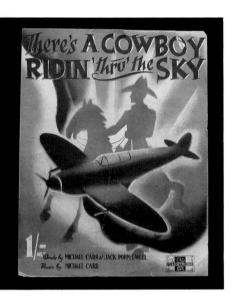

Wake, friend, from forth thy lethargy! The drum/Beats brave and loud in Europe, and bids come/All that dare rouse: or are not loth to quit/Their vicious ease, and be o'erwhelmed with it./It is a call to keep the spirits alive That gasp for action, and would yet revive Man's buried honour, in his sleepy life:

from "An Epistle to a Friend, to Persuade Him to the Wars" by Ben Jonson

above right: James Gray. top right: Carroll "Red" McColpin. right: Arthur Roscoe. far right: The Eagle Squadrons memorial in Grosvenor Square, London.

ON BECOMING AN EAGLE

AMERICAN FIGHTER PILOTS had been serving with the Royal Air Force since the first year of the war. Their numbers remain a disputed issue since in order to circumvent the U.S. Neutrality Act many assumed Canadian or South African nationality.

Charles Sweeny, a wealthy American businessman living in London in 1940, had noted the growing number of American volunteer fliers coming to England and began organizing them into a cohesive fighting unit—the Eagle Squadron. Approved by the British Air Ministry in September 1940, the Eagles were to operate within their own exclusive squadrons in RAF Fighter Command, numbers 71, 121 and 133. The first of the Eagles, 71 Squadron, was formed with Hurricanes at Kirton-in-Lindsey, in Lincolnshire.

In the United States a clandestine organization known as the Clayton Knight Committee helped and advised prospective candidates to become Eagles. Then, from Canada, the fledglings had to run the transatlantic gauntlet of U-boats before actually becoming Eagles in Britain. And there were other obstacles. James A. Gray joined No. 71 Squadron via the Clayton Knight organization. "It was a curious situation. I didn't have to register for the draft . . . so I didn't have a draft notice . . . so I wasn't trying to avoid the draft, which a number of the chaps were. I had been flying out of Oakland Airport where I soloed, and then went to the University of

California where I joined the Civil Pilot Training Program and got myself another hundred hours or so of flying time. About then, word was circulated around Oakland Airport that the British were recruiting for the RAF. It was sort of subrosa, though, because they really weren't allowed to. I had applied to the Army Air Corps and been turned down, and I was really eager to fly with an air force—any air force. So, I signed up. I took some exams from a retired Air Corps major who was a medico down in Berkeley. Then, I was assigned to Bakersfield on July 1, 1940."

Four schools were set up for training pilots in the United States, as a part of the British Refresher Training Course: at Dallas, Tulsa, Glendale and Bakersfield. They provided eighty percent of the ultimate total of 243 Eagle Squadron pilots. Jim Gray recalls his fourteen-day voyage from Halifax, Nova Scotia, to England: "It was a boat which used to ply the Caribbean. About five days out of Liverpool, a huge storm developed and our old banana boat just couldn't keep formation with the convoy of some eighty or so ships. The deal was that everyone would keep formation on the slowest ship in the convoy. About eight knots. Well, the commodore of the convoy radioed that everyone was on their own and, for about four days, we were just that. On our own. We were a little nervous because some time earlier, a ship in another convoy had been torpedoed and had gone down with some prospective Eagle types on it. Eleven were rescued but five were lost."

Safely in London and still officially civilians, the new Eagles were quickly fitted for

94

Now fades the glimmering landscape on the sight,/And all the air a solumn stillness holds.

from "Elegy Written in a Country Churchyard" by Thomas Gray

above right: Vic Buono and Art Roscoe, 71 (Eagle) Sq. far right: Eugene "Red" Tobin, killed on 71 Squadron's first sweep over France, after an attack by ME 109s on September 7, 1941. below right: Sam Mauriello at rest.

RAF uniforms at Moss Bros. Clothing Store, and given the most junior rank of pilot officer. From Number 3 Personnel Reception Centre at Bournemouth they were sent to Number 56 Operational Training Unit (OTU) at Sutton Bridge, Norfolk. Graduating as a fighter pilot, Jim Gray was posted to 71 Squadron, Martlesham Heath, Suffolk, its new base, in December 1941. The squadron had seen action since February 5, 1941.

Other American pilots had already been flying and fighting with the Royal Air Force, Red Tobin, Shorty Keough, Andy Mamedoff, Billy Fiske and Hack Russell among them. Fiske died in the Battle of Britain, and Russell had been killed over the beaches of Dunkirk. Mamedoff, Keough and Tobin were all killed later in the war.

Problems plagued the Eagle Squadrons from the beginning. The RAF was extremely wary of American leadership of any of its squadrons. A British officer, Squadron Leader Walter M. Churchill, was put in charge of 71 Squadron. The unit was part of No. 12 Group, RAF, which was under the command of Air Vice Marshal Trafford Leigh-Mallory, who had made no secret of his distaste for American fliers in the Royal Air Force. Even the Air Officer Commanding, RAF Fighter Command, Sholto Douglas, expressed reservations about the Eagles to the visiting Commanding General, U.S. Army Air Corps, Henry H. "Hap" Arnold. The future seemed precarious for the Eagles; and in America, the FBI had been making it difficult for the Clayton Knight Committee to operate, and had made it known that the Neutrality Act would be

strictly enforced. Then, however, Winston Churchill himself intervened in support of Charles Sweeny's original Eagle Squadron concept, which the British Air Council was now opposing. And, in a fortunate decision for the Eagles, 71 Squadron was transferred out of Leigh-Mallory's 12 Group and posted to Martlesham Heath as a part of 11 Group. At last the Eagles were down in the main battle zone and seeing action.

The fortunes of 71 Squadron improved and, with the increasing numbers of American volunteer fighter pilots en route to England, two additional Eagle Squadrons were soon formed—121 at Kirton-in-Lindsey and 133 at Coltishall. Many of the Eagles, and not exclusively those in 71, were to become leading aces in the U.S. 8th Air Force, Don Blakeslee, Don Gentile, Richard Peterson, and Howard "Deacon" Hively among them.

Jim Gray: "Bob Sprague and I were out on an air-sea rescue duty after a big raid on Düsseldorf. A lot of the bombers were strewn out across the North Sea, so we went to try to locate them and escort Walrus amphibians or ships that might pick the crews up. While we were on this duty, we encountered some ME 109s. We were at two thousand feet and a couple of them were flying down below us, so Bob says 'Hey, let's go down and get 'em.' So down we went. Well, some other 109s joined in the fray and I was kind of circling round when one got on my tail. I shook him off but, as I turned out of it, there was another 109 on Bob's tail, all set to do some damage. Luckily, I was able to position myself well and sent the German splashing into the sea, and the other

Where did you come
from, baby dear?/
Out of the everywhere
into here.

from "At the Back of
the North Wind"
by George MacDonald

109s withdrew. We continued our patrol after that. Bob's number two was a fabulous guy called "Deacon" Hively who would later achieve fame with the 4th Fighter Group at Debden. This was his first operation."

No. 71, the first Eagle Squadron, was getting a lot of attention. But it would not be the first choice of Carroll "Red" McColpin, who considered himself a careful and professional pilot. He wanted to fly and he wanted to fight. But he also wanted to live. In his opinion, there was a certain playboy-adventurer element in 71 Squadron that he didn't trust. He believed that survival in combat depended on the other pilots as well as himself. "I reckoned some of these guys were not proper people. There was a particular gang from Los Angeles in 71 that raised hell, wrote bad checks, got in trouble with the females and wanted to drink more than they wanted to fly—all that kind of stuff. So, from OTU I flatly refused a posting to 71 Squadron. Instead, I joined a British squadron."

But after a period of flying Hurricanes with No. 607 Squadron in the north of England, McColpin was posted to No. 121 (Eagle) Squadron. He saw a lot of action with 121 and earned a reputation as one of the very best of the Eagle pilots. Recognized for his courage and skill in air fighting, he was one of the first American recipients of the British Distinguished Flying Cross. He was then summoned to see Air Chief Marshal Leigh-Mallory, who had moved from 12 Group to the command of 11 Group. Despite his doubts about the American pilots, Leigh-Mallory now had a job for McColpin to do. He was to be promoted from

pilot officer to flight lieutenant, and was to take command of B Flight, 133 Squadron.

McColpin, at twenty-seven, brought a rare maturity to the youthful Eagles. While not doubting that his age and experience contributed to his survival and success, there were other factors that he counts as crucial. "You could still use luck. Every once in a while a part would break or fail on your airplane while you were flying, but you could eliminate or reduce your need for luck by making sure your plane was 100 percent ready to go. Then, as double insurance, you'd always make sure you knew where you were going to land in any emergency."

McColpin's policy was careful planning, and he followed certain personal rules. They included not living it up in the pubs and clubs—all part of maintaining the peak physical condition in which he prided himself. He had first-rate eyesight, good hearing, physical strength . . . and endurance. Four hundred fighter missions without once being hit and never losing a pilot when leading his flight proved the wisdom of his philosophy. His success as flight commander eventually led to his promotion to commander of 133 Squadron. His men admired and respected his leadership qualities. McColpin was once gratified to overhear one of them say, "Well . . . I'll go with McColpin any place he'll go." "Amen" was the response of the other pilots in the room. But despite this vote of confidence, there was still an occasional voice of dissent, as when his pilots became aware that pilots in other squadrons were getting quicker promotion. McColpin told them bluntly that he

99

So nigh is grandeur to our dust,/So near is God to man,/When duty whispers low, *Thou must,*/The youth replies, *I can.*

from *Voluntaries* by Emerson

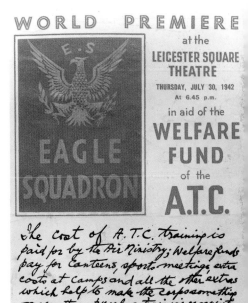

far left: The officers' mess at Kirton-in-Lindsey, Lincolnshire. left: A tattered wind sock on the airfield at Kirton. below left: The watch-office tower at Kirton, 1990.

THEY SHALL
RENEW THEIR
STRENGTH AND
MOUNT UP ON
WINGS LIKE EAGLES

On Memorial at Falcon
Field, Mesa, Arizona
where RAF and
American pilots were
trained in WWII

would transfer them if they wanted out, but they should remember one thing: The other outfits were taking the casualties. Did they want to be live pilot officers or dead flight lieutenants?

In the spring of 1942 the Eagle Squadrons were well established, with 71 Squadron at Debden, 121 at North Weald and 133 at Biggin Hill. These were the best, most prestigious stations, in the forefront of Fighter Command's offensive. Under the commands of Gus Daymond, Chesley Peterson and McColpin, the squadrons had become seasoned and fully effective. They were great favorites of the press, and Hollywood showed interest with a new motion picture, *Eagle Squadron*. Introduced by the popular war correspondent Quentin Reynolds, the cast included Robert Stack, Diana Barrymore, Jon Hall, Eddie Albert, Nigel Bruce, Leif Erikson, John Loder . . . and the Eagles themselves. Most of the action was filmed at the actual bases of the Eagle Squadrons in England, but the filmmakers hadn't appreciated or accounted for the reality of war. Every time a pilot was lost, the script had to be rewritten and previously exposed footage had to be scrapped. In the end the filmmakers gave up and moved the production back to Hollywood. The resulting movie was a schmaltzy, romanticized disaster. It was too much for the assembled Eagles to stomach and most of the pilots walked out of its London premiere, even though the King was present.

After the United States' entry into the war, the transfer of the Eagles into the U.S. 8th Air Force was eventually agreed on and,

by September 1942, was under way. Some Eagle pilots were wearing U.S. OD uniforms alongside others still in RAF blue. Transfer to the Army Air Force meant better pay; however not all of the Eagles would move over to the 8th, despite this and the generally improved conditions available in American service. Jim Gray recalls that there was and is a general misconception about the pilots having to transfer over. "They gave us the opportunity to transfer or not. I opted not to. Everybody thought you had to transfer over to the American Air Force at a certain point if you were American. Not at all. There were about six or seven of us that didn't transfer—Art Roscoe, Leo Nomis and Jimmy Nelson among them."

It wasn't the same for everyone. Red McColpin: "I knew that a big mission to Morlaix was coming up, but I'd been ordered to transfer to the USAAF. *Ordered*. I kept delaying it week after week. We were down at Biggin Hill, but 133 was being moved up to Great Sampford, near Debden. The mission was being laid on . . . then off . . . then on again. I decided I wouldn't go and leave the outfit until the mission was over with. I was gonna lead that mission. Then General 'Monk' Hunter called up from Fighter Command Headquarters of the 8th Air Force and said, 'I understand you haven't transferred,' and I said, 'Yes sir.' He just said, 'Well, you get your butt in there and transfer, right now!' To which I came back, 'Sir, I'm waiting for this Morlaix mission and I'm trying to keep enough boys in here to run it, 'cause it's a big one.' 'To heck with that . . . you get in there and transfer,' Hunter replied. 'Well, sir,' I

Many of the Spitfires used in the Battle of Britain were privately sponsored. Individuals, villages, towns, cities and companies raised money to buy the planes for the RAF. These donated "presentation" aircraft bore names usually suggested by the donor. In most cases the name appeared over the engine cowling or just beneath the cockpit rail. A Spitfire named "Dorothy" was bought by women all over Britain with that name. Another fighter, called "Gingerbread," was purchased by red-haired men and women, and was flown by a red-headed Australian pilot. "The Dogfighter" was presented by a kennel club. London police gave "Bow Street Home Guard." Prisoners of war contributed a Spit called "Unshackled Spirit," and Hoover Ltd donated "Skysweeper." The city of Southampton gave "R. J. Mitchell" in honor of the Spitfire designer, and the London community of Hendon presented the

above left: Art Roscoe at 56 Operational Training Unit, Sutton Bridge in July 1941. above right: Tommy McGerty. far left: Bob Sprague. left: Forrest "Pappy" Dowling at North Weald in 1941.

'Griff' on the GREMLIN

Half the Authors' Royalties from this book are being devoted to the R.A.F. BENEVOLENT FUND

by D. J. MARSHALL & F. V. G. ROYCE

Illustrated by LEN KIRLEY   3/6

said, 'You understand that I'm in the Royal Air Force, sir, and I have an ops instruction here which says we are going to Morlaix when they lay it on. I'm the CO here, and I've got my squadron on the line.' With that he snorted and hung up. About an hour later I got a call from an air marshal in the group. 'McColpin, do you take orders from me?' I said, 'I certainly do, sir. Yes sir.' That's how I came to transfer over.''

The Morlaix raid, when it came, was a disaster. It was a sad way for the Eagle Squad-

rons to bow out of the RAF. Gordon Brettell, a British pilot, was placed in command of 133 Squadron, and led the Morlaix mission on September 26, 1942, in Red McColpin's place.

The Morlaix raid required the Eagles to escort American bombers hitting the Brest Peninsula, flying out across the widest part of the Channel, over a heavily defended area, and back again. By this time 133 Squadron was at Great Sampford in Essex, waiting to be absorbed into the USAAF . . . but would still fly the mission. To that end, the unit was sent to Bolt Head, a forward base located between Dartmouth and Plymouth in Devon. Here, its pilots were to refuel, be briefed for the mission and join the other two squadrons flying it, 401 and 412 (Canadian). On the flight down to Bolt Head, the weather was bad and getting worse, threatening the impending mission.

Without McColpin's discipline, the pilots of 133 Squadron were overly casual in preparing for Morlaix. Most didn't bother to attend the briefing. Only Brettell and one other pilot were briefed for the raid. In it the Met officer gave a tragically erroneous bit of information—a predicted thirty-five-knot headwind at the mission height of 28,000 feet. Further, no one knew precisely when the bombers were to take off, or their precise rendezvous time with the fighters. The pilots lounged under the wings of their Spitfires and waited. McColpin's key word, "planning," certainly did not apply. The take-off was a mess. There were near-collisions; pilots didn't get proper instructions about radio channels; some even left maps and escape kits behind.

Flying with auxiliary fuel tanks, thirty-six Spitfires headed out to meet the bombers. There was no sign of them, and the fighters continued on course and called by radio for news of the big friends. The predicted thirty-five-knot headwind had been a major miscalculation. Both bombers and fighters—miles

service with "Hendon Pegasus." It was probably the name Spitfire which captured the public imagination, leading to the establishment of the various "Spitfire Funds." If that is so, it was most unfair to the marvelous Hawker Hurricane which, in fact, flew in far greater numbers in the Battle of Britain, and accounted for more than 80 percent of the German aircraft destroyed in that battle. It was in May 1940 that the question of the price of these aircraft arose in relation to the collection of donations to sponsor their construction. The Ministry of Aircraft Production then announced a nominal round figure of £5,000 for either aircraft, and funds were soon organized all over Britain and the Commonwealth. The largest single donation came from Queen Wilhelmina of the Netherlands, who presented the sum of £216,000 on behalf of the Dutch East Indies, to purchase an entire squadron of 43 Spitfires. More than 1,000 such aircraft produced between June and September 1940 bore a presentation

left: Hurricanes of 121 (Eagle) Squadron at Kirton-in-Lindsey.

apart—were being whisked along by a one hundred-knot tailwind. One of the pilots later commented: "It all added up to a streaking catastrophe." Miles ahead of the fighters, the bombers had unknowingly crossed the Bay of Biscay above a blanket of cloud and, on reaching the Pyrenees, discovered their problem, dumped their bombs and swung back to the north on a reciprocal course, meeting the Spitfires head-on. The fighters turned north as well. By this time, all of the aircraft had vanished from the radar plots in England, and communications between bombers, fighters and their various bases was a shambles. Having been airborne for two hours and fifteen minutes, the Spitfire pilots believed they were near home again and began to let down through the cloud cover. A coastline appeared which they assumed to be England. It was, in fact, the French coast, and they passed over Brest harbor and through a massive flak barrage. In moments, ten Spitfires were lost, four pilots killed and six downed and captured, among them the CO, Gordon Brettell. Two other Spitfires failed to return to Bolt Head. Morlaix was a most unfortunate final mission for the Eagles.

Twice Debden had been the headquarters of 71 (Eagle) Squadron and, on September 29, 1942, it became the base of the newly-formed 4th Fighter Group, 8th USAAF. The 4th was made up of the three former Eagle Squadrons. In the presence of Major General Carl Spaatz and Air Chief Marshal Sir Sholto Douglas, the Union Jack was hauled down and the Stars and Stripes run up. Sholto Douglas, who had expressed reservations about them in the beginning, had only praise for the transferring American pilots:

"We at Fighter Command deeply regret this parting. In the course of the past eighteen months we have seen the stuff of which you are made. We could not ask for better companions with whom to see this fight through to a finish. Of those who died, those sons of the United States were the first to give their lives for their country.

"Like their fathers who fought and died with the Lafayette Squadron so will these Eagles who fell in combat ever remain the honored dead of two great nations."

So parted the Eagles and the RAF. It had not always been a comfortable relationship, but it had laid foundations for Anglo-American cooperation in air fighting, had seen seventy-three enemy aircraft destroyed and hatched the 4th Fighter Group of the 8th Air Force. The 4th at Debden became the highest-scoring fighter group in the USAAF. A German propaganda statement called them the "Debden Gangsters."

The Eagles are still remembered by the British. A returning veteran was surprised to get a free taxi ride when revisiting London in recent years. He asked why. Back came the driver's answer: "You were an Eagle. You already paid."

legend. Other "fund-generated" Spits included "Lima Challenger," "Kenya Daisy," "Adele Astaire," "Royal Tunbridge Wells," "Manchester Air Cadets" and "Royal Observer Corps."

Out of the chill and the shadow,/Into the thrill and the shrine;/Out of the dearth and the famine,/Into the fulness divine.

from "Going Home" by Margaret E. Sangster

Something attempted, something done,/Has earned a night's repose.

from "The Village Blacksmith" by Longfellow

far left: P/O John Butler Ayre. left: Bob Mannix.

SPECIAL OPERATIONS

GRADUALLY, the tide of the European air war turned. In 1940, the British had fought it almost entirely on a defensive basis. Early in 1941, there were offensive raids across the Channel by aircraft of RAF Fighter Command, operations with code names such as Circus, Rodeo, Rhubarb and Ramrod. These had mixed success, but at least the war was being taken to the enemy, which encouraged both the RAF pilots and the citizens of Nazi-occupied Europe. By 1943, in conjunction with the "round-the-clock" bombing offensive by the USAAF and RAF, aggressive fighter missions were being flown continually. Many of these missions were unusual in their nature and result. Some were exceptional.

Major Pierce McKennon was a scholarly young American, an accomplished concert pianist . . . and a fighter pilot. An interesting combination. Leader of the 335th Fighter Squadron in the 4th Fighter Group at Debden, he was a popular man and much in demand at parties and dances for his piano playing of swing and boogie. But away from the relaxed atmosphere of the Officers' Club and out from behind the piano, McKennon was a leader who would tolerate nothing less than the best from his men. One of them, a Lieutenant George Green, did not conform and was guilty of sloppy flying and a variety of other offenses. One more and he was to be transferred to another outfit.

On March 18, 1945, the 335th made a routine attack on Prenzlau airfield. As usual, flak was their main problem and the squadron came under heavy fire. McKennon's Mustang lurched and he knew it had been hit. Although the plane was still flying and the controls were still responding, his engine instruments gave warning of the seriousness of his situation. The oil-pressure needle was at zero. The engine had been hit and, at any moment, he knew it would seize or catch fire. The time had come to say good-bye to poor old *Ridge Runner*, so at four thousand feet he slid back the canopy and prepared to jump.

Later, in a letter to his mother, he described the incident: "I almost got myself killed getting out of the aircraft. I got caught on something in the cockpit when I was only halfway out. The plane was in a dive and the slipstream was so strong that it held me against the fuselage. The plane was going straight down when I finally tore myself loose. I figured right then that this was my last ride because in the position I was in, it was ninety-nine out of a hundred that I would hit the tail, and you can't do that and live. Anyway, I missed it by a couple of inches. My 'chute opened OK and the landing in a small field wasn't too hard."

But Pierce McKennon's adventure was just beginning. As he struggled to shed his parachute he saw another Mustang circling overhead and then coming in to land. Some other guy must have been hit . . . but why the hell was he trying to put it down on this tiny patch? After the Mustang's third attempt to land—wheels down—McKennon understood. It was a rescue. As the aircraft finally touched down, bounced and skidded to a halt, McKennon ran for it. Overhead, twenty-four other P-51s formed a protective circle. As he reached the Mustang, McKennon was amazed. The pilot was the "unsatisfactory" George Green.

Green was shedding his flying gear to make extra room in the small cockpit. Not a word passed between them. Without hesitating, McKennon jumped onto the wing and reached into the cockpit to release the drop tanks—which Green hadn't bothered or remembered to jettison—and adjusted the flaps for a very short take-off roll. As they prepared the fighter for take-off, German soldiers appeared across the fields. "Strafe those Huns," Green yelled into his radio. A Mustang dropped down, guns blazing.

Their prop wash scattered the discarded parachute pack, dinghy, flight jackets and

far left: An RAF parachute release box. below left: A remaining RAF sign at Goxhill, 1990. below: An RAF Air Diagram poster issued during WWII.

War is a crime against humanity . . . and its punishment.

—Anonymous

Prosperity is a great teacher;/adversity is a greater./Possession pampers the mind;/ privation trains and strengthens it.

—Hazlitt

Mae Wests. McKennon was jammed uncomfortably into the bucket seat with Green on his lap. It had been a tight squeeze getting both of them into the cockpit, and it would be even more difficult getting out of the tiny field. Wheel brakes held down, throttle open . . . sixty inches of manifold pressure . . . then more. They were off across the grass, bumping and bucking. At Debden a comfortable nine hundred yards of runway and a take-off speed of 150 MPH was the norm . . . here it would be much less. Somehow, they staggered into the air, wheels skimming the trees. McKennon was going home.

The flight back to Debden was easy, if uncomfortable. McKennon pummeled the back of his rescuer. "You crazy, crazy bastard," he kept shouting. At one point, Green, on oxygen, forgot that McKennon had no such supply. McKennon lost consciousness. Having just rescued him, Green was now killing him through oxygen starvation. A quick application of Green's mask brought McKennon around and, from then on, they took turns using the one mask. Two and a half hours after the miraculous rescue/escape, they were back at Debden, cramped, stiff and elated.

Alan Geoffrey Page, who had been shot down and badly burned in the Battle of Britain, was back on operational flying status in 1943 despite his injured hands. The agonizing months in the East Grinstead Cottage Hospital as a plastic surgery "guinea pig" had left him bitter and determined to get even. Another fighter pilot, James MacLachlan, felt the same way. A cannon shell from a ME 109 had

shattered his left arm, which had had to be amputated. His flying career seemed over. But like Geoffrey Page, he was set on getting back at the enemy. Mac was fitted with an artificial limb, its "hand" a complex metal clamp designed to fit perfectly onto the throttle and controls of a fighter aircraft. When Page was posted to the Air Fighting Development Unit a Wittering, he met Squadron Leader MacLachlan for the first time. He recalls their unique partnership. "The one-armed pilot was supposedly resting from a long tour of night intruder operations. These had consisted of sitting over enemy airports in the darkness, waiting for the German bombers to return from their night's work over the British Isles. In this he'd had considerable success. But, bored by his enforced 'rest,' he began to devise new ways to hit at the enemy.

"Among the aircraft supplied to the Wittering fighter assessment unit were two Allison-engined Mustangs—fast, low-level fighters, which caught Mac's eye. Somewhat reluctantly, Fighter Command granted him permission to use one of the Mustangs on a lone raid into the Continent. His idea was to penetrate the German fighter-defense belt and get into those areas where Allied airplanes had not been seen before . . . in broad daylight and at extreme low altitude. He had the Mustang painted a dark green to blend in with the French countryside. He perfected his low-level navigation in hours of practice flying around England at treetop height. I watched all these preparations with great interest.

"One day Mac took off in the green Mustang to carry out his first raid. Several hours

In the wings of our planes was mounted a 16 mm movie camera, which started taking pictures as soon as the guns were fired. If no other pilot could verify your claim, the films would bear witness to your marksmanship. The films were processed on the base and copies made. One was immediately rushed to Eighth Air Force Headquarters, where assessments were made; one was spliced together with an appropriate heading giving the pilot's name and claim, along with other movies taken from other pilots of the same date, and this was shown on the next day to the group. A movie room had been set up in the back of the photo lab so that pilots could observe the previous day's shooting. I couldn't wait this long. That night I went to the photo officer's room to ask about my film. Did it show any strikes? His answer discouraged me: "Not a thing, Johnny. There wasn't even a picture of a German plane on the film."

from *The Look of Eagles* by John T. Godfrey

left: Major Pierce McKennon of the 4th Fighter Group, Debden, with his P-51 Mustang, *Ridge Runner.*

Year 1945		Aircraft		Pilot, or 1st Pilot	2nd Pilot, Pupil or Passenger	Duty (Including Results and Remarks)	Du.
Month	Date	Type	No.				(1
—	—	—	—	—	⋯	⸻ Totals Brought Forward	
2	28	P-51	A	Self	136	RAMROD - Ingolstadt	
3	2	P-51	A	"	137	RAMROD - Genthin	
3	3	UC-64		"		X-country.	
3	4	P-51	A	"	137	RAMROD - Stuttgart	
3	5	P-51	A	"	137	RAMROD - Hamburg	
3	6	P-51	A	"		Local	
3	7	P-51	H	"		X-country - Chartres (Franc	
3	8	P-51	A	"		X-country - Tangmere	
3	9	P-51	A	"		Sqd. Ballo?	
3	12	P-51	A	"	140	RAMROD - Swinemünde	
3	13	P-51	2	"		Local	
3	13	P-51	2	"		Local	
3	13	P-51	2	"		"	
3	16	P-51	2	"		"	
3	16	P-51	2	"		"	
3	17	P-51	A	"		"	
3	18	P-51	A-M	Green & Hyse	16 141	RAMROD - Berlin	
3	22	P-51	A	Self	141 2	RAMROD - Rutland	
3	23	P-51	A	"		Gun Test	
3	24	P-51	A	"	141 3	Fighter Patrol. Munster Area	
3	25	P-51	2	"		Local	
3	25	P-51	2	"		"	
3	26	P-51	A	"	141	RAMROD - Plauen	

GRAND TOTAL [Cols. (1) to (10)]

.....................Hrs.....................Mins. .

TOTALS CARRIED FORWARD

NGINE AIRCRAFT		MULTI-ENGINE AIRCRAFT						PASS-ENGER	INSTR/CLOUD FLYING [Incl. in cols. (1) to (10)]	
NIGHT		DAY			NIGHT					
DUAL	PILOT	DUAL	1ST PILOT	2ND PILOT	DUAL	1ST PILOT	2ND PILOT		DUAL	PILOT
(3)	(4)	(5)	(6)	(7)	(8)	(9)	(10)	(11)	(12)	(18)

2 landings - one by Berlin. Flak got me and George picked me up.

| | | | | | | | | | | 2:00 |
| (3) | (4) | (5) | (6) | (7) | (8) | (9) | (10) | (11) | (12) | (18) |

The course home was easy to remember, 260 degrees would take us to the coast of England.

from *The Look of Eagles*
by John T. Godfrey

left: Pierce McKennon's logbook noting the eventful March 18, 1944. above: George Green and McKennon reenact Green's daring rescue of his boss.

Many a battle have I won in France./When as the enemy hath been ten to one:/Why should I not now have the like success?

from *Henry VI, Part 3* by Shakespeare

later, I watched him climbing stiffly out of the cockpit, a disappointed man. After crossing the French coast he had been seen by enemy fighters. The cockpit hood configuration of his early-model Mustang allowed such poor rearward visibility that, had he stayed to fight, he wouldn't have stood a chance.

"Later, I approached Mac and offered to have a go. 'So you think it's a good idea too, eh? Thank God someone else thinks so. Nothing but opposition from everyone ever since I started,' was his response. We discussed the problem and agreed that the solution was to take *two* Mustangs. 'Two Mustangs! That's it.

Must get another aircraft,' he said.

"The commanding officer of the unit was a hard nut to crack, and would probably view our idea as the lunatic scheme of two cripples. But I underestimated my new partner. With a wave of his artificial hand, he dismissed the commanding officer. 'To hell with him. I'll get permission from Fighter Command, and then he'll have to lend us the second plane.' It worked and we got my machine ready to go.

"We practiced extreme low-level flying for hours. We each had to learn how the other would react under differing circumstances. Having no radio made it even more difficult. But Mac found that his one arm was fully occupied flying the airplane and navigating without adding the push buttons and transmitting switch of a VHF radio set.

"At last we felt ready to go, but we needed the right weather conditions over the route . . . preferably a complete cloud layer at about three thousand feet. As we would be skimming low over the French fields, any prey would be flying above us and easy to spot if silhouetted against the cloud. The visibility must be good for obvious reasons and little or no wind blowing. A strong wind would add navigational difficulties and probably produce bumpy conditions, causing added fatigue on what would already be a tiring flight. Putting a toothbrush, razor and a stout pair of walking shoes (it would be a long walk home from where we were going) into our aircraft, we took off from our inland base for Lympne airfield on the south coast. There we would remain until our weather requirements were fulfilled. It was also necessary to arrange for Typhoon fighter-bombers to carry out diversionary procedures.

"On an overcast June day in 1943 I was sweating with fear, knowing that bullets would be flying in my direction within the next hour. The hands of my watch pointed at 0855. 'Your aircraft is ready, sir.' The flight sergeant's face betrayed nothing of his thoughts. I wondered how mine looked to him. A voice behind me called, 'All set?' Turning, I saw Mac grinning at me. His warm personality had a cheering effect on my depressed spirits. 'Let's get cracking.' Saying this, he juggled with the clawlike mechanism that was attached to the end of his artificial arm. 'Fine pair we are,' I thought. 'Going off to tackle the enemy with only one good hand between the two of us.'

"The operation itself was simple enough. Escorted by a squadron of Typhoon fighters, our two Mustangs would fly across the Channel at wave-top height, until we were just off the enemy coast. The Typhoons would then climb up, firing their guns, and simulate a dogfight. Unnoticed, we hoped, our aircraft would slip in over the French coast and proceed at low level to the Luftwaffe night-fighter airfields south of Paris. As soon as we had destroyed some of the enemy air force, all we had to do was fly back two hundred miles, assuming German day fighters or antiaircraft fire didn't interfere with our plans. It was almost three years since I had been in combat with enemy aircraft in the Battle of Britain. In my last fight I had been shot down in flames and spent two painful years in the hospital. Fear was my other companion on this flight.

No one ever reaches a high position without daring.

—Syrus

The burnt child dreads the fire.

from *The Devil Is an Ass*
by Ben Jonson

We are McIndoe's Army,/We are his Guinea Pigs,/With dermatomes and pedicles,/Glass eyes, false teeth and wigs. But when we get our discharge/We'll shout with all our might— "Per Ardua ad Astra, We'd rather drink than fight."

from "The Guinea Pigs' Song"

left: An RAF Mustang similar to those used by James MacLachlan and Geoffrey Page in their special operations flown from Lympne.

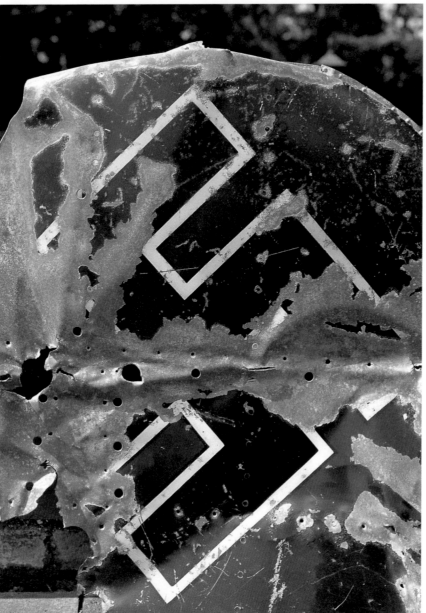

"In pairs the Typhoons taxied out over the grass of Lympne airfield, turned into the wind and took off. Soon they were joining up in squadron formation overhead, circling and awaiting our two Mustangs. I sat strapped in my cockpit watching Mac's immobile aircraft. Then his propeller began to turn, followed by a bursting roar as the Allison took life. I forgot my fear as I concentrated on the job of starting my own engine. The next five minutes were fully occupied with positioning and taking off my heavily-laden fighter from the small airfield. As soon as the wheels retracted I leveled off at a hundred feet, and went into a tight turn to catch up with the other Mustang, also turning about a mile ahead. The Typhoons were not our problem; their task was to position themselves on us. The English coastline flashed beneath as I caught up with MacLachlan. Gently we dived down to about twenty feet above the waves. I could see the Typhoons settling into position slightly above and to either side of us. So far so good.

"No sooner had we comfortably settled on course than all the old fears came flooding back. Would a barrage of light enemy flak, with its horrid orange tracer balls, come out to meet us as we crossed the French coast? If my aircraft got hit, would it burst into flames the same way my Hurricane had exploded on that previous occasion? This time I would not be at fifteen thousand feet with the opportunity to bail out. I would be roasted alive at this low altitude before I could ever crash-land the burning plane. My imagination even recalled the smell of my own burning flesh after such a long passage of time. Fine sort of person you

114

are, I thought. Scared stiff even before the first shot has been fired.

"Perhaps it was the seagulls that kept me from completely losing my nerve and turning for home. Aware of the approaching formation, they arose from their undulating watery couch right in the path of our flight. Unable to alter course I watched fascinated as their flapping white wings were poised ahead of us, then suddenly slipped past, only to be replaced by others. One bird striking the propeller blades would cause enough damage to ensure a watery grave. Miraculously, time passed without collision. Behind us we left a trail of squawking feathered aviators ruffled by our lightning passage.

"Suddenly I saw a murky gray outline on the overcast horizon. Enemy coast. The Typhoons began to climb away, leaving a sense of unutterable loneliness around our two Mustangs. In a flash the coastline had come and gone without any enemy action.

"MacLachlan's low-level navigation was a masterly achievement, when you consider that he had only one hand to fly his aircraft and hold a map in, which needed constant turning as the miles raced by. Soon we were over the rooftops of Beauvais, heading south towards Rambouillet. The Seine had passed quickly beneath us and, apart from the momentary thrill of flying under some high-tension electric cables, the French countryside remained peacefully serene.

"Three enemy aircraft appeared fifteen hundred feet above us and ten miles ahead. Important little tasks filled the seconds that passed as we rapidly closed the gap between ourselves and our slow-moving prey. Camera gun to be switched on—ah, yes, gunsight and gun button to *fire*, fine pitch and . . .

"Gunfire ripped out over the peaceful woods beneath and the port aircraft burst into flames from Mac's withering blast. I watched our dying enemy fly along in a flaming mass and dive in a seemingly slow and dignified manner into a house on the edge of the forest. We destroyed the two remaining aircraft and moments later we sighted another one. MacLachlan attacked and the unfortunate victim dived steeply to earth. It was my privilege to finish him off on the way down and the wreckage was strewn over a large field.

"We flew on to Brétigny and spotted German night fighters near their base. Two of them were preparing to land as we closed in behind. Mac shot at the one farthest away from the airfield and pieces flew in all directions from the JU 88. Once again it was my task to finish a job that needed little completion. The aircraft disintegrated on striking the ground. Incredibly, the observer in the second JU 88 had noticed nothing and his pilot continued his landing approach. As he held off a few feet above the runway, Mac struck again. The Junkers hit the concrete in a blazing sheet of flame and skated drunkenly down its full length. All the flak gunners around the airfield must have witnessed the fate of their countrymen. But it was our lucky day and we slipped through the stream of innocent-looking orange balls that rose lazily from the ground in our direction. Joining up together, we headed for England.

"Delighted with the success of our first

Birds of a feather will flock together.

—Minsheu

O Lord—if there is a Lord;/save my soul—if I have a soul./Amen.

"Prayer of a Skeptic" by Ernest Renan

above left: An original wartime tobacco tin. left: Partial rudder section from a German fighter downed over England. below: Wing Commander Geoffrey Page, 1989.

sortie, Mac and I waited impatiently for ideal weather conditions to permit a second attempt. It was to end tragically.

"Once again we set out with a Typhoon escort, but crossing in over the French coast Mac must have been hit by machine-gun fire. His aircraft climbed steeply from our treetop height and, at one thousand feet, his canopy opened. But he presumably changed his mind

above: S/L James MacLachlan. right: An extraordinarily low pass by an RAF Mustang over an English fighter station.

about bailing out, for the aircraft then glided toward a small field. His approach speed was far too fast. With wheels up the Mustang touched the ground three quarters of the way across the field. It plowed into an orchard, shedding its wings before coming to rest. I orbited several times at a low height, but there was no sign of life in the wreckage. I contemplated trying to land in the field to go to Mac's aid, but realized the impossibility of landing wheels down in such a confined area. Reluctantly I dived at the scene of the crash to register some gun-camera photographs, and heartbrokenly headed for home. Years later I learned that Mac had survived the actual crash, but had died three weeks later in the hospital. His body lies buried in a small French graveyard."

Fw 190D

Out there, we've walked quite friendly up to Death:/Sat down and eaten with him, cool and bland,—Pardoned his spilling mess-tins in our hand. We've sniffed the green thick odour of his breath,—/Our eyes wept, but our courage didn't writhe./He's spat at us with bullets and he's coughed/Shrapnel. We chorused when he sang aloft:/We whistled while he shaved us with his scythe.

from "The Next War" by Wilfred Owen

THE
VILLAGERS

"WE WON'T SAY VERY MUCH until we've done something. We hope that after we've gone, you'll be glad we were here."

So said 8th Air Force Lt. General Ira Eaker to the British people. Nearly fifty years later, the gratitude of the villagers who lived alongside the American airmen and their airfields is still evident. Today, many memorials have been erected on or near the sites of former U.S. bases.

Until war brought a different style of life, Bottisham was a sleepy rural village in the East Anglian countryside. For Bottisham and its neighboring communities of Little Wilbraham and Swaffam Bulbeck, the most exciting local event previously had been the village fête. That was about to change abruptly. So it was for scores of other East Anglian villages when the American invasion came. At Bottisham, though, there was a special relationship between villagers and airmen; a relationship that, since the war, has been strengthened and cherished on both sides of the Atlantic. In part, this can be attributed to the location of the main airfield domestic site within the village itself. Nissen and Maycrete huts were side by side with village houses.

As Station 374, Bottisham became home for the 361st Fighter Group, USAAF, on November 30, 1943. Before that it had been an RAF fighter station. The villagers had become accustomed to aircraft and the eccentricities of those who flew them by the time the Americans arrived. Gone were many acres of farmland. Well-used country lanes were cut and closed. Properties were requisitioned for military use.

Just down the road from the airfield, Bottisham Hall had been home to the Jenyns family for generations. Realizing its potential desirability to the War Office, the Jenyns wisely offered their home for military use before it was taken from them. In return for this patriotic gesture, the family was rewarded with official approval for one elderly member to remain in residence in one of the wings. What Grandma Jenyns thought of the often rowdy activities of her housemates is not recorded. She shared Bottisham Hall with the 361st who made it their Officers' Mess. Surprisingly, when handed back to the family after the war, the house was still in good shape with no significant damage. Only two small broken portions of marble fireplace remind one of the American occupancy. As the officers had stood by the fire drinking and smoking, they discovered that smooth marble was useless for striking a match. The simple solution was to chip off bits of the mantel to provide a rough surface. Outside the house there is further evidence: a moldering squash court, grassed-over foundations of hutted encampments and faded traces of white "blackout" bands painted on trees in the driveway. Other nearby trees bear carvings: WALT—WISCONSIN and EMILY AND JACK 1944 are messages from the past. Elsewhere in the village, traces of 8th Air Force wall art have survived until recently in the Maycrete huts and have been preserved for museums: a GI astride the cowling of a Thunderbolt, the Statue of Liberty, a flying tractor and a transatlantic liner. And plenty of stories still abound.

Jack Heath, then a farm laborer in his

You see them in the "local" anywhere/In town or country near a fighter station/In flying boots and scarves— their ruffled hair/Like schoolboys out for a jolly celebration:/Eight in a car for four had raced along/And miracles were wrought to bring them here./To pass an hour with banter, darts and song And drink a pint or two of English beer,/And talk of "binds" and "dims" with lots of natter/Of "ropey jobs" and "wizard types" and "gen"/Amid much

above left: The ops room at Steeple Morden, home of the 355th Fighter Group. left: A decaying hut near the site of the old main gate at Steeple Morden. below: Steeple Morden resident Cecil Savage.

Ninth USAAF P-47 Thunderbolts line up for take-off on a mission in which they will operate as dive-bombers, hitting rail and road targets near Louvain, Belgium, April 26, 1944. Lt. H. W. Collins flags them off.

mid-twenties, witnessed the airfield activity from Frog End Farm. Jack liked to spend his leisure time in the local pubs, where he got to know several of the Yanks. He remembers Cookie, Big Finn and Mexican Pete, who, with their fellow airmen, frequented The Hole in the Wall, The Greyhound, The Carpenter's Arms, The King's Head and The Swan. Over pints of Greene King, the villagers rubbed shoulders with the Americans. The company of these colorful Yanks could be a pleasure;

but when they were full of beer, not always so. "Old Pete," recalls Jack, "was a big, unpleasant chap with a pockmarked and sallow complexion. And with a few pints inside him he became even more unpleasant and always ready for a fight. One evening I was riding home on my bike and he came at me from behind with a bottle. Wallop! He landed me one and sent me over the handlebars onto the road. Then he set about my mate and cut him over his eye. Suddenly, he dropped the bottle and it rolled toward me. Right, I thought, now it's your turn. But just then two other Yanks turned up and restrained him."

Pubs were the center of village social life and since there was no other local entertainment, it was natural that the Americans would patronize them. Many of the villagers' memories are associated with times spent drinking with the GIs. At The Carpenter's Arms, landlord Tom Middleditch and his wife, Gertie, welcomed the young airmen warmly. Big Finn took advantage of Middleditch's hospitality and in a memorable binge, drank thirty-two pints of beer—eighteen in a morning session and a further fourteen during

laughter glasses chink and clatter./Deep underneath was hid the real men,/Who saw their comrades fall out of the skies,/and knew too well the look in dead men's eyes.

"In the Local"
by W.A.G. Kemp

You must look into people as well as at them.

—Chesterfield

In this world a man must either be anvil or hammer.

from "Hyperion" by Longfellow

above: Bottisham Hall, 1990. above right: A bit of 361st FG wall art now preserved. right: One of the last traces of 361st FG occupation of Bottisham village in 1943–44. center right: An 8th AF emblem painted on a hut wall in Bottisham.

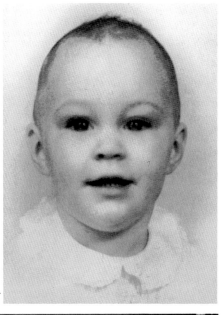

THIS STREET IS SITUATED ON WHAT WAS PART OF BOTTISHAM AIR BASE AND IS NAMED IN HONOUR OF COL. THOMAS J. J. CHRISTIAN JR. COMMANDER OF THE 361ST FIGHTER GROUP US. EIGHTH AIR FORCE. WHO. WITH MEMBERS OF HIS COMMAND. FLEW FROM HERE AND GAVE HIS LIFE IN THE DEFENCE OF FREEDOM DURING WORLD WAR II.

UNVEILED BY COL. CHRISTIAN'S DAUGHTER,
MS LOU CHRISTIAN WILSON FLEMING. ON 16 OCTOBER 1988.

LEST WE FORGET.

above left: Col. and Mrs. Thomas Christian. above center: Baby Lou Christian. above: Lou Christian Wilson Fleming, 1990. far left: Col. Thomas Christian. center: A plaque dedicating Thomas Christian Way in Bottisham village. left: A P-51D Mustang restored and painted to replicate *Lou IV*, the aircraft flown by Col. Christian from the Bottisham base.

123

With vacant stare in the market square, Tricked out in a lilac suit,/The villager stands with great hands/And chaffs with a raw recruit./The heat comes down on a sleepy town/Like a blanket over the head,/And a church clock beats in the silent streets/Saying "Dead, dead, dead."

The hour of seven is just like heaven,/The moment of wishful drinking!/Giggling wenches on bar-room benches/Can guess what the boys are thinking./Shropshire lads look a bunch of cads/As they jingle the week-end cash,/And girls on munitions in certain conditions Regret they were once so rash.

from "Rural Sunday" by Michael Barsley

the evening. This impressed the folk of Bottisham and led to one of the Yanks offering an inviting challenge to Jack and his pals: "We're gonna teach you Limeys how to *really* drink!" "Well," Jack replied, "if you've got the money, we've got the time!"

Not all English villagers, though, recall that things were quite so convivial between them and their American visitors. Cecil Savage of Steeple Morden, home to the 355th Fighter Group, remembers: "Of all the bombs they dropped . . . well, they should have dropped one here in the center of Steeple Morden. They make all this fuss about memorials and the like, bit it weren't like that then . . . oh no! Most of the people here were quite unfriendly to the American boys. At least, that's my impression. Why, they wouldn't even open the church, village hall or the like for the boys to go sit and relax in their time off. Just down at Litlington, though, I remember it was a different story. The lads seemed welcome there. The Congregational church was opened up for them whenever they wanted, but Steeple Morden? No. Do you know, the ladies in the village were even afraid to talk to

STOP
MISSION RETURNING
NO VEHICLES PERMITTED ON PERIMETER TRACK UNTIL THIS SIGN HAS BEEN REMOVED

the lads for fear of what others might say, and if any of them had invited the American boys in for tea, well . . . they'd be accused of being loose. The gossip would soon get around that so-and-so had had a Yank in her house and that she must be after some nylons."

If some Steeple Morden residents could be accused of a coldness bordering on hostility to the Yanks, they at least could not be accused of the savagery of some of the American MPs to their fellow servicemen, as witnessed by Cecil. "Oh they had wickedly long truncheons and beat the Yank airmen absolutely mercilessly when they rounded them up from the pubs at closing time. It was all quite unnecessary. Once, and I saw this myself, an MP pulled his pistol and shot one of the poor boys in the leg—as if he were a rabbit—just because he tried to run off."

War brings out the best and worst in human nature, civilian and military, and it is easy to imagine the upheaval and resentment that ensued when both groups were thrown together. But often the passage of time filters out unpleasant memories, leaving the happier ones. Cecil Savage's account shows that the American airmen were not always welcome in English villages. But whether memories are good or bad, it remains that the local population played an important part in the lives of the U.S. servicemen, who in turn brought some color to the austere wartime lives of their hosts.

Jock Wells and his pals rushed from school each day to watch the American planes up at the Bottisham base. Apart from the thrill of seeing the aircraft take off and land,

there was the added attraction of candy and gum. "Us lads knew where all the local chickens would lay their eggs, so we regularly collected them up and took them to the airfield. One of the dispersal points was up against a lane and the Americans would pass a long telescopic pole through the coiled barbed wire. On the end was a net and we'd put the eggs in it, and in return would come back a net full of candy and gum."

Memories of exciting crash landings . . . of a GI shooting rats on the blister hangar roof . . . of the locals scavenging for food in the Americans' rubbish pit . . . of the weekly dances endure for Jock and others from Bottisham and the neighboring villages. "They were mostly happy times for us, but on one occasion the reality of war came home. We had "adopted" a particular pilot called Geigerson and his fighter—a Thunderbolt named *Contrary Mary*. We used to wait for him to come back, but one day he didn't. Just after D-Day he was lost shooting up a flak train, but the memory of him standing on the wing of his plane, emptying his pockets of candy after a mission and throwing it across the wire to us kids will always be with me."

Jack Heath remembers a head-on collision between a Mustang and a Thunderbolt near the airfield. He recalls seeing the flaming wreckage falling into a cornfield, setting the standing corn alight, and the panic as he and the other farm workers struggled to save their valuable Allis-Chalmers combine harvester from the burning crop. More important, men they had known and befriended had died violently and horribly as they watched. Usually

There is an hour in each man's life appointed/to make his happiness, if then he seize it.

—Beaumont and Fletcher

above: Sgt. Bert Spence teaches an English child, Edwin Aylott, how to hit a baseball.

above: 361st FG wall art preserved at Duxford. above right: The Bottisham airfield site, 1990. center right: Jack Heath. far right: Jock Wells. below right: A Bottisham Maycrete hut, demolished in 1990.

death was more remote than that. Pilots and aircraft simply didn't come back—as if they had flown off to another place.

There were other losses. In all, the 361st lost eighty-one aircraft during its time in the European theater, including that of its highly respected commanding officer Colonel Thomas Christian, who was posted missing in action after a strafing attack on August 12, 1944. After he had left his home in Texas for England, his young wife bore him a daughter, Lou, whom he would never see. He named all of his fighters after her. At Bottisham Hall, Colonel Christian had shared a room with his old friend and deputy commander of the 361st, Joseph Kruzel. Writing to Lou of her father, in later years, Kruzel recalled:

The friendship and high regard I held him in grew even deeper as we worked together to assemble the group and prepare it for combat. When we got to Bottisham he and I shared the big master bedroom suite at Bottisham Hall. We also shared thoughts about our loved ones back home. He wanted so much to see you. We shared, too, the excitement and sad times which go along with wars, but I got to know a man who was an absolutely outstanding leader and as concerned about his enlisted men as he was his officers. He also appreciated the importance of maintaining good relations with the local community and, in my view, managed to do so. I saw in him a sense of confidence, discipline, fairness and maturity you rarely see in a man of

twenty-seven. Had he survived the war, he would, I am convinced, have become one of the U.S. Air Force's outstanding leaders. He was, to me, 4-star general officer material.

The qualities that Kruzel recognized in Thomas Christian are remembered with admiration by many in the local population around Bottisham. In 1988, a company called Bellway Homes developed the former communal site of the 361st into a new residential area and joined with the villagers in naming a road there Thomas Christian Way. Beside the road a memorial was erected and dedicated in his honor.

In an emotional pilgrimage to Bottisham to unveil the memorial to the father she had never known, Lou Christian Wilson Fleming experienced the same warmth and friendship the villagers had shown her father forty-four years earlier. It was a deeply moving ceremony for Lou, especially when a Mustang roared low overhead in salute. Until that visit she had known little of her father. All her mother had told her had been "he was a hero . . . a good man . . . he would have been proud of you."

Until her trip, Lou had been unable to bring herself to read through a trunk full of letters written by her parents to each other. They had been together barely eight months before the war took Christian away. Among the relics of her late father was a letter posted in Bottisham on August 11, the day before his death.

. . . Sorry to hear about your backing into the painter's car. How is the old

126

jalopy (oops!) holding out? Did you ever get any more tires? What are the prospects of a new one after I get back? Are they still making them? What models etc?

Golly, doesn't Lou have to have something to "chew" on now—or does she still work on that thumb? If so, maybe you should break her of it—shouldn't you? I'm glad you're not giving in to her when she cries for attention (but I'll bet you do lots of times!) She has got to be disciplined tho. It probably <u>was</u> just her tooth bothering her.

Yes, darling, our love is the "forever and ever" variety and its not a bunch of nonsense. It just <u>is</u>. I may not be able to say it as romantically 50 years from now as I have tried all these past five years but it will always be in my heart that way. Its the perfect <u>completeness</u> of it that continually inspires me. So very few things <u>are</u> complete when you stop to think about it.

The letters, the pilgrimage, the memorial and, above all, the villagers helped Lou come to terms with grieving for her father—". . . a sad but necessary experience." After the dedication ceremony she commented: "It's a poignant moment and I have learned more and feel closer to my father now than I ever have." As the Mustang flew low overhead she added: "It's an unforgettable experience. I feel like my father is flying that plane and I feel so close to him and to the village of Bottisham."

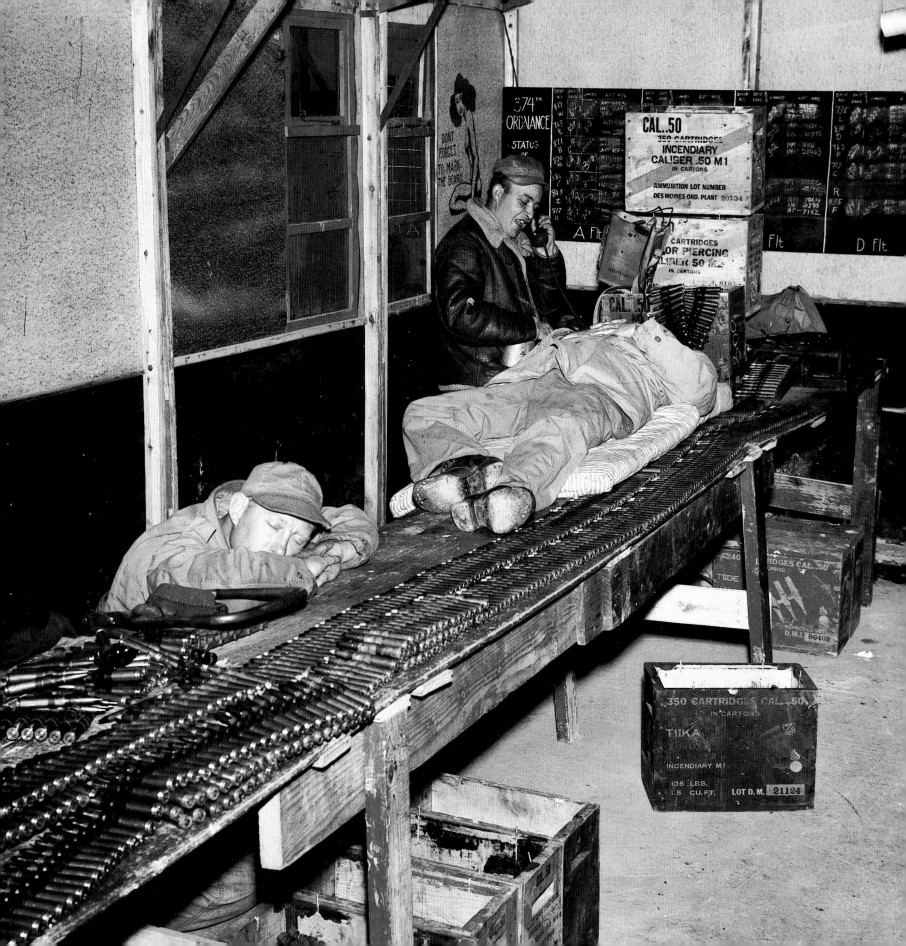

LITTLE FRIENDS: THE BEGINNING

THE DAYLIGHT ATTACKS by RAF Bomber Command in the early years of the war had been no more than token forays. At night, though, its bombers had been raiding targets in Germany as well as northern Italy, and during the Battle of Britain it had pounded the assembling German invasion fleets in France. From the outset of the war, the RAF had seemed more comfortable with night operations. Its daytime raids on targets just inside France and Belgium drew heavily on the resources of RAF Fighter Command. The bomber formations escorted by Hurricanes and Spitfires of 11 Group on what the RAF called "Circuses" were often costly exercises. These were the early days of protective fighter escort.

On April 16, 1941, a mission was launched by Blenheims of 21 Squadron against the heavily defended Luftwaffe fighter field at Berck-sur-Mer. Their escort was made up of 601 Squadron Hurricanes and 303 (Polish) Squadron Spitfires. The Spitfires provided top cover while the Hurricanes flew close escort. Outbound, the flight was uneventful although a formation of Messerschmitt ME 109s was observed at higher altitude. The forces did not engage in combat.

Delivering their bombs on target, and damaging or destroying seven of the new ME 109Fs on the ground, the Blenheims turned for home with their escort, unhindered by flak or enemy fighters. their return across the Channel was also without incident until they reached the English coast at Dungeness. With the advantages of height and sun, a formation of 109s of Werner Mölders' JG53 tore through the British fighters, with cannon and machine guns blazing. The weavers, flying to protect the rear of the RAF formation, were the first to be picked off. Two of the Polish airmen were shot down. Pilot Officer Waskiewicz was hit and sent plunging into the Channel while Pilot Officer Mierzwa's Spitfire exploded on the pebbled beach near Dungeness lighthouse.

The RAF pilots broke in all directions. Wing Commander "Minnie" Manton, who had recently been appointed to oversee operations such as this one, was having an unfortunate indoctrination. Wounded, and with his Hurricane badly holed, he prepared to bail out. The Luftwaffe had even removed the hood for him. But then a glance at the sea made him reconsider. The airplane did seem controllable. With enough altitude to glide back across the coast, he would try to put the battered kite down somewhere. He had spun down from the combat area and a quick check confirmed that no one was on his tail. He managed to get the Hurricane down in a farmer's field and was lucky to survive as the aircraft cartwheeled across a drainage ditch and tore itself apart. His Sutton seat harness had been damaged in the attack and Manton was pitched forward and knocked unconscious. A gashed forehead, shrapnel wounds, severe bruising and a chipped spine were to keep him off ops for some time.

The rest of 601 Squadron was having a

There set out, slowly, for a Different World,/ At four, on winter mornings, different legs . . ./*You can't break eggs without making an omelette/*—That's what they tell the eggs.

from "A War"
by Randall Jarrell

I never raised my boy to be a soldier/I brought him up to be my pride and joy./Who dares to lay a gun/upon his shoulder,/And teach him how to kill another mother's boy./I brought him up to stay at home with me. There would be no war to-day,/if every mother would say/I never raised my boy/to be a soldier.

—Traditional, North Country

left: Weary USAAF armorers asleep at their workbench after loading many linked belts of .50 caliber rounds for the P-51 Mustangs of their fighter group.

right: A Maycrete hut at Merston. above right: Test pilot and former RAF fighter pilot Neville Duke. below: Heather and gorse on the airfield site at Martlesham Heath. below right: A Hurricane control grip. center: Two RAF fighter manufacturer's plates. far right: Captain Jack Ilfrey, 20th Fighter Group, Kings Cliffe.

Boys will be boys.

—English proverb

hard time too. Its commanding officer, Squadron Leader John "Peggy" O'Neill, was hit and forced to bale out into the sea. Whitney Straight, an American pilot in 601, circled overhead to guide rescue boats to O'Neill's dinghy in Rye Bay. As O'Neill was being rescued, Group Captain Theodore McEvoy, station commander of 601 and 303's Northolt base, was crash-landing his damaged Hurricane on the Dungeness beach. McEvoy was not an operational pilot and had just come along to observe.

As suddenly as they had come the Messerschmitts disappeared, leaving behind two dead and four wounded RAF pilots, and five aircraft destroyed, for no loss of their own. "They slized us to beets," said a wounded Pilot Officer Strembosz on returning to Northolt in his crippled Spitfire.

The British bombers had escaped the attack without loss and the results of their bombing on Berck-sur-Mer had been good, even though the operation had been a disaster for their fighter escorts. However, a lesson had been learned about fighter-escort tactics from this debacle. Having the fighters tied so closely to the bombers was a mistake, and flying fighter squadrons in archaic "air-display" formations was suicidal. And finally, the need was recognized for effective rear-cover fighter protection for returning bomber formations whose escorts were low on fuel. But the value of the Circus missions that pioneered the fighter-escorted daylight bombing raids into occupied Europe was questionable. The cost in bombers, fighters and crews was unacceptable in relation to the limited success of these

Please understand there is no depression in this house. We are not very interested in the possibility of defeat.

—Victoria R.I.

Put your trust in God, my boys,/and keep your powder dry.

—Colonel Valentine Blacker

Unfaithfulness in the keeping of an appointment/is an act of clear dishonesty. You may as well/borrow a person's money as his time.

—Horace Mann

left: A German HE 111 bomber crew en route to England.

133

escort missions.

Neville Duke, later to achieve fame as a test pilot and holder of the World Air Speed Record, had just joined 92 Squadron at Biggin Hill when the Circus missions began. He recalls: "Stirling bombers were being used for these daylight raids, usually flying in threes with Spitfires for escorts. On one occasion, though, 92 Squadron provided top cover for nine Blenheims which were bombing Haze-brouck marshaling yards. I was glad, and a bit

Lt. R.L. Schlieker, 357th FG, was killed while flying *"Floogie II"* on escort, January 13, 1945.

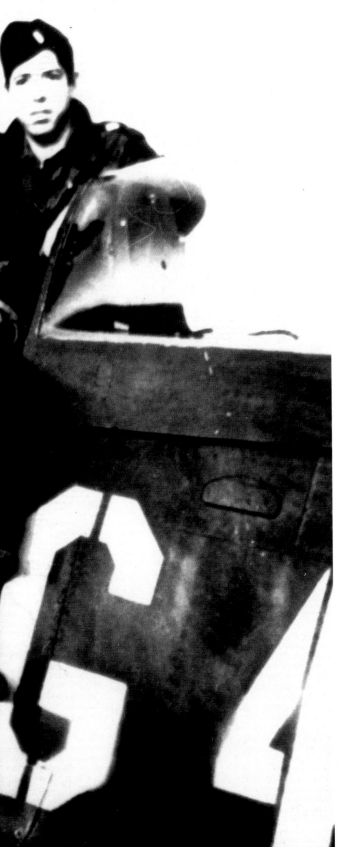

relieved, when I got down again after this show. We were at twenty-five thousand feet and there were a lot of 109s about—too many, in fact, for my liking. One of them managed to latch onto my tail and suddenly I saw tracer going over my hood. I was able to get out of his way by turning hard and climbing—only to be jumped by eight more of his friends. I used all the dodges I could think of, but only managed to get away from them when I was well out to sea. To add insult to injury I was then attacked by a Spitfire . . . fortunately without result."

The next time out, Neville got a confirmed ME 109 kill in a dogfight over the Channel between Dover and Calais. In the twisting maneuvers, he became disoriented and was climbing while inverted, unable to distinguish between the blue of the sea and that of the sky. Then a 109 was framed in his gunsight; he fired and the German went into a slow spin toward the sea . . . and Neville was reoriented. By the end of that day he had been on ops three times.

In the next year, the escort operations of RAF Fighter Command produced mixed results. One pilot commented: "Circuses? They were never half so much fun as any circus I had ever been to, but whoever dreamed up the idea was certainly a clown!" The RAF was paying a heavy price in its new offensive role, including the deaths of the outstanding fighter leaders Brendan "Paddy" Finucane and Victor Beamish, and the loss of the legless legend, Douglas Bader, boss of the Tangmere Wing. As a young man in 1931, Bader had been involved in a flying accident that result-

None of us has ever doubted/he was indeed the best of us,/more skillful in the art of living/than the rest of us.

His death was no pitiful drama/laboriously enacted before our eyes./He died remotely beyond the horizon/as a comet or a meteor dies.

The cabled news was brief/but it shattered our world like shrapnel,/splintering our lives/with all the violence of a bursting shell.

We said (more from fear than from conviction) "He would feel nothing, it was so swift,"/and with this comfortable fiction/ gave fear short shrift.

Our unquestioned leader/it was so like him to go before us into the mapless region of death/thereby diminishing the terror for us.

For however we may recoil/from the invisible torrent/we shall not be entirely fearful to follow on/into the unfathomable canyon where he has gone.

"20th Century Requiem" by Patricia M. Saunders

135

ed in the amputation of both his legs.

Shot down over France on August 9, 1941, Bader was fortunate to survive. One of his artificial legs had become lodged in the damaged cockpit of his fighter, trapping him. Finally, he managed to break free of the prosthesis and bail out safely, but into captivity. "Buck" Casson was flying with 616 Squadron of the Tangmere wing under Bader's command and he too, was shot down and captured that day. Casson remembers: "On this operation it was a novel experience for us to have ample height for attack, instead of being in the role of underdog." But despite this advantage, Casson and Bader were downed by Adolf Galland and his formidable JG26 wing. Galland's admiration of Bader led him to ask Reichsmarshall Hermann Göring for permission to contact the Royal Air Force to request that a spare set of prosthetic legs be dropped by parachute near Galland's French base. Radio contact was made with the RAF on an international SOS wavelength and the English were informed of Bader's capture and the request for his artificial limbs was made. Shortly thereafter, Galland's base and other targets in the St. Omer area were bombed by the RAF, who later notified Galland's unit that, in addition to bombs, they had dropped the requested spare legs. The Germans then located a large box near their airfield. The box had been painted with a red cross and German lettering: THIS BOX CONTAINS ARTIFICIAL LEGS FOR WING COMMANDER BADER, PRISONER OF WAR. When taken into German custody at Galland's St. Omer base, Casson was informed that Bader was also a prisoner. Refusing to

It's easy to be nice, boys,/When everything's okay./It's easy to be cheerful When you're having things your way./But can you hold your head up,/And take it on the chin,/When your heart is nearly breaking,/And you feel like giving in?

It was easy back in England,/Amongst the friends and folks,/But now you miss the friendly hand,/The joys, and songs, and jokes./The road ahead is stony,/And unless you're strong in mind, You'll find it isn't long before/You're lagging far behind.

You've got to climb the hill, boys/It's no use turning back,/There's only one way home, And that's off the beaten track. Remember you're an American,/And when you reach the crest, You'll see a valley, cool and green;/America at her best.

You know, there is a saying/That sunshine follows rain,/And sure

acknowledge that he knew Bader, Casson would only admit to having heard of him in the service. "Quite honestly, I just couldn't believe it." Neither could anyone else in Fighter Command.

A year later, on August 19, 1942, at Dieppe, RAF fighter units fought hard and well in the famous raid, but more significantly, fighter units of the U.S. 8th Air Force saw action in the ETO for the first time. It marked the start of an illustrious campaign.

From the beginning of American air operations in England, "Monk" Hunter, commanding general of VIII Fighter Command, was hampered by the limited operating range of his aircraft. Assigned to accompany the 8th Air Force's B-17 and B-24 bombers then being organized for deep-penetration raids into Germany, his then-current fighters carried insufficient fuel to cover such distances. The early Spitfires with which the first 8th Air Force fighter groups were equipped couldn't do the job, nor could the new Thunderbolts or the early Mustangs. Even the innovative P-38 Lightning was to prove incapable of such long hauls. What the bombers required was total fighter protection, all the way there and all the way back.

At Bovingdon, near London, the technical experts of 8th Fighter Command were working on a system of long-range drop tanks for the fighters. Different types were tried, including resinated-paper 205-gallon tanks and metal tanks that could be pressurized. Technical snags, shortages and slow delivery from the United States caused a delay of several months before drop tanks were available in

quantity for the Thunderbolt. It was not until midsummer of 1943 that drop tanks became standard operational equipment, extending the fighter radius of action by about eighty miles. The concept called for the fighters to use the fuel in their external tanks first, then dumping the empty containers. The ungainly pods would consequently no longer inhibit the performance of the fighter in combat. The fighters' range would be extended further in time, and, ultimately, the ultra long-range P-51D Mustang would become available in large numbers; but for the time being the escort capability was to be a narrow one.

The American fighters took their bombers as far as they could until forced to withdraw, usually somewhere near the Dutch-German border. Flak, the weather and enemy fighters continually threatened the bombers and their escort. Aware of the fuel limitations of 8th Air Force fighter escorts, the German interceptors often shadowed the massive American formations, waiting for the moment when the escorting fighters would have to turn for home and the bombers were left untended and alone. At this point in the war, the main German fighter units were still well equipped, well organized, well led—and determined.

The Americans soon realized that the defensive fire of the bomber formations would not, in itself, protect them. Close fighter escort from home base to target and back was the only way to operate. Newly-arrived P-38 Lightnings soon demonstrated their superior range to that of the drop tank–fitted P-47s, which then equipped most 8th Air Force fighter units. On November 13, 1943, the Lightnings escorted a force of B-24s to Bremen. In a fierce air battle the 48th Fighter Squadron of the 14th Fighter Group shot down seven German fighters. Though other American fighter groups lost seven P-38s on this mission, not a single B-24 was lost to enemy fighters. The point had been made. If our fighters could stick with the bombers all the way, our losses to enemy fighters could be minimized.

Long before the range problem was resolved, American bombers were being sent to attack targets deep in Germany and were incurring intolerable losses. As the bomber force struggled back from the target area to fighter-escort range where the rear-cover wing of Thunderbolts or Lightnings would pick them up, the sight of these "little friends" was as welcome as the longed-for first glimpse of the English coastline.

"Hub" Zemke's 56th Fighter Group, the "Wolfpack," was one of the outfits assigned to escort duty in the early days of the mass daylight bombing raids. One of Zemke's pilots, Walker "Bud" Mahurin, recalls that altitude, as well as range, was a vital consideration to the Thunderbolt pilots: "At heights above thirty thousand feet the P-47 could out-turn and outrun any Messerschmitt 109. Below that, though, it was still a pretty good match, but its rate of climb was less than impressive. Conscious of the critical altitude factor, and in a belief that less weight equaled more altitude and a better climbing performance, Zemke once stripped out of his P-47 every item of equipment he considered superfluous—the

armor plating, bullet-proof windscreen ... even the relief tube. When he had finished, the revetment where his airplane was parked looked like a junkyard. With his new "light-weight" P-47, he led the 56th on another escort mission. Over German-held territory, he had a scare. A .50 caliber bullet slammed into his cockpit, entering where the armored windscreen had previously been. It narrowly missed his head and tore through the back of the cockpit. The bullet had been fired by a B-17 gunner testing his weapon. Back on the ground Zemke put all the junk back on his airplane again."

In the late summer of 1943, a force of B-17s raided Münster and discovered to its cost what could happen if a planned fighter shield was not in place. Fighter cover had been intended and was to be provided (in fact, by the Wolfpack) but a slight navigational error en route made the Thunderbolts late for their rendezvous with the bombers. Catastrophe resulted for the lead bomber wing, comprising the 100th, 95th and 390th Bomb Groups. In minutes the 100th was almost entirely destroyed; half of the 390th was shot down, as was a quarter of the 95th. Twenty-nine B-17s were lost—nearly all of them to German fighters. In human terms, the loss equalled two thirds of the casualties suffered by RAF Fighter Command in the Battle of Britain—but this time the losses had been inflicted in a matter of minutes. With adequate fighter protection these losses would certainly have been fewer. Clearly, the attrition rate of the American bombers was unacceptable and could not be tolerated regardless of bombing results.

left: The wallet of 2nd Lt. Roy E. Wendell, 78th FG, 84th FS, Duxford. Wendell was killed March 13, 1944, in the crash of his P-47C while on a local camera gunnery training flight. above: A popular airmen's pub near RAF Church Fenton.

THOSE GIRLS

"Will you walk into my parlour?"/Said the spider to the fly:/"Tis the prettiest little parlour/That ever you did spy."

from "The Spider and the Fly" by Mary Howitt

A source of innocent merriment!/Of innocent merriment.

from *The Mikado* by W. S. Gilbert

right: September 1942. On leave in London, GIs are rowed on the Serpentine in Hyde Park by American Red Cross girls.

IT WASN'T ALL BLOODSHED, boredom and booze. There were . . . distractions. In one form or another, the female of the species featured as prominently in the life of the fighter pilot as the airplane in which he went to war. Pinup or wife, sweetheart or mother figure, all played a part in boosting morale and normalizing an otherwise abnormal existence. Unlike other experiences of war, the memories of those girls remain mostly pleasant. Apart from the wives and sweethearts though, the image of one girl persists with many American and British servicemen. Jane, the comic-strip cutie. Along with Betty Grable and Vera Lynn, she ranks as one of the best-loved girls of the war years, especially among the fliers.

Jane was everybody's girlfriend. She was leggy, curvaceous, a scatterbrain . . . and a sensation. She oozed sex appeal—yet was naïvely unaware of it. In fact, she was a fantasy girl, the creation of cartoonist Norman Pett, and she appeared nearly every day in the London *Daily Mirror*. Readers invariably turned to see Jane's capers before scanning the news. The headlines could wait. What had Jane been up to? No wonder one member of Parliament referred to the Allied Forces, in a House of Commons speech, as "Jane's Fighting Men." Her success was astounding, yet the storyline was entirely predictable. She would always lose her scanty clothes, or most of them, in this particular cartoon strip.

The model for Norman Pett's "Jane" was, in fact, Chrystabel Leighton-Porter, an attractive and vivacious young blonde. Given the success of the cartoon, there was a demand for Jane to appear in person and a stage show

140

KINGSTON EMPIRE

Proprietor - KINGSHOT THEATRES, LTD.
Direction - - - - STANLEY WATSON

Phone: KINgston 3131

6-0 | MONDAY, MAR. 31ST, 1947 | 8-15

Twice Nightly

NO PERFORMANCE ON GOOD FRIDAY

LEW & LESLIE GRADE present

"JANE OUT OF THE MIRROR"

PERSONAL APPEARANCE OF

JANE

THE FAMOUS CARTOON GIRL of the DAILY MIRROR

MAX & HARRY NESBITT

THE POPULAR ENTERTAINERS AND SONG WRITERS

EDDIE

MICRO-PHUN

LITTLE

was conceived. It was considered to be quite risqué, but despite complaints from those who safeguarded public morals the shows were put on almost daily in theaters around Britain. Her "act" was portrayed through windows positioned across the stage to suggest the boxes of her comic strip. The audience saw Jane and her little dachshund Fritz as shadows against a white screen.

With the rationing and shortages of wartime Britain, pretty clothes were hard to find, an ironic problem for a girl best known for her state of undress. Her creator's frequent failure to meet his newspaper deadline, however, ensured that Jane was never short of one item. Pett's tardiness with the artwork caused the *Daily Mirror* to threaten to drop the series, which they eventually did. There was such an outcry that the cartoon was immediately brought back, its absence explained in a single drawing of a flustered Jane and the words: "Give me a break boys, I've lost my panties!"

143

The reaction was swift and overwhelming. The offices of the *Mirror* were deluged with undies.

At the height of the Blitz bombing, Jane was putting on nightly shows in London. The servicemen loved them and flocked to each performance. Every night as she concluded her show she would invite a male in the audience to join her on stage in a song-and-dance routine. Often he would be an American airman. Both Jane and her real-life model, Chrystabel . . . had a special affection for Americans. "They were wonderful. So full of life and so much fun. In fact, the Yanks fell in love with England . . . with English girls . . . and with me," Chrystabel remembers. Many proposed to her. "Of course, every one of them had a ranch back home, or a newspaper or oil empire. At least they all said they had."

It was an RAF fighter pilot, however, whose proposal she eventually accepted: Flying Officer Arthur Leighton-Porter, who flew Typhoons in 182 Squadron. But the marriage was a hush-hush affair. Her image as a pinup and as "everyone's girl" would have been shattered had news of the marriage leaked. Consequently, her wedding became one of the best-kept secrets of the war. Jane's eventual postwar "marriage" to the character Georgie Porgie when the cartoon series ended caused an uproar and even made the BBC news.

Chrystabel recalls that the well-heeled American fighter pilots were a great hit with the girls in Jane's theater company. "Some of them would get our tour dates and follow us around the country to all the different venues in one great gang. After the show they'd have taxis lined up to take us on to a club, or for a meal and some music and dancing. In London it would be the Savoy, where they had made a basement ballroom safe from the bombs falling above as we danced."

When they had bribed the bandleader to play "As Time Goes By" for the last time, it was taxis home for Chrystabel and her girls to whichever hotel happened to be "home" for

Day, too, broke silently.
Before the blackbird,
Before the trouble of
traffic and the mist
unrolled,/I shall
remember at the dark
hour turning to you
For comfort in the cold.

from "At the Dark
Hour"
by Paul Dehn

Here in the lounge of
this hotel/We struggle
for our holy ground,
Our faces play
discretion well,/Our
deepest anguish breaks
no sound;/the spirit's
sole confession here
Swims in the crystal of
one tear.

from "The Tear"
by Stephen Haggard

right: From the notes of a
WAAF Aircraftwoman II
flight mechanic. above
right: WAAF armorer
trainees positioning a
Browning machine gun into
the wing of a Hurricane
fighter. above center: Kath
Preston at the White Hart,
Brasted, in WWII. above far
right: Kath Preston, 1990.
far right: The "Wolf
Wagon" bus at the 357th
FG Leiston base.

STARTING & RUNNING.

Hurricane I (Merlin II)

NOTE. The procedure & figures given below apply
to this a/c only & may vary on other types
Therefore before running a strange a/c.
Reference should always be made to the relevant AP.

(Ground Handling Notes now available - AP 6013 (Hurricane I).

1. Nose into wind, chocks in position, fire extinguisher
airscrew barrier.

2. GUNS 'SAFE'. UNDERCAR. 'NEUTRAL'. BRAKES 'ON'
SWITCHES 'OFF'

3.

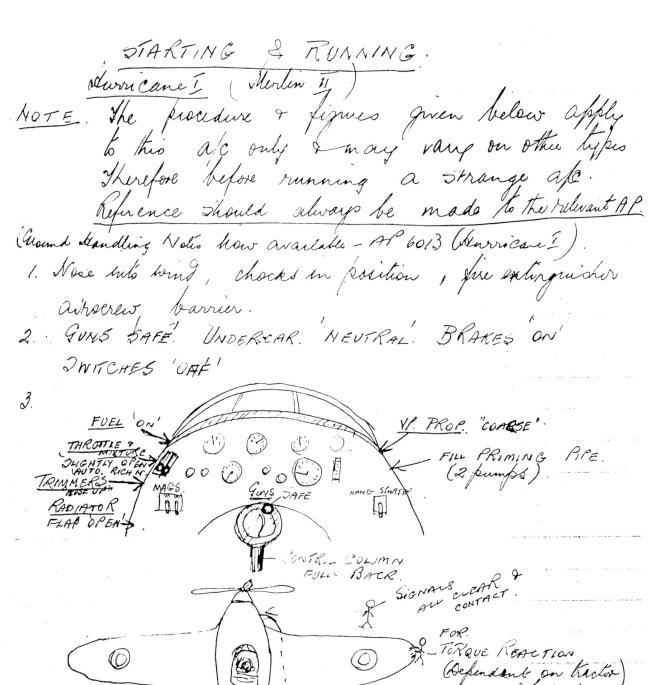

right: The famous chorus of London's Windmill Theater visiting Debden's 4th Fighter Group.

that week. But, like thousands of other wives in wartime, she had to get on with life aware that her husband was in constant danger. And, since the marriage had to be kept a secret, she couldn't confide in anyone about Arthur. The moments they could spend together were few. Their leaves rarely coincided and wartime travel was difficult. On-base visits by wives and girlfriends were not encouraged by RAF station commanders. As Major James Goodson of the U.S. 4th Fighter Group put it: "Marriage tempered a man too much and the cautious pilot is doomed. I've never seen a fighter pilot get married and keep on the way he was. He gets careful, thinking about his wife. The first thing you know he's thinking about her and a Hun bounces his tail."

There were, of course, other girls in the lives of the fighter pilots, and a special one in the life of Harley Brown of the Kings Cliffe-based 20th Fighter Group, USAAF.

The excitement and novelty of being in a strange country and flying fighters was matched by only one thing: the English girls. With so many of the English servicemen away at war, the coast was clear for the American pilots, who moved in with gusto. They brought an easygoing and flattering breeziness to the art of dating. These Yanks were really something. What British serviceman could compete with the money, the accent, the uniform? Descending on the cities, towns and villages of Britain, the Americans launched an attack with candy, nylons, nail polish and perfume. It was called "shack-up material" and, while such aids to conquest were not always successful, the young Ameri-

can serviceman was rarely offended or discouraged by a firm refusal. There was sure to be some other honey anxious for his attentions. But Harley Brown needed neither money, perfume, nylons nor accent to win his girl. It was just plain old-fashioned love at first sight.

On leave from their first base at Goxhill, Brown and two friends had crossed the River Humber for a day out in Hull. There, they went to a typically English tea room for refreshment.

"We were standing there waiting for an empty table when I noticed two English girls dressed in the National Fire Service uniforms having their tea and crumpets. One was a brunette and the other the most beautiful blonde I had ever seen. I told my two buddies, the heck with waiting for an empty table! We approached their table and asked if we could join them. What two girls could say no to three handsome young pilots standing there in their new uniforms with the silver wings and shiny gold bars? While getting acquainted we learned that the girls were telephone operators in the NFS and on their afternoon break. Before they had to go back to work I had gotten the blonde's phone number and address. During the next two weeks, every time I could get a day or even a few hours off, I'd call her and head for Hull."

Harley Brown's blonde was Peggie Blaymires. Their relationship was to survive his subsequent posting south to Kings Cliffe. When the war in Europe ended Harley went back to the United States on three months' rest leave. Although he and Peggie were en-

148

In every mess I find a
friend./In every port a
wife.

from "Jack in His
Element"
by Charles Dibdin

gaged by this time and had made plans for a
wedding, the relationship seemed to be going
the way of so many wartime romances between English girls and American servicemen—nowhere. A return to the UK for Harley
was now out of the question and Peggie could
not get to America. But somehow their relationship lasted. They remained in touch and
in love until, in June 1946, Peggie got to New
York and the couple was married. Forty-five

years later Harley's little Yorkshire lass is still
the most beautiful blonde he has ever seen.

It was the girls in the services who figured most immediately in the lives of the Allied fighter pilots. Driver, plotter, clerk or
nurse, the girls in uniform were often more
than just that to the fliers. Friendships and
romances flourished between the pilots and
the girls working together on the same
stations.

Edith Heap was only twenty years old
when she volunteered to join the Women's
Auxiliary Air Force the day after war broke

out. Aircraftwoman Heap enlisted as a driver and reported for duty at RAF Yeadon in her home county of Yorkshire. Posted later to Debden in Essex, she drove lorries and tractors, and laid out flarepaths for the Hurricane fighters at the RAF station. She enjoyed her work.

"We were all so young and naïve, and although a lot of the boys were knockouts, we hardly knew how to treat the opposite sex because we had all been segregated at school. Holding hands or perhaps a peck on the cheek was enough to send us into ecstasies, and most of what went on was just light-hearted chat and a sort of banter we'd developed to keep the boys in order."

At Debden Edith met twenty-year-old Denis Wissler, a pilot officer on a short-service commission flying Hurricanes with 17 Squadron. By the time of the Battle of Britain she was remustered and had become an operations room plotter, while Denis was in the thick of the fighting.

"When the controller had vectored the squadron toward the enemy, we would hear shouts of 'Tally-Ho' over the RT and a running commentary from the pilots. We listened to 'Blue Two going down in flames,' without knowing whether he had managed to bail out."

On September 24, 1940, Denis was shot down by a Messerschmitt ME 109 over the Thames Estuary. He managed to make it back to Debden, where he crash-landed on the airfield. He was admitted to Saffron Walden Hospital with an arm wound and Edith visited him there frequently. He returned to duty

and, shortly after, his squadron was posted away to Martlesham Heath on the Suffolk coast. By this point he and Edith were in love and from then on they wrote to each other every day and met whenever their duties allowed.

They managed to get a twenty-four-hour pass together. "We went to Cambridge, but the Garden House Hotel there was full, except for a double room. Denis came out and told me that he had declined the double room and asked if that was right. I said yes, and wondered later if he would have asked me to marry him if I had said no. We eventually found single rooms at the Red Lion at Trumpington. We had dinner and lots of chat. It was getting late and Denis came to my room and sat on the bed and asked me to marry him. I said yes of course and Denis ordered a bottle of champagne, which the manager brought up. I was surprised that he didn't say anything about Denis being in my room, definitely not done in those days. And, after all of the bubbly, we went to our respective beds." Once they had the approval of Denis's commanding officer and their families, the wedding date was set for January 4. Then came November 11.

Although Denis's squadron had moved to Martlesham Heath, it was still controlled by the ops room at Debden, where Edith was a plotter. "Just before we came off watch at 1200 hours, there was a cry of 'Blue Four going down into the drink.' I was paralyzed with fear. I *knew* who it was, and I *knew* what had happened, but I allowed myself to hope. When we left Ops, I didn't bother with lunch, but went up to Motor Transport to talk to old

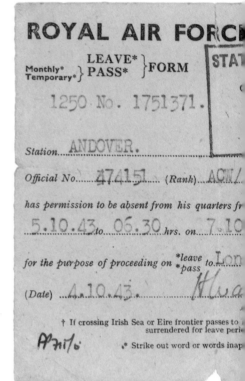

He has not even seen
you, he/Who gave you
your mortality;/And
you, so small, how can
you guess/His courage
or his loveliness?

from "War Baby"
by Pamela Holmes

left: Royal Air Force
personnel taking tea at a
NAAFI wagon on a fighter
station in England.

friends. Later, I got the news. Yes, it was true, He was missing. No parachute observed."

When men like Denis failed to return, some pilots looked for comfort from mother figures like Kath Preston, landlady of The White Hart at Brasted. The pub was a popular haunt of the Biggin Hill pilots and she had quickly learned to recognize the symptoms of a loss when "her" boys came in.

"Sometimes the usual crowd would come in and perhaps they would be a bit sub-dued. Then you would realize that a face was missing and the best friend of the missing man was sitting alone in the corner, drinking."

In situations like that Kath knew to say nothing. They didn't want to talk about the missing man. No other subjects were taboo, however, between Kath and her pilot customers. In her mid-thirties, she was a woman of maturity and experience to these very young men. They would take her into their confidence about their problems and their love

lives. Kath was always there to listen as a trusted and respected friend. She was fun too. A joke, a kind word, a game of darts and a four-penny pint of mild beer on the house was her way of entering into the spirit of things. It could not have always been easy for her though. Her husband Teddy was away in the navy and she feared for his safety—a kind of fear that Jane, Peggie and Edith shared.

In her own way Kath was serving her country by cheering Biggin Hill's "Few." She contributed immeasurably to the morale of those pilots and is still remembered by them today. Doubtless there were other Kaths in the lives of the fighter pilots, but none could surpass the warmth, affection and caring of Kath Preston. No wonder they loved her.

Girls, friends, wives, lovers, whoever they may have been, almost every Allied fighter pilot had his often short life enriched by a Jane, an Edith, a Peggie or a Kath. He needed her.

above far left: A WAAF meteorologist. far left: WAAF Cpl. Evelyn "Tiggy" Lowe stationed at Foulness in 1943. center left: Mrs. Eleanor Roosevelt, calling at Debden, meets Col. Edward Anderson and Major Gus Daymond, June 11, 1944. below: A dance at Debden.

VERY SPECIAL DELIVERY

above and above right: The former headquarters of the Air Transport Auxiliary at White Waltham.

"RECKLESS," "colorful," "aggressive," "egotistical," "flashy" . . . all were descriptives commonly associated with World War II fighter pilots. But there were others, and very different types, who flew the Mustangs, Spitfires, Typhoons and Hurricanes in a noncombatant role, out of the limelight. They were the men and women delivery pilots of the Air Transport Auxiliary (ATA), an organization of which Lord Beaverbrook, Churchill's minister for aircraft production, later said: "They carried out the delivery of aircraft from the factories to the RAF, thus relieving countless numbers of RAF pilots for duty in battle. They were soldiers fighting in the struggle just as completely as if they had been engaged on the battlefront."

Petite and attractive Diana Barnato was as far removed from the archetypal battlefront soldier as one could be. Granddaughter of the diamond-mining magnate Barney Barnato and daughter of the famous racing driver Woolfe "Babe" Barnato, she selected war work as a Red Cross Voluntary Aid Detachment (VAD) nurse, a suitably feminine occupation for an ex-debutante. But a chance meeting with the chief flying instructor of the newly formed ATA, while out riding in Windsor Park, was to change her life.

Diana had learned to fly during 1937 at the Brooklands Flying Club and had soloed after only six hours of lessons. "I really hadn't a clue what I was doing and waggled the stick around as if stirring a pudding. I always remember that as I was getting ready to taxi out for my solo, a little man came running over and hung onto the edge of the cockpit staring up at me. He had a hideously burned and disfigured face, and called out, 'Miss Barnato, Miss Barnato, please don't fly. Look what it's done to me.' Well, I took off anyway although, in fact, he did me a very good turn. Later, whenever I got in a tight spot, I thought of that man and his little face looking up at me. It had been a salutary experience, even though I ignored him at the time.

"After a mere ten hours of flying I couldn't afford it anymore on my own pocket money and had to give up. Later, when I was invited to take a test for the ATA, it seemed my flying experience of a few years before was hardly sufficient qualification, but they said I was 'promising' and asked me to come and have the test anyway."

At this time there were only eight ATA women pilots in the service and, despite the exploits of famed aviators like Amy Johnson and Amelia Earhart, flying was not considered an occupation appropriate for females, least of all in wartime. With that in mind, Diana was not hopeful about passing her test. Then a riding accident delayed her taking the test, and it was a further six months before she took it, passed and joined up as a trainee pilot. She was taught to fly again, from scratch, and was given the rank of first officer. In her smart navy-blue uniform with its gold-embroidered wings, Diana was eventually posted to No. 15 Ferry Pilot Pool at Hamble in Hampshire. Of all the ATA airfields, Hamble was very much in the front line, and yet its complement of pilots was exclusively female.

Sandwiched between Southampton Water

commodore's room and operations block, 1990. below right: The hangar interior.

above: First Officer Diana Barnato-Walker. right: First Officer Maureen Dunlop

and the River Hamble, it had the balloon barrages of Portsmouth and Gosport on one side and those of Eastleigh and Southampton on the other—posing considerable hazards to all pilots in the region. It was not just light aircraft such as Tiger Moths which these Hamble girls flew. Their proximity to the Hamble Spitfire building and repair facility and the Eastleigh Spitfire factory meant that the girls handled primarily fighter aircraft. But they were also required to deliver Hudsons, Mitchells, Blenheims and Oxfords, as well as Walrus and Sea Otter amphibians and many other types. The girls had to be adaptable. One moment they could be expected to fly a Blackburn Roc . . . then a Proctor and then a Mitchell. During the 1944 invasion period they were delivering upwards of twenty fighters a day—Typhoons, Tempests, Mustangs and Spitfires—directly to the forward airfields on the south coast, from where RAF squadrons flew them straight into action over France.

Diana recalls a typical day at Hamble: "We would be waiting around for the weather to clear—writing letters, playing bridge, listening to the wireless, sewing. Suddenly the loudspeaker would blare out 'All pilots to report to Operations Room for their chits.' Everyone would immediately drop whatever she happened to be doing and go to the hatchway to be briefed for her job for the day. There would be a mad scurry into the lockers for maps and helmets . . . a visit to Met for the weather information . . . then off to the Maps and Signals Office for the latest news about stray balloons and airfield serviceability. If a pilot got a type of aircraft she had not flown before it would be off to the library for a book of 'handling notes' which would tell her all she needed to know about flying that type!"

The girls trudged out to the taxi aircraft, lugging parachutes and overnight bags, and one of their number would have been assigned the duty of taxi pilot, ferrying the girls by Anson to their starting points and collecting them all again at the end of the day.

Home for Diana was a rented cottage, shared with one of the other girls. "We all got on well together, we had to. There was no bitchiness and we worked together well as a team under the guidance of Commander Margot Gore." This team of women at 15 FPP was a multinational one with girls from Denmark, Poland, Argentina, South Africa, Chile, Australia and the United States alongside the British contingent.

It was the American girls who formed the largest foreign group. A New York businesswoman, Jacqueline Cochran, had begun to recruit likely women candidates for the ATA. Among them was a twenty-year-old office clerk, Emily Chapin. With just a minimum of flying hours she bravely traveled to England by cargo boat across the U-boat–patrolled Atlantic and joined the ATA in August 1942. Soon she qualified as pilot with the rank third officer and was attached to the Hamble-based No. 15 Pool.

Apart from the hazards of the English weather, balloon barrages, inexperience on so many aircraft types and unfamiliar terrain there was also the unexpected. Emily was only just airborne in a Spitfire when a defective

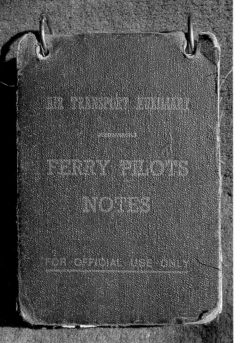

latch caused the hood to blow open. Unable to close it, she came in for an emergency landing, but with her wind-blurred vision she misjudged the approach. The Spitfire dropped on one wheel and the wing scraped along the concrete; it then bounced hard onto its other wheel, severely damaging the other wing. By the end of the runway the airplane was a wreck and Emily was badly shaken but unhurt. Shortly after this incident, the unpredictable weather claimed Emily's American friend Mary Nicholson, who flew into a mist-shrouded hillside and was killed instantly.

When Jacqueline Cochran later contacted Emily about a new organization being set up in the States for women pilots, she decided to go home and join the Women's Air Service Pilots—WASPs for short. Reluctantly the ATA released her. Emily Chapin and her compatriots gave selfless and invaluable service to Britain in her hour of need.

During World War II 174 ATA pilots were killed—men and women. Tanya Whittall, Dora Lang, Honor Salmon and Pat Parker, all from 15 FPP, Hamble, were among those who died, as well as Mary Nicholson. Amy Johnson was also among the ATA casualties. If combat fighter pilots were heroes, then these girls were surely heroines. They were certainly exceptional women doing vital work. The ATA,

however, was not an exclusively female organization. Its male pilots were generally men with flying experience, who if over twenty-five, were too old for operational RAF service. Many were World War I fliers, some were prewar airline captains, club pilots or barnstormers. Some were disabled but all were united in purpose and in their love of flying. It was sometimes joked that ATA really stood for "Ancient and Tattered Airmen."

When war broke out, Len Biggs was one of those considered too old to join the RAF for flying duties. The Air Ministry didn't even bother to reply to his applications. He was discouraged, but knew that as a healthy thirty-five-year-old he had something worthwhile to offer his country. One day he happened to hear on the radio that pilots under fifty, with a minimum of fifty hours' flying experience, were required for work of national importance. As an ex-club pilot, he qualified and immediately applied and was told to go home and await instructions. Six weeks later he was at White Waltham and in ATA uniform as First Officer Biggs.

Len was posted to Whitchurch, near Bristol, where his unit was delivering Beaufighters to and from the Bristol aircraft works. He remembers: "The Beaufighter was not the easiest of airplanes to fly, but it was exciting.

Believe only half of
what you see
and nothing that you
hear.

—Dinah Mulock Craik

above far left: Diana Barnato-Walker, 1990. far left: Diana's pilot notes. center left: The control room at ATA headquarters, White Waltham. center right: The control room, 1990. above: Len Biggs, 1990.

159

right: Diana Barnato-Walker preparing to deliver a Spitfire. below: An Anson brings ATA ferry pilots to an aircraft factory where they will pick up aircraft for delivery flights to RAF squadrons.

Many pilots were scared to death of them, but if in difficulties I'd rather be in a Beau than anything else. When you put her through the gate there was this massive surge of sheer power and you'd leap into the air. It had immense strength too. One of our pilots, 'Timber' Woods, hated Beaus and one day spread one all over Sealand aerodrome. He made the most frightful landing you can imagine—the tail section broke off, the engines shot out and he was left sitting in what remained of the center section. If it had been anything other than a Beaufighter he'd have been dead."

Sometimes the ferry pilots would show the fighter boys how things were done. "On one occasion we had a pilot on our Pool deliver an urgently needed Spitfire to a fighter squadron. The weather was dreadful. So bad, in fact, that the fighter pilots were all grounded. Who could this be, they asked, flying on a day when they, the real 'ace' pilots, were all grounded? Well, this particular pilot was an elderly gentleman with a gray beard and, to give them something to think about, he produced a walking stick, struggled arthritically from the cockpit, and limped away before an astonished audience."

Humor, of course, played an important role in maintaining morale. "On the Hurricane, the radiator was slung in the center, so that when on the ground the propwash kept it cool. On the Spit though, it was offset so that you had to be careful when taxiing or running the engine up on the ground that you didn't overheat. One day, I was taxiing a Spit round the perimeter track when I came across a truck parked in my way. It was impossible to go round it off the track because it was winter and the ground was very soft, so I revved the engine to attract attention. After ages they moved, but by then the temperature had shot up and up so that when I finally parked I was furious. I complained to the ground crew and said that I was boiling and my temperature had shot up to a hundred and twenty degrees! Later I was in the watch office complaining about the truck when two medical orderlies dashed in excitedly carrying a stretcher and breathlessly inquired, 'Where's this pilot with the high temperature?' "

Like Len, Diana Barnato flew most fighter and twin-engined types during her time with the ATA, but regretted not getting her hands on all of them. "The RAF only had a few of some aircraft and the rarer ones which came through the ATA were all flown by those we called 'type catchers.' Everything else, though, seemed to appear in her log book and before she reached her twenty-second birthday she had flown no less than 260 Spitfires. They were mainly delivery flights of brand-new airplanes, or transiting flights of Spitfires to be modified, or the return of repaired aircraft for squadron use. To Diana and the other girls of 15 FPP, such flights were routine. But there was one very special delivery.

During 1944, Diana had married Wing Commander Derek Walker, DFC, a Typhoon pilot who had been appointed assistant to Air Vice Marshal Coningham, VC, the Air Officer Commanding, RAF 2nd Tactical Air Force. When Derek phoned one day to say that he had a Spitfire that urgently needed delivering to Belgium, the opportunity of spending some

Oh, what a blamed uncertain thing/This pesky weather is;/It blew and snew and then it thew,/And now, by jing, it's friz.

—Philander Johnson

The taxi Anson's piled with flying kit,/Each ferry pilot cons his morning chit,/When from the weather office comes the cry/That to the west black clouds bestride the sky./Then out "Met's" head is thrust from windows wide/This dark portent to ponder or deride;/'Tis dull, 'tis dark, the cloud's precipitating,/No weather this for us to aviate in!/But one more bold by far than all the rest/Out to the runway taxis, gazes west,/Raises an eyebrow, casts his eyes about,/Wriggles his corns, his shoulder blades, his snout./Instinct at work—will it be wet or fine?/What does this Flying-Weather seer divine?/He turns about and trundles back to "Met"/To tell them that it really will be wet.

—Anonymous ATA pilot

ATA Ferry Pool buildings remaining in 1990 at Hamble near Southampton. top right: The Bugle Inn, a Hamble pub well known to the ATA pilots.

time together on leave in newly liberated Brussels seemed too good to miss. Diana remembers: "Although France and the Low Countries had been liberated, the official policy was that these places were still out of bounds to ATA women. It was said that there were still pockets of German resistance, and that facilities were basic and primitive and not fit for females. The girls at Hamble were upset to say the least. We really wanted to get over there and, with Hamble so close, it was doubly frustrating. When Derek phoned to ask if I would fly the Spitfire PR VII [a photoreconnaissance Mark VII] to Evers, near Brussels, I was thrilled, but said I could only do it if he got special permission. In due course he produced a letter signed by AVM Coningham and I booked some days leave. Meeting Derek at Northolt near London, I took MD174 and flew in formation with him down to Tangmere, Derek in his personal Spitfire. Outbound from Tangmere, we crossed over the Channel and when we reached the French coast I could see a stretch of sandy beach which was completely covered by bomb craters. It was an awesome sight. The experience of this flight, in formation with my husband, was exhilarating and we subsequently spent a wonderful few days in Brussels. On the day we were to leave, the airfield was fog-bound. There was no hope of getting back, so I got permission to extend my leave for a couple of days. Even then, on the day I was due out, the weather was still poor, but Derek said it might not be so bad once we were airborne. So we took off and I formated on Derek and stuck close to him in thick cloud, fog and haze. My Spitfire was to be returned to England, complete with rolls of exposed film still in the cameras, the airplane having been flown over enemy lines and the pictures needed back in London. Derek told me not to put down in France if I had a problem, but to head back for England if I could. I had a little bit of difficulty staying with Derek anyway, because the RAF flew at higher revs and boost than ATA pilots and, in any case, we always flew alone. Never in formation! When I looked away from Derek's Spitfire for one second he was gone. He'd vanished into cloud and I was on my own. Looking around I saw a plane in the distance and, thinking it was Derek, flew off to see. It was a Dakota going the other way. So I had to sort things out for myself. I had no radio and even if I had, I wouldn't have been able to use it because we never flew with radio in the ATA. I went down low to have a look and try to see where I was. Down on the deck I ran into some thick clag of cloud and I knew I had to climb to get over the hills around St. Omer. I reached the coast eventually and, in looking down, I could see what I was sure was that same pockmarked sandbar I'd seen on the way in. Confidently setting 317 degrees, I calculated that Dungeness would be my landfall in seven and a half minutes. There was sea fog just above the deck so I went over it and after seven and a half minutes I glanced down to see that there was still water between the gaps in the low yellow fog. It was a heart-stopping moment. Where was I? What had gone wrong? I concluded that my point of departure from the Continent must have been much farther north than I had imagined and that 317 degrees could be tak-

The WASPs (Women Air Force Service Pilots) were the first women military pilots who served the Army Air Force between September 1942 and December 1944. They flew more than 60 million miles in 77 different types of military aircraft, from trainers, pursuit fighters and transports, to four-engined bombers. They ferried 12,650 aircraft from factories to points of embarkation for the battlefront, and combat-weary planes to repair depots. Their other routine and hazardous duties included target sleeve towing, searchlight, chemical and smoke laying missions, radio-controlled flying, basic and instrument instruction, engineering testing, administration and utility flying. They paved the way for American women who now serve as military pilots. Approximately 25,000 women applied to get into the WASP— 1,830 were accepted, 1,074 graduated—all had previous flight training. Thirty-eight WASP pilots were killed while serving.

—from *Join Up*, official publication of the Combat Pilots Association

163

below and right: American
WASPs (Women's Air
Service Pilots).

ing me up the North Sea where I would soon vanish when the petrol ran out. But if I had left the French coast farther south then I was possibly flying up the middle of the English Channel. So I turned west for a few minutes more, and then on to due north so that I would be able to get to the south coast of England. I flew just above the sea to avoid the yellow fog and thought I would climb above it when I knew I must be over land and then bail out. Contemplating the awfulness of my predicament, I suddenly saw a white gleam dead ahead. The white cliffs of Dover! No. It wasn't Dover. Where was this? Bognor Regis. Yes, that was the Bognor gasometer. I don't suppose anyone before or since has been so glad to see the Bognor Gasworks, but at least I knew now where I was. Tangmere was just a few miles inland and the fog was so thick that I flew up river to Chichester, round the cathedral and into Tangmere. As I taxied up to the watch office I could see a Spitfire parked outside. It was Derek's! White-faced, he asked me what had happened. All of England was fogged in. He had been told on his radio that Tangmere was the only aerodrome open. How had I found it? 'Oh, no problem,' I told him."

Not all of Diana's flights were so dramatic but there were other worrying moments. On one occasion, a large fuselage portion of the Typhoon she was ferrying fell off in the air, leaving nothing beneath her feet. She managed to land the unstable airplane, but it was still a write-off. The watch office clerk, known to the girls as "Ned in the shed" scolded her as she taxied the crippled Typhoon in, "Whatever are you doing, Miss Barnato, bringing me

only half an airplane!"

Flying a new type, or a modified mark of an otherwise familiar plane, could be disconcerting. A Ford-based RAF Mosquito squadron had taken heavy losses and now, to add to their unease, were about to be re-equipped with a new type of Mosquito. It was Margot Gore's girls at Hamble who were to deliver the new kites and Margot had a confidence-boosting trick up her sleeve for the RAF pilots.

"We were all told to look our best— smart uniforms, lipstick, makeup and our hair done so that when the boys saw all these pretty young things climbing out of their new mark Mossies, they'd know that they could *certainly* fly them. But there was a master stroke to Margot's plan. One of our number, Lois Butler, was a grandmother, although still in her thirties. Lois arrived last and we girls stood around chatting to the RAF pilots, craning our necks and straining our eyes for the straggler. 'Where's Grandma?' we asked. Grandma? The reaction was as planned. A *grandma* flying Mosquitos? Soon, Lois arrived, landed, climbed out and took off her flying helmet, shaking her hair out as she did so. The effect was perfect. If young girls and grandmothers could fly these new beasts, anyone could."

By the end of hostilities and the standdown of ATA, its pilots had completed a staggering 309,011 aircraft movements and collected CBEs, OBEs, MBEs, George Medals and other decorations in recognition of invaluable and heroic service. The unofficial and fitting motto of the Air Transport Auxiliary was *Aetheris Avidia*, "Eager for the Air."

OTHER FRIENDS

"THEY KNEW why they were here," remarked a senior RAF officer of foreign fighter pilots in the World War II Royal Air Force. His comment was a tribute to the exceptional determination of those non-British airmen who formed an important element of Fighter Command. Airmen from at least thirteen nations took part in the Battle of Britain and this tally increased as the war progressed. Czechs, Poles, Belgians, Dutch, Free French, Norwegians and at least one Icelander took part, in addition to other English-speaking nationalities including Canadians, Americans, South Africans and New Zealanders. But it was mainly the non–English speaking nationals of whom it was said that "they knew why they were here." Almost without exception they had escaped Nazi occupation, had left behind families and loved ones, had endured dreadful hardships in their efforts to reach England . . . and none knew if or when they would be going home. Half a century later Kazimierz Budzik still has the keen eyes and quick reflexes of a fighter pilot. It is easy to imagine him in the role.

Commissioned as a second lieutenant in the Polish Air Force the day war broke out, Budzik had a depressingly short career as a fighter pilot in his native country before fleeing the Nazis to continue the fight from France. There he flew Potez and Dewoitine fighters from Pol air base near the Pyrenees until France fell. The French helped to get him and other Poles to Casablanca via ferry, and then to Gibraltar, from where he was finally able to sail for England by convoy.

At Liverpool, Budzik was sent for training and then posted to No. 308 (Polish) Squadron, flying Spitfires. He joined an air force that was just going on the offensive, a course perfectly suited to his temperament. Born in Lekawica, a district of Kraków, it was appropriate that Budzik should have been posted to 308, the City of Kraków Squadron. It was based at Northolt near London and was primarily engaged in bomber-escort missions and offensive sweeps over France.

Modest to a fault, Budzik dismisses any suggestion of heroism. "Heroes? I don't know what they are. There were brave deeds done, of course. Mostly, though, heroes were born out of spur-of-the-moment actions. Most of the time I was concerned with self-preservation, like everyone else." But his log book tells its own story. Two operational tours of duty . . . tally upon tally of ops flown . . . dogfights . . . night-fighter patrols . . . strafing attacks . . . dive-bombing missions . . . bomber-escort missions . . . being shot down twice . . . and a score of kills or probables to which this exceptional man reluctantly admits. As he jabs a finger at an entry in his log, the memory of a particular combat prompts comment: "Probably I should have claimed that one. I know I hit him . . . yes . . . that 190 was mine. I know it." Even his commanding officer urged him to claim it, but Kaz wouldn't bother. What did it matter? That he'd got it was important to him. He didn't need to advertise the fact. Tomorrow there might be another. Perhaps he'd count that one. Reflecting on that particular

combat, he commented on the tendency of the Polish pilots to become impatient and overexcitable in air combat. "We always, always opened fire much too early. The English seemed to have more patience and self-control, waiting until they had got in close or maneuvered into the best position before opening fire." That tendency may have cost Budzik and his fellow Poles a considerable number of victories. With precious few seconds of ammunition, the available rounds were soon gone in a careless, out-of-range hosing of the sky.

As an exclusively Polish squadron, 308 used their native tongue during RT conversation in the air. "Most of us knew little English and, in any case, if in a tight corner or shouting a warning of danger, we'd be fumbling around for the right English words and someone would have soon been dead." Quick reactions were, of course, fundamental to fighter piloting. As Kaz put it: "You had to do it before you had thought about it." But one young Pole posted to Budzik's squadron, Pilot Officer Jan Wiejski, just didn't have those lightning reactions. Budzik, by now an old hand, saw that the new boy was not up to it. " 'Now, look here,' I told him. 'Why not see the CO about a transfer to another squadron? You just won't make it otherwise. Bombers, or Coastal Command perhaps is your thing.' " Wiejski knew that Budzik was right. But he'd not change now. He'd see it through. Sadly, Budzik's judgment proved correct.

"We were escorting bombers, but the operation just didn't go properly to plan. On the way back we saw a group of FW 190s. I was

below and left: Kaz Budzik in 1990. above: The Polish Air Force pilot wings.

one of the last in my section of six aircraft and, watching the 190s, we didn't see another group of them coming from behind. Suddenly, something in my mirror. A flash. Instinctively, I swerved and pulled around tightly toward our attackers and was head on to about ten . . . maybe twenty . . . 190s. The next few seconds were spent just trying to survive. I did, but the rest of my flight, five aircraft in all, were shot down. Among them was Jan Wiejski. It was his first operational trip. He didn't stand a chance."

As the war continued, the German fighter opposition over France, Belgium and Holland seemed to diminish. When there was a dogfight, it would be over in seconds. In and out. Attacking or evading. That was the battle. Often the two opposing formations would climb and circle miles from each other, vying for the advantage of height or sun. Then it would suddenly be over. The German formation would dive away without a shot being fired. It was frustrating for the boys of 308 to return to base without having pressed the gun button.

Once the Normandy invasion got under way, however, that frustration ended. As an element of the 2nd Tactical Air Force, Budzik's squadron was deployed in the ground-attack/close-support role. Flying Spitfire XIVs equipped with cannon and bombs, there was a lot of satisfaction in knowing that they were delivering real damage to the enemy. "I flew what must have been dozens of flights during the struggle for the Falaise Pocket. I don't mind admitting to a feeling of glee and excitement because, on the ground, I could see

Jerries by the score looking up at me . . . terrified. Some of them had their hands above their heads as I roared over them. I remember thinking, Now, you bastards, how do *you* like it? It was a different story in 1939, though. They showed Poland no mercy then, but here they were now, begging for it. It was a wonderful experience."

About this time Budzik's squadron aircraft were being fitted with a new gyro gunsight. This remarkable innovation greatly

increased the accuracy of shooting and made automatic corrections for deflection, largely eliminating human error—but not Polish impatience and excitement. Budzik was to discover this to his cost.

"They fitted these sights, but they never trained us how to use them. Instead, we had to find out for ourselves. Well, for air-to-ground work . . . no problem. You just put the dot on

If you strike a thorn or rose,/Keep a-goin!/If it hails or if it snows, Keep a-goin!/'Tain't no use to sit and whine'/Cause the fish ain't on your line;/Bait your hook and keep on tryin.'
Keep a-goin!

from "Keep a-goin!" by Frank I. Stanton

Such indomitable courage and determination cannot go unrewarded, and when this war is won we must see that Poland is again restored to her former liberty and freedom, which her sons fought so valiantly to maintain.

—F/L D.M. Crook, DFC

above far left: Sgt. Pilot Rudolf Zima of Czechoslovakia, 310 (Czech) Sq., Duxford. below far left: F/L Jeorge Solak, a 9th AF fighter pilot in September 1944. left: An RAF Polish squadron Spitfire. overleaf above: Flt. Sgt. Emil Samuelsen. overleaf below: The Norwegian Airmen's Memorial at North Weald. overleaf far right above: Helen and Kaz Budzik during WWII. overleaf far right below: The military medals awarded to Budzik.

the target and simply hit it. You couldn't miss. Of course, by this time, intervention by German fighters was comparatively rare. We just got on with our lovely job of bombing and shooting things up on the ground. Then, one day, there was a shout of 'Focke Wulf' over the radio. 'I'll get him!' I called, diving after him absolutely flat out. He was in my sights . . . rrrrrrmmp . . . nothing. Not a single hit. Problem was that these wonderful new gyro sights needed a second or two to settle. I hadn't allowed for that. My impatience and excitement wouldn't let me. But now the chase was on. Down on the deck we were streaking for Germany. I wouldn't let him get there. No. Was that smoke or exhaust fumes I could see trailing out behind? Well, it soon would be smoke. In my sights . . . gyro settled now . . . *fire!* Nothing. All my ammo had gone in that first burst that had missed. But at least I had learned about gyro gunsights."

But it was the ground-attack role that proved to be the most dangerous for Budzik. "After the invasion, we had been flying from Ghent in Belgium and were tasked to carry out a dive-bombing attack on Walcheren island off the Dutch coast. As we approached the target a terrific amount of flak came up from all directions. When that happened, we learned that we could tease the gunners by holding off just out of range of their guns; then we'd judge the moment to dive when the fire had slackened off, or maybe we'd fool the gunners into thinking that we were going away. Often this ploy worked quite well. But on this occasion I remember I was trembling with fear. Everyone experiences fear, but for me the

fear went once we had committed ourselves to the attack—although the trembling soon returned. I was leading my section in when suddenly *wham!* I quickly turned the aircraft around and, despite the damage, I managed to get it down in a crash landing. Once I was down everything seemed so quiet, and yet, as I got out of the cockpit there was the sound of a ground battle all around me—heavy gunfire, rifles and machine guns. I quickly got myself to a ditch and thought that this was not a good situation for a fighter pilot to be in. Then some civilians turned up. From a distance I shouted to them, 'Go away!' and waved my pistol around to reinforce my request. I was worried that they might turn me over to the Germans. But then a woman among them shouted in English, 'Are you British?' 'No, Polish. Where are the British?' I answered. Back came the reply, 'Down the road. We're waiting for them.' Once identities and allegiances had been established the civilians came closer and a man with a bicycle approached and said he'd take me to the British lines. I hopped on the bike and went off with him, but before I did, I produced my pistol again and told him I'd shoot him if he was taking me to the Germans. He didn't, so I didn't have to shoot him after all, and gave him cigarettes instead of lead."

Almost immediately, Budzik was back flying ops and very soon was shot down again. Once more it was ground fire and once more he survived. He luck held. He had survived through two tours of duty, but after two crash landings he was sure he wouldn't be lucky a third time, though he kept his fears to himself. So many friends had gone and his turn was surely coming. "By this stage of the war I was really nervous about flak. Quite jumpy. But then I had reason to be. Twice it had nearly killed me. Even so, to a certain extent we fighters could get out of the way of flak—not like the bombers. Once, while escorting Mitchells over Le Havre, the flak was too intense for us so we simply moved off away from the bombers which were attracting the gunfire. Suddenly, one of the B-25s in the center of the formation took a direct hit and went down, but the formation just ploughed right on. The most amazing thing was to see another bomber slide into the position from where the other aircraft had just been lost. To me, that took guts."

The war was coming to an end; Budzik would survive, and Helen, a pretty young Polish WAAF, had agreed to marry him, though they shared the sadness of being unable to return home to a free Poland. He was awarded the Polish VC (the Virtuti Militari), the Polish Cross of Valor four times and the Polish Air Force Medal four times. His portrait by Slawa Sadlowska appeared in her 1947 *Album of Polish Airmen* side by side with the fellow pilots he revered.

Kaz Budzik was lucky. It was not just his skill that kept a fighter pilot alive in World War II. Luck played a major part. Shooting prowess and airmanship counted for nothing when catastrophic aircraft failure occurred, and a great number of pilots were killed in such accidents rather than in combat. One was Flight Sergeant Emil Samuelsen of the Royal Norwegian Air Force.

Samuelsen was considered to be one of

The visible atmosphere in the room was cloudy with tobacco smoke which seemed to reach its optimum height a foot or so from the ceiling where it appeared to flatten out and drift in horizontal layers until someone passed through it and then it appeared to follow whoever did so for a moment. There was wireless somewhere in the room, for I could hear music coming from near where I was standing. There were two of our Polish pilots here . . . both non-commissioned and their names were so difficult to pronounce that we simply called them "Zig" and "Zag." They didn't seem to take any offence at this abbreviation.

from *Clouds of Fear*
by Roger Hall, DFC

Norway's most capable military pilots. Born in Tjølling in 1918, he grew up in a large family and seemed set for a career at sea when the war changed the course of his life and Norway fell to the Germans in 1940. He was serving as assistant engineer on a whaling factory ship, the SS *Kosmos II*, and instead of returning home to occupied Norway the *Kosmos* sailed for England, where Emil discharged himself from the ship's company and enlisted in the Norwegian army. Army life did not suit him, though, and by August of that year, inspired by the exploits of "The Few," he transferred to the Royal Norwegian Air Force for pilot training.

He was sent to Canada to the "Little Norway" training facilities for Norwegian airmen at Toronto and Moose Jaw. There he earned his wings. Along the way, though, there was the drama of an emergency landing with wheels retracted on a Dakota. Unhurt, Samuelsen was commended for his skill in saving the aircraft.

From Canada, Emil followed the well-trodden route to an operational unit via an operational training unit: 58 OTU at Grangemouth. On August 19, 1942, he was posted to North Weald in Essex to No. 332 (Norwegian) Squadron, flying Spitfire Vs, where he performed well and showed great promise.

On January 27, 1943, flying one 332's new Mark IX Spitfires, Samuelsen was doing a routine air test. He was seen to perform a 250 MPH aileron-reflex check over North Weald and to fly straight and level across the field shortly after. Then, climbing to complete a 400 MPH test, he was lost to view as the Spitfire entered cloud. Moments later it reappeared in a high-speed vertical dive, clearly out of control.

At Brick House Farm, near Matching Green, the occupants heard the roar of the stricken plane directly overhead. The impact, when it came, was devastating. Plaster came down from ceilings, windows cracked and pictures fell from walls. Then silence.

Emil's Spitfire had missed the house by yards, but sliced instead through the roof of a nearby barn. When rescuers approached the smoking hole, it was apparent that there was no hope for the pilot. The impact had driven the Spitfire deep beneath the earthen floor of the barn, taking Emil Samuelsen with it. It was a tragic end for a man described by Hans Jörgen Jörgensen, his boyhood friend, as "among the cream of the cream of Norway's youth."

At Honor Oak Crematorium, London, nearly the entire complement of 332 Squadron turned out for Emil's funeral; the coffin decorated with the Norwegian flag and a wreath from King Haakon VII. After the war his ashes were returned to Larvik on the shores of Oslo Fjord and close by his birthplace. Unlike Kaz Budzik, he had gone home.

The story of Emil Samuelsen has a postscript. In 1989, the cement screed floor of the repaired barn at Brick House Farm cracked and caved in. As it was dug out for repair, pieces of metal shining in the bottom of the hole—a wheel, cannon shells and bits of wing—were revealed. Poignant reminders of one life lost among the many who were Britain's "other friends."

Over the grave/A sloppy squad/Ragged salvo gave./Two fields away/A mild old horse./Peewits quavered, altered course/As echoes, rolling, died./There was a small human gesture made./Back in the cosy Mess/We drank his death.

from "Polish Airman" by Stuart Hoskins

left: Norwegian pilots training in England, 1941. above: F/O J. S. Hamilton, 412 Sq., RCAF, at Tangmere in May 1944.

A GERMAN
ESCORT PILOT

IN 1940-41 some fortunate Luftwaffe fighter pilots on the Channel coast of France were living well in the comfort of requisitioned châteaux. Most, though, were living in the field under canvas. But, early in the war, they were buoyed by easy victories and confident that the impending fight with the Royal Air Force would be yet another quick skirmish with conclusive results. That illusion was quickly shattered. There would be no walkover and the German pilot would have a lot to worry about.

The British pilot was fighting for the survival of his homeland. He had the psychological advantage—and powerful incentive—of flying and fighting above his own country. For the German there was the daunting prospect of overflying the sea to England, followed by combat over alien territory and then another flight back across water—possibly with a battle-damaged airplane, certainly low on fuel and maybe wounded. Most of the German units operated from fields that were little more than commandeered farm meadows. Ulrich Steinhilper flew Messerschmitt 109s with the 1st *Gruppe*, JG52, from such a field.

"The mustiness of the tent and the dampness of the dawn were smells I well remember from those days at Coquelles, living in tents, British bell tents we had recovered from the beaches of Dunkirk. Pulling back the coarse army blankets I got up and felt the chill of the air; it was the end of September and already the dawn was cold. I washed and pulled on my uniform trousers and shirt, leaving off the collar—today as on most days I would be flying early and there was no place for the formal collar and tie in the cockpit of my fighter. Although the army boys called us '*Die Schlippssoldaten*' (the Necktie Soldiers) nobody with any experience flew in a collar and tie.

"Helmet Kuhle, the squadron leader, was suffering from blocked eustachian tubes in his inner ear and, as a result, he couldn't fly. He'd tried many times over the past few days, but as soon as we started to gain altitude the pain would become unbearable and he would have to break for home. So this morning, September thirtieth, I was to lead the small group which would represent our squadron—just four of us. Our *Gruppe* had entered the Battle of Britain with thirty-six experienced pilots in the three squadrons. Now there were just a handful left.

"For those who could eat prior to a flight there was food and hot coffee, but for many now breakfast consisted of a chain of cigarettes, each one lit from the butt of its predecessor. I hated the waiting. I could feel the acid bile building in my stomach and an awful nausea which seemed to wash through my whole body—nerves and accumulated battle fatigue. We had been flying day in and day out for weeks and the stress was beginning to show. More and more cases of '*Kanalkrankheit*' (Channel sickness) were being reported and it was no wonder: A tour of duty for the bomber crews was twenty-five missions.

174

By then we fighter pilots had flown over one hundred, the equivalent of four tours without a rest.

"How many flights would we make to-day? Eight was the most we'd managed in one day so far. Incredible. We were to fly as escorts again, in line with the new policy of total protection for the bombers, a policy which found no favor with the fighter squadrons. We felt we had proved beyond all reasonable doubt that our machines were at their most effective in the *Freie Jagd* (free hunt), not shackled inflexibly to the lumbering bombers without even any means of communicating with them. But Hitler had become obsessed with the bombing of England in reprisal for

above left: Ulrich Steinhilper in WWII. below left: Steinhilper in 1990. below: German NCO fighter pilots of the 2nd *Staffel*, JG52 in 1940, on the Channel coast of France.

We never thought we'd
be beaten. We thought
it might have gone on a
bit longer. But the
Battle of Britain as such
. . . it stopped. We
didn't win anything. I
don't think we won any
battles. But we did buy
time . . . a little
valuable time which
enabled our Bomber
Command to get ready.
Don't forget, it's the
only time in history
two air fleets had ever
met each other, and the
change of a whole war
happened. If we'd lost
that air battle, you
could have said the
world today would be a
different place.

—Denis David

right: The tiny, cramped
cockpit of an ME 109F,
1941.

attacks on German cities and so we were hobbled guarding our bombers.

"I walked out with the other three pilots along the line of aircraft, each one protected by straw bales and covered with camouflage netting. I arrived at Yellow 2, my aircraft, and ran my hand along the leading edge of the wing, easing the leading edge slat out to see if it functioned OK. I needn't have. Peter, my mechanic, would have checked her over thoroughly and I knew she was as ready as she could be. Walking around to the wingroot I looked at the sky and chatted with Peter as he helped me strap on my equipment: life jacket, yellow sea-water dye container, life raft, but no pistol (earlier in the month we had been forbidden to carry sidearms). Apparently many airmen, alone and seasick in the Channel and at the limits of their endurance, had taken what our high command saw as the 'easy way out'—shooting themselves in the head, rather than slowly dying with stomach and lungs full of the Channel. Bending forward to attach the parachute harness straps I felt as though I would be sick, but I quickly straightened up, knowing the feeling would soon pass.

"Dropping down into the familiar surroundings of the cockpit, I fastened the harness straps which held me firmly in my seat. I performed the few checks necessary and waited as Peter wound the handle of the starter, feeling the aircraft gently rocking on its wheels as the flywheel gathered speed and energy. At the right moment I pulled the handle which would engage the starter and the big DB 601 turned a couple of times and then fired. In seconds the control panel was alive as the gauges began to register and climb to the normal readings. Warning lights winked out as the engine settled to a steady pace. My left hand firmly on the throttle, I finished the pre-take-off checks and signaled Peter to pull the chocks away. I told myself I would feel all right in a few moments. I could see the others coming out to line up with me on my left and right. Then it was time to go. A last check either side of the huge cowling, a wriggle of the body to get comfortable in the straps, a feel of the rudder with each foot and a firm grip on the stick with the right hand.

"Easing the throttle lever forward in one smooth action was, and always will be, one of the most exhilarating feelings I have ever had. 'A firm boot' begins to press in the middle of the back and the pressure stays there as the aircraft accelerates faster than a sports car. I keep the stick well back to hold the tail wheel on the ground. The 109 has a tendency to yaw on the main wheels if the tail is raised too quickly. Keep her in a straight line with the rudder, maintaining a steady pressure on the rudder to counter the swing due to torque. Watch the ASI [air speed indicator] as we approach take-off speed, then relax the stick a fraction, and as one movement, the tail rises as the main wheels leave the ground. Retract the gear and the indicator lights wink out—at last. As always, the nausea passes.

"Our *Schwarm* of four climbed away along the coast to where we are to meet with the bombers; *Feldwebel* Sigi Voss is my *Rottenhund*, with the second *Rotte* being led by Karl Ruttger with *Unteroffizier* Kurt Wolf as his number two—four of five pilots who had survived a very sticky situation over London three days earlier. Because of this we were still in a confident mood and ready to take on anything. Maybe overconfident. As we crossed the Channel, we were released from the main formation to undertake a *Freie Jagd*. This couldn't have been better for us as we believed our tactics had been too timid and were hungry for the chance to vindicate our theory—and a little impetuous because of it.

"We crossed the Sussex coast at about 0930 hrs (10:30 UK time) and having gained plenty of height, we spotted a squadron of Hurricanes climbing below us among other formations. They were flying in three vic formations in line astern, very orthodox by our standards. I judged that they must have been somewhat inexperienced and decided to attack. Over the RT I gave instructions that I would attack the leading formation, Voss the next, Ruttger and Wolf the third. I was conscious that there were many other formations of enemy aircraft in the area, but we were hungry for action and thought that our height and speed would see us through unmolested.

"On my order, we dropped into the attack, picking up terrific speed in the dive and dropping below and behind the Hurricanes. We were able to hit them from slightly below with complete surprise. I gave the order '*Nach Angriff in Linkskurve sammeln*' (After the attack, assemble in left curve). We were not sure exactly what happened. We think that one of the others pressed the transmission button on his radio at the same time as me, but the actual effect was that the first two

177

below: Early in the French campaign, members of 1st *Gruppe*, JG52. Karl Rüttger looks over the shoulder of Fw. Sigi Voss. Kurt Wolf sits on the table reading a book. Lothar Schieverhöfer is also seated reading. Ulrich Steinhilper (wearing a wrist compass) stands in the foreground.

words of my instructions were cut off, leaving just the order '*In Linkskurve sammeln*' (Assemble in left curve). I went on firing for a good few seconds, sweeping right through the vic formation, not realizing that the others were breaking off almost immediately. They were understandably annoyed that they hadn't been able to fully press home their attacks, particularly in light of our shared feelings about officers who apparently risked

all to raise their own personal scores.

"There was little time to debate what had happened because some of the other enemy fighters had seen our attack and turned upon us with great fury. Our small formation was broken up with me and Voss making it home and Ruttger limping in alone a while later. I witnessed Wolf's fate, seeing him hit by numerous shells from an enemy fighter in a beam attack . . . almost invariably fatal be-

cause of the lack of armor on our sides. His aircraft began to burn immediately. We had paid dearly, our only consolation being that we had hit the enemy very hard, myself claiming my fourth victory, albeit with little enthusiasm.

"The morning mission had certainly given me cause for reflection. I had let my own impetuosity and that of my young colleagues overcome common sense. We had attacked with good results which would certainly have been better had we not had the mix-up on the radio; but I'd seen Kurt Wolf shot down. I was sure that he'd been killed and his death was weighing heavily on my conscience. My managing to get all of our people back in the evening went some way in assuaging my feelings of guilt. It had been a mission which went badly wrong with serious losses for the Luftwaffe, hardly any of which were attributable to enemy action.

"Another escort duty, tied to the bombers as their protection. Once more I was to lead, with four aircraft from the squadron. During the morning another machine had been fixed and we were able to replace the missing Kurt Wolf. Our brief was to assemble with squadrons from our *Gruppen* and others, to escort JU 88s to London, flying blind high above the clouds, relying on their navigation. They were using the experimental '*Knickebein*' radio beams and should have hit the target with great accuracy. We missed London completely, passing it somewhere to the left. It was almost certainly a case of the leading bomber flying down the beam on course, but missing the

intersecting beam which was to warn him that he was almost on target.

"The whole bomber *Gruppe* (about thirty aircraft) flew on, and only turned for home when we had used about two thirds of our fuel. And even then they didn't take the shortest course, but set off in the direction of the Isle of Wight where the Channel is at its widest. We couldn't leave the bombers because they were being constantly harassed by enemy fighters, and so the object became to conserve fuel as much as possible. However, it isn't easy to fly straight and level and give proper protection [at the same time], so the precious fuel reserves were running low.

"The fighters held their positions and as we began to cross the Channel we could see that the bomber force was still intact. Now it became a matter of survival for the fighters. At last we could break away and I ordered my *Schwarm* to drop to sea level where the wind resistance was lower. We literally wave-hopped, hoping that our fuel gauges were wrong and that we would have just enough to get to France. One after another our comrades came on the radio to report that their red fuel-warning lights had come on. Below us we could see the gray, uninviting waters with waves running very high. We knew that if we tried to land the aircraft in such rough water, our chances of survival were slim. So, as fuel ran still lower the orders were to try to gain a little height and jump. At least this gave an improved chance of survival, although not much better.

"One after another the fighters plowed into the waves of the Channel or rose in a last

How grand is victory, but how dear!

—Boufflers

Fortune and love befriend the bold.

—Ovid

He who fights and runs away/May live to fight another day./But he who is in battle slain, Can never rise to fight again.

—Goldsmith

We make our fortunes and we call them fate.

—Disraeli

The Battle of Britain was just as important as the Battle of Waterloo and the Battle of Trafalgar, and, indeed, as the fight against the Spanish armada . . . in that it saved this country from invasion. And, had we lost that, God knows what sort of state we would be in today.

—Raymond Baxter

Even the lion has to defend himself against flies.

—German proverb

desperate effort to gain height before the pilot bailed out. Our track across those wild waters became dotted with parachutes, pilots floating in their life jackets, and greasy oil slicks on the cold water showing where yet another 109 had ended its last dive. Our air-sea rescue people tried their best, but it was so hard to locate men in the high waves. Most that were located were already dead, victims of exposure or drowning. The next day I saw a secret memorandum which reported nineteen pilots drowned. Only two were recovered by the *Seenotflugkommando*.

"My group of four survived and just made it to Boulogne where we refueled. All along the coast near Boulogne we had seen 109s down in the fields and on the grass, some standing on their noses. Our losses had been huge, the penalty for having been chained to the bombers and for not being able to communicate with the bomber leader. When we four flew into Coquelles, the ground crews went wild with joy. They had written us off with the others and were pleased that we had made it back.

"By September 30, 1940, there were few of the original thirty-six pilots left in our *Gruppe*. The survivors who were still flying were under great stress. Each of us knew by a quick perusal of the casualty list that our time must come soon."

A month later Ulrich Steinhilper was shot down over Kent. "Unfortunately, on this day I didn't have my new Yellow 4, which had an automatic pitch-control propeller . . . because the airplane was having an overhaul. But we had more planes than pilots, so I used my good old Yellow 2, which was a bit slower but had already earned me five victory stripes on the tail. Peter, my mechanic, was happy. His neglected favorite had another chance. 'Maybe, *Herr Oberleutnant*,' he said, 'you will be more fortunate with this one. With the new airplane you don't seem so lucky.' They were his last words as he closed the hood.

"We assembled over France with about fifty ME 109s, twenty of them carrying bombs to London in the fighter-bomber mode. We were to protect them. When their bombs were dropped we would turn together for home with the aim to get back to Calais as quickly as possible.

"Together with my *Rottenhund, Feldwebel* Lothar Schieverhofer, I was at the top right in the formation—the nucleus of it being the fighter-bombers. They flew a tight formation, while for protection we flew at different heights and to the sides. Suddenly, one of our pilots, Rabe, shouted into the radio: 'Eleven o'clock high! Vapor trails. Same flight direction.' Yes, they were there. To the left and above, British fighters . . . waiting in a higher and superior position. They were just biding their time for when we were in our weakest tactical situation. The two-fighter *Rotte* was designed [for mutual protection], but in a curve this was useless because while turning we could not protect each others' tails. Clearly, the moment to attack was when we turned for home. In the meantime, we just kept our eyes on them.

"From my position I had a pretty good view. It all looked quite attractive and peaceful, these white and silver condensation stripes, straight lines in the blue sky. First they were mathematically parallel, but then they started to boil out to end in very thin smoke. But no time to admire vapor trails. I had problems. Old Yellow 2 had been parked for days and during these cold October nights water must have collected in the propeller-pitch change mechanism. Now, at altitude, that water had frozen and locked it solid.

"The suburbs of London were below and it became imperative that I know soon whether we would make our turn to the left or the right. In the presence of the British fighters, and with my propeller problems, it was essential for Schieverhofer and me to be in the best position. Apparently the squadron commander had similar worries. 'Right or left turn?' he asked over the radio. The wing leader answered: 'After Bombs Away, turn right.' Excellent. This was just what I needed. I would be right at the inside of the turn and afterward would not be at the end. It was a relief because it is always the poorest rabbits who are shot by the hunters.

"Then, 'Bombs Gone.' We dived down with the fighter-bombers, but as we did so all hell broke loose. And, as usual, everyone was speaking and shouting into their radios at once so that nothing could be heard but a crazy whistling noise. This noise of interference really got on one's nerves, but above it all, one pilot shouted 'My bomb is still on . . . please slow down.' An angry voice came back, 'Well, pull your emergency bomb lever.' After that, nothing. Just the whistling. But now what was going on? Below they started the turn . . . to the left! Terrible. I was now in a

There's still no letter . . ./In my troubled mind/I seek a reason, and quickly reasons find,/Indeed they tumble in, to be discarded/Each as it comes . . . It could be that/You're very busy; missed the evening post;/Or else it's held up in the mail. A host Of explanations . . . Yet that gnawing fear O'errides them, still keeps dinning at me that/You just don't want to write. And vainly I/Attempt to thrust aside the thought; deny/It with your last note, and the one before./But no. I must resign myself to wait/A day. Surely then I see your hand— Writing and envelope. And life is sweet, until Still no letter.

"Still No Letter"
by John Wedge

position well to the right of my *Rottenhund*, who had followed the radio chatter and cleverly chosen his position to the right of me. And now we were turning to the left.

"We'd had it. About four or five fighters dived toward Schieverhofer with a lot more speed than we had. 'Watch it,' I shouted, and made a protecting turn to shoot behind his tail. But what was he doing? Instead of a dive away, he turned toward me and started to shoot behind my tail. A quick look back and I saw why. It was just like a staircase of Spitfires which led right up into the sun. The first one already had eight little guns winking at me from its wings and I slammed the 109 into a steep dive. Schieverhofer was on his own now and would have to fend for himself.

"Then, *bang*. My over-revving motor had caused the supercharger to explode and the control column shook. However, the airplane remained operational, though I would have to be careful. I was certainly losing oil from the damage and had to get lower for more engine power. I slipped into a milky soup of cloud, let the control go back a bit and right away shot up into the blue again. I was almost blinded by the sudden change in light and my compass was running wildly with all this stamping on the rudder pedals. I knew, though, from the position of the sun, that I was on the right course and so went back into the murk. At once I was through it again. Below was land and the Thames estuary. So, even with all my terrible speed I hadn't got very far.

"But then I couldn't believe my eyes. I was right in the middle of some Hurricanes flying in a loose formation in the same direction. I was slightly above them and they didn't see me. Quickly I switched on my Revi gunsight, but flying through the clouds had caused ice to collect on my windscreen and everything was distorted. I tore off my gloves to adjust the metal aiming piece and at the same time removed my oxygen mask. Now I knew real fear. With the mask off, my airplane smelled like a steam locomotive. A glance at the instruments . . . one hundred thirty degrees Celsius. I must have been hit in the radiator. Right away I forgot about shooting anyone else down and was just glad they hadn't seen me.

"I turned the ignition off and went into a glide, calling the ground radio station with my position and predicament. They heard me and alerted air-sea rescue. Good. Now I was down to five hundred meters. Near a little town below, light antiaircraft guns opened fire. So, ignition on again and get some height. Into the clouds. Here the engine was running OK, but the oil temperature was rising visibly. Once more ignition off and into a glide. Now I could see Pegwell Bay off Manston and radioed my position.

"Down to two hundred fifty meters and I had to switch on again in a hurry, but even at low revs the engine shrieked. It was metal against metal now. Maybe full throttle would help? Yes, that helped all right. The engine just stopped dead.

"I had to jump. First, I wanted to make a final radio statement. 'From *Eule 2A*. Engine has stopped. Am bailing out.' It was crazy how loud I sounded in the quietness around me.

'Poor Yellow 2. This is now your very last minute,' I said, tearing off my helmet, headset and mask. I pulled the hood lever but nothing happened and I couldn't move the handle another millimeter. Damn. At two hundred fifty meters and two hundred KMPH I had to get out quickly, so I pulled open the cabin roofing. With a rumble it flew off to the rear. Pushing up I was suddenly out into a storm, somersaulting past my fighter. After my escape I didn't care how many somersaults I did or which direction they were going . . . only to get the parachute open. I looked for the D-ring and pulled and a small silky thread came up between my legs.

"Incredibly, the drogue chute had wound itself around my leg and when the main chute opened it felt as if my leg had been torn off. The rearward tumbling stopped with a suddeness; then I was hanging by my left leg turning round and round with my leg as an axle. Finally, this also ended and I was in the right position. I could still move the leg but it was extremely painful. Just at that moment I saw my Yellow 2 head straight into the soft-looking ground right in the middle of a herd of cows which were running off in all directions, their tails raised in the air. At once its ammunition started to go off—a kind of ridiculous salute of honor.

"Now I was lucky. Just at the end of a swing on my parachute, I landed quite gently on my right leg on the soft ground. For my injured left knee it couldn't have been better. Now I stood on English soil. The sky above was dark gray and a light drizzle fell. Down here it was hard to believe that moments earlier I had been floating up there in the brightness of the sun. One thing was certain. From now on, and for quite a long time, I would no longer be the master of my own fate. A feeling of hopelessness almost overwhelmed me and made me want to cry. Above I could hear the howling engines of my returning comrades with whom I had so recently been in radio contact. Now, how helplessly far away from them I was."

Though he might not have thought so at the time, Ulrich was a lucky man. He was, at least, alive. For his dwindling band of fellow

Alone, alone, all, all alone,/Alone on a wide wide sea!/And never a saint took pity on/My soul in agony.

from "The Rime of the Ancient Mariner" by Samuel Taylor Coleridge

A caricature of a wounded German airman POW drawn in the Royal Herbert Hospital, Woolwich, by another German POW.

The eyes believe themselves;/The ears believe other people.

—German proverb

One by one the flowers close,/Lily and dewy rose/Shutting their tender petals/From the moon.

from "Twilight Calm" by Christina Rossetti

below: Ulrich Steinhilper in a ME 109 again, at Biggin Hill in 1990. below right: A manufacturer's plate from the first German aircraft (a HE 111 bomber) shot down on English soil in WWII. far right: The highly refined cockpit of a FW 190 fighter, 1941.

airmen, survival was quite unlikely. The Battle of Britain was all but over, but the raids would go on into November and December. And those who got through 1940 on the Channel coast and then went on to the Eastern Front had an even slimmer chance of surviving the war. Captivity had its compensations.

In the camps, first in Britain and then in Canada, Ulrich was reunited with a number of old colleagues—men who had long since been written off as killed over England or the Channel. Kurt Wolf, whom Ulrich was sure had been killed, was there. Despite the fearsome attack on his Messerschmitt, Wolf had survived with a single bullet in his right leg and had parachuted down near Rye on the Sussex coast. For Ulrich it was wonderful to find that Kurt was alive. There too was his friend Schieverhofer. Shot down in the same combat with Ulrich, he had landed on the grass aerodrome

at Penshurst, Kent. The victor, Pilot Officer Peter Chesters of 74 Squadron, had landed his Spitfire there and taxied alongside to have the unique experience of taking his adversary prisoner.

In the four-month period of the Battle of Britain a total of 551 Luftwaffe fighter pilots were killed or taken prisoner.

There existed in the Luftwaffe what the RAF christened "Spitfire snobbery." It is now apparent that Hurricanes were the backbone of the RAF during the Battle of Britain and certainly accounted for the majority of German aircraft that were shot down or damaged. However, Luftwaffe pilots insisted that virtually everything they shot down was a Spitfire and invariably claimed to have been the victim of a Spitfire. This is well illustrated by an incident involving the late Robert Stanford-Tuck. Flying a Hurricane, he shot down a German fighter that fell close to Tuck's airfield. He promptly landed and jumped onto a truck that sped out to pick up the German pilot. As they arrived, the German was introduced to Tuck and he complimented him on the fighting capabilities of his Spitfire. Tuck explained that he had been flying a Hurricane but the German insisted that he'd been shot down by a Spitfire.

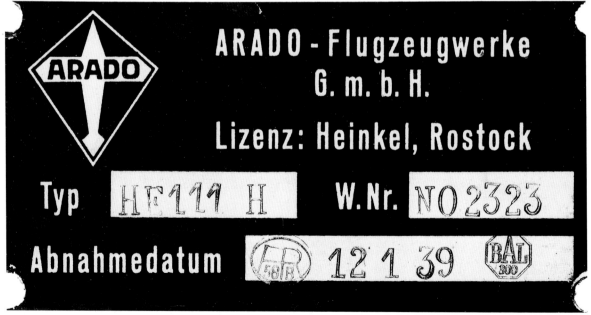

AT LIBERTY

FOR THE ENGLISH PILOT "leave" usually meant time at home with his family, but for his American counterpart there could be no such comfort. Off duty, he would spend his time, money and emotion however it suited him . . . at liberty to enjoy himself on a "48." Home leave was something to be looked forward to only after a long tour of duty in England—he would have to try to unwind on occasional three-day passes to London or one of the other "liberty towns."

On base, the American could relax briefly in an officers' club or aero club, where he could read, have a beer or play cards. Informal in furnishings and tone, these clubs were often given names by the pilots who used them; The Auger Inn for example, at the 353rd Fighter Group's base near Raydon.

Sometimes, if lucky, a Yank would be befriended by a local family, welcomed and fed as one of their own. It was a unique experience for both guest and host. With few exceptions, these Americans had never before been outside their country, some never having crossed the border of their home state. Equally, many of their English hosts had never before met foreigners.

A forty-eight-hour pass was eagerly awaited by the American fighter pilot. It meant a time-out of war and, often, a trip to London, where the action was. For the pilots of the East Wretham–based 359th Fighter Group, it was a fourteen-shilling round-trip adventure. One of them takes us along for the ride: "You stood on that train from Thetford all the way to London, your feet numb in the drafty corridor, the windows steamed so that even the bleak Suffolk landscape was hidden in the November curtain of cold. There was the jerking, stopping, backing, starting and there was the inevitable twenty-minute stop at Ely. You cursed the heat lever over the seat. It never worked.

"But then it was April, a half year later. You left your overcoat in the belly-tank crate that served as a wall locker, stuffed some shaving articles in your musette bag and hopped the five fifty or the nine or eleven o'clock bus from the gate. You were taking off on a 48 to London. It was spring and you felt eager.

"No tickets now at the fourteen-bob-the-round-trip rate. In April 'forty-five, you began getting reverse lend-lease travel warrants to any point in the UK. You waited on the platform for the train to pull in from Norwich, buying a *Daily Express, Mail, Post, Sketch* or *Illustrated.* Then you read the signs—THERE'LL ALWAYS BE MAZAWATTEE TEA—and watched a farmer herd two goats off the Bury train through the passengers. And you looked over the local civilians, the British officers and the scores of American airmen, a few of them with all their gear starting the trip back to the States. Local trains from Swaffham and Watton arrive with school kids in shorts and high wool stockings, clutching their books like school kids anywhere. Thetford is a small town, but its station carried life in and out by day and night: girls from Knettishall, Scottish officers in kilts, clean-shaven GIs starting on leave and returning ones un-

186

pressed, unshaven and unwell.

"There was the morning a few months after D Day when your train was an hour late and then you saw why. A hospital train steamed in to pick up a score of U.S. wounded, casualties headed for the States. There was no ceremony. No coffee with doughnuts and brave smiles. The wounded just stared right back at those who stared at them, their eyes dull and tired . . . .

"You sat in the compartment and slept most of the way. That is, you sat when there was a seat. One of the eight that could be crowded into each compartment. Opposite you was a minister who smiled in a kindly, professional way; three gunners from the B-17 field near Bury, invariably sleeping; two civilian women next to you reading a cheaply covered book and holding boxes and babies; a civilian smoking steadily, his pipe acrid and penetrating, tobacco shreds sprinkled unnoticed on his well-worn coat. You read the signs on the train: IF DANGER SEEMS IMMINENT, LIE ON THE FLOOR, advised the poster next to the watercolor of the cathedral. IT IS DANGEROUS FOR PASSENGERS TO PUT THEIR HEADS OUT OF THE CARRIAGE WINDOWS warned the message over the door with the window you opened by working a heavy leather strap.

"Italian POWs were standing and sitting around the freight cars at Brandon, smoking and waving, but mostly just watching and joking with each other. The civilian next to you explained that land around Ely was all under water a long time ago, and that the cathedral was raised on the only high ground in the vicinity. You see planted fields slipping by. CARELESS TALK COSTS LIVES . . . You reach Cambridge and know your trip is two-thirds done, only two stops now and you'll be at Liverpool Street Station—London. The train picks up speed through the canals and pastures the other side of Cambridge and finally you pass the rowhouses, each with its vegetable garden facing the railroad track, an air-raid shelter in the garden, and each with laundry out on the lines. Ten minutes now . . . You are up on an elevated track banked on both sides with the ruins and debris of bombed-out apartment houses, factories, churches and office buildings. You know then you are in London.

"Liverpool Street Station . . . 'Tickets please.' The station is noisy with hissing steam from your train, the familiar voice of the girl announcer and the crowds of people heading for the tube. It is unlike any American train station, for there are no hilarious meetings or emotional good-byes. Everyone is intent upon his own journey; to the London man or woman the train is not a novelty, it is a God-sent chance to get away to the country for one night of solid sleep away from the bombs, V-1s and V-2s. To the GI arriving, the train is no novelty either. It has been a boring, uncomfortable means of getting to the city where he plans to stay awake . . . .

"Your pass is almost up. You get to the station at eight o'clock and find a seat. Then you joke with the girl you met or brought along and maybe try a cup of scalding tea in the canteen. You're on the eight twenty. Now you find sleep easy, and you no longer have to keep your uniform pressed or clean. *You* are

"Good show!" he said, leaned his head back and laughed./"They're wizard types!" he said, and held his beer Steadily, looked at it and gulped it down/Out of its jam-jar, took a cigarette/And blew a neat smoke ring into the air./"After this morning's prang I've got the twitch;/I thought I'd had it in that teased-out kite." His eyes were blue, and older than his face,/His single stripe had known a lonely war/But all his talk and movements showed his age./His whole life was air and his machine,/He had no thought but of the latest "mod,"/His jargon was of aircraft or of beer./"And what will you do afterwards?" I said,/Then saw his puzzled face, and caught my breath. There was no afterwards for him, but death.

"Fleet Fighter"
by Olivia FitzRoy

above left: The "library" of the 364th Fighter Squadron at Leiston. far left: Zeke Roepke, Merle Olmsted and Ray Morrison on the day that ice cream was first sold in the Leiston PX. left: Bing Crosby entertaining airmen of the 78th Fighter Group at Duxford.

I slept and dreamed
that life was Beauty;/I
woke, and found that
life was duty.

from "Beauty and
Duty"
by Ellen S. Hooper

above: Coombe House, the
Red Cross-run "rest home"
near Shaftesbury, Dorset.
right and above right:
Coombe House stables in
1990 and during WWII. far
right: The ballroom at
Coombe, 1990.

unshaven and tired, and you smoke and read the London papers . . . Lakenheath, Brandon, Thetford.

"Forty-eights to London were a little different each time you went. You remember some of the sights and sounds, and the flat English countryside divided by trees, hedges and waterways. You will never forget the voice of the girl calling trains at Cambridge and the shafts of light cutting through the steam in Liverpool Street Station."

In London, the attractions were much the same for the serviceman as for any tourist—the Thames, the Houses of Parliament, St. Paul's and Buckingham Palace all featured on the "places to go–things to do" list for the American aviator. Off the list, nightclubs were popular, The Washington, The Nuthouse and the American Melody Club among the favorites. The American Eagle Club at 28 Charing Cross Road was a regular haunt of U.S. pilots. They often visited Rainbow Corner, the Red Cross–run club on Shaftesbury Avenue. Other attractions included the "Piccadilly Lilies" who plied their trade by day and night, targetting the well-paid American fliers with precision.

The American officer in London could take his meals at an exclusive eating house known as Willow Run. Located in the Grosvenor House Hotel, Willow Run provided the Yank with food that would make him feel at home and that he knew would surpass the stodgy, indifferent and meager meals available in English restaurants. Pork chops, mashed potatoes, ice cream, sweet corn, pancakes, fried chicken and steak were offered—

luxuries to help the Americans forget the frugality of wartime Britain. Featuring chefs—whose culinary careers had been postponed by the draft—from some of America's most interesting restaurants, the "Run" served delights from the menus of Boston's Kenmore, the El Paso Hilton, Rand's Bakehouse of Morgantown, West Virginia, and the Sabinal (Texas) Chicken Shack.

Another way to relax on R&R was at the large country houses that had been turned over to the U.S. Air Force for use as "rest homes." The Air Force understood the importance of such interludes in restoring war-weary fliers to combat-ready condition. One such facility was Broadlands at Romsey, the country home of Earl Mountbatten. Exhausted and flak-happy types were delivered by B-17s to nearby Stoney Cross airfield for a week away from the battle front. Coombe House, at Shaftesbury, was a rest home run by American Red Cross girls. One of them, Ann Newdick, wrote of her life at Coombe House—"the Flak Farm," as U.S. airmen called it:

"It's January in England, so the morning sun is rare and welcome. Breakfast is bacon and eggs. Apparently the grapevine knew it too because half the house is up for breakfast, 20 or so combat fliers disguised in sweaters, slacks and sneakers. Plans are afoot for golf, tennis and shooting skeet in the back yard, but the loudest conversation and most uproarious kidding centers around the four who are going to ride to the hounds in a country fox hunt. On a rainy day there's almost as much activity at Coombe House—the badminton court in the ballroom is our chief pride. But

All life, all love's his fee/Whose perished fire conserves my spark, Who brought the brightening day for me and for himself, the dark.

from "The Infinite Debt" by Rachael Bates

Music is the universal language of mankind.

from *Outre-Mer* by Longfellow

Goodbye ladies, O ladies sweet, goodbye, No more the gentle flowers,/Another life I'll try./No more the scented evenings,/The tussles in the hay,/It's time that I was leaving To live another way.

from "To Certain Ladies, On Going to the Wars" by Henry Treece

Carrying my gas-mask to school every day buying saving stamps remembering my National Registration Number/(ZMGM/136/3 see I can still remember it)/avoiding Careless Talk Digging for Victory/looking for German spies everywhere/Oh yes, I did my bit for my country that long dark winter,/me and Winston and one or two others,/wearing my tin hat whenever possible Singing "Hang Out the Washing on the Siegfried Line" aircraft-recognition charts pinned to my bedroom wall/the smell of paint on toy soldiers doing paintings of Spitfires and Hurricanes,/Lancasters and Halifaxes/along with a Heinkel or a Messerschmitt plunging/helplessly into the sea in the background/pink light in the sky from Liverpool burning fifty miles away/the thunder of daylight Flying Fortresses high overhead/shaking the elderberry tree/bright barrage-balloons flying over the docks/morning curve of the bay seen from the park on the hill/after coming out of the air-raid shelter listening for the "All Clear" siren/listening to Vera Lynn Dorothy Lamour, Allan Jones and the/Andrews Sisters/clutching my father's hand tripping over the unfamiliar

nevertheless, the Army calls it a Rest Home. It looks as English as the setting for a Noël Coward play, but even as you approach the house you discover that actors and plot are American. You meet a girl in scuffed saddle shoes and baggy sweater bicycling along a shaded drive with a dozen young men. You'd guess it was a co-ed's dream of a college house party—not a military post to which men are assigned and where girls are stationed to do a job. We have so much fun that we usually forget its military purpose, and so much the better, because this house party is a successful experiment to bring combat fliers back to the peak of their efficiency.

"There are four of us here, American girls sent overseas by the Red Cross. Never in our wildest dreams did we expect such a job. At first we felt almost guilty to be having such a good time. I was talking about what a picnic it was to one of the boys. 'That's the way it should be,' he said with authority. When I looked again I remembered that he was a medical officer who'd been at Coombe for about six weeks. In our conversation, I found out that he was Captain David Wright, Psychiatric Consultant for the Eighth Air Force. He had spent his six weeks in careful observation to decide the value of Rest Homes. 'Coombe House and the others like it,' he said, 'represent the best work of preventative medicine in the ETO. Very definitely Rest Homes

are saving lives—and badly needed airmen—by returning men to combat as more efficient fliers.' A remarkable per centage of men who finish their tours have had a chance to be in Rest Homes sometime during their combat tour. There isn't any one word to describe the varying states of mind of combat fliers when they are just plain tired. Tired because it's hard work flying a P-38 or navigating a B-24 or shooting out [of] the waist window of a Fort. Tired as anyone is after intense mental and muscular strain—intermittent though it is, the lulls in between are not long enough for the flier to get past the let-down stage before he plunges into danger again.

"At first the Air Force ran these Rest Homes alone. After two had been established, a large part of the responsibility was transferred to the American Red Cross to make them as un-military as possible. Army Quatermaster outdoes itself on food, and 'Cooky' in the kitchen does it to perfection. Fried chicken, steaks, eggs and ice cream are regular items on the menu, all served by pretty waitresses. 'Irish Mike' and Cooky, and all the rest of them are contributions of the Red Cross which disguise the technical and military nature of Coombe House almost beyond recognition, and we four American girls show no obvious solicitude for anyone's morale. We turn down an invitation to play bridge if we want to dance with someone else. Lack of

kerb/I walk over every day/in the black-out.

from "Autobiography"
by Adrian Henri

When they have gone, the room/retains its temperature of doom, the smell of waste;/of stubbed out fags, stale tea/and that sharp memory/of the flushed faces of the young hung, for ever, hung.

from "NAAFI at the Drome"
by Bruce Bain

far left: Preparing for a Spitfire beer run. left: Unicycular prowess on a 56th Fighter Group hardstand.

Fare thee well and if
forever,/Still forever,
fare thee well.

from "Fare Thee Well"
by Byron

Here's a sigh to those
who love me,/And a
smile to those who hate
me;/And, whatever
sky's above me,/Here's
a heart for any fate.

from "To Thomas
Moore"
by Byron

Army demands and freedom from regulations help create the free and easy tempo of the place. The whole feeling is one of such warmth and such sincerity that men come away knowing they have shared an experience of real and genuine living."

Rest homes and 48s were in stark contrast to the experience of the RAF fighter pilot. As one wife put it: "My husband could have been up at twenty thousand feet in the morning fighting the Germans . . . then home to lunch with me. It was almost unreal." While this nearly-cozy: "home-for-tea" war in which the RAF operated in 1940 and 1941 may have helped their morale in a limited way, they too needed to unwind occasionally, at parties, pub crawls, clubs and shows. It was the same for all airmen—they all needed to let off steam in a variety of outlets on and around the RAF fighter stations. One such was a "tradition" devised by Squadron Leader Geoff Warnes of 263 Squadron: a weekly "thrash." Believing in the value of such off-the-base gatherings for keeping a good squadron spirit, Warnes made Friday-night attendance compulsory for his pilots. The venue was the Golden Lion in Weymouth and *no* excuses for absence were accepted. On one occasion, a Flight Sergeant Proctor failed to appear and was hauled before his CO the next morning to explain himself. He thought he had a good enough reason for being absent—a date with a WAAF and a visit to the local cinema. Warnes was incensed. Women, Proctor was told, had two places—in the bedroom and the kitchen. Never, repeat never, were they to interfere with the Squadron Night Out. In future, he

would be present on Friday nights. For Proctor, it was the end of a romance before it had begun. But Warnes' embargo aside, the women of the Auxiliary Air Force were part of the on-and-off duty lives of the RAF. Sergeant Dennis Todd, another 263 Squadron pilot, describes his experience.

"I had been changing some equipment at Stores when a WAAF officer appeared. 'Don't you salute officers, Sergeant?' she snapped. 'I'm not wearing my cap, Ma'am,' I said. 'Put it on and salute in the proper manner,' she demanded. I did so only to be ordered to give her my name and squadron number. No sooner had I got back to dispersal than Warnes called me to his office. A mild ticking-off then followed, with him confiding that he really didn't agree with the existence of 'Petticoat Bosses,' but [that] we had to tolerate them all the same. The following week the squadron was at a dance in one of the seafront hotels at Weymouth and one of the bedrooms and been turned over to us for a cloakroom. Sometime during the evening I realized that I had left my handkerchief in my greatcoat and went to the room to collect it. I opened the door and switched on the light. Then I heard something and realized I was not alone. Going round the end of the bed, I discovered there on the floor a Canadian pilot and *my* WAAF officer in a very embarassing situation. But I didn't salute. I didn't have my hat on and, in any case, she was improperly dressed."

Todd remembers another incident at Warmwell: "A pair of WAAF's knickers [black, elasticated bloomers, often referred to as Blackouts, Passion Killers or Wrist Break-

194

ers] were put to use on the airfield as a windsock until, one day, when a signal came in from Fighter Command to ' . . . take down the WAAF's knickers.' "

Every squadron had its favorite local pub. Today, many of these places survive and are famous for their wartime associations. They are remembered and sought out by returning veterans. One of the most famous is The White Hart, at Brasted, which was frequented by Biggin Hill pilots during the war. Officers and other ranks would use separate pubs. At Biggin Hill, officers went to The White Hart; NCOs and airmen preferred The Jail in Jailhouse Lane. A favorite for Tangmere pilots was The Unicorn in Chichester. They also crowded a waterside establishment at Bosham called The Ship. The men at Hornchurch patronized The Good Intent. At North Weald it was The Crown in Epping, and at Fowlmere, The Chequers. Each pub had its own character, an ambiance in which the pilots felt comfortable and relaxed. The Yanks also enjoyed what was for them a new experience, English pub life.

Fighter pilots spent much of their leave time in England's pubs and clubs, and memories of them abound. One evening a group of 92 Squadron pilots were at the White Hart celebrating Biggin Hill's one-thousandth. They were warned by the village policeman that they were drinking after hours and must leave. The pilots then carried the lawman into the street and dumped him there. They filled his helmet with beer and wouldn't let him go until he had drunk it all. Surrounded by a dozen fighter boys he had little choice.

Some fighter pilots spent their leisure time as if there was no tomorrow. For many, there wasn't.

My Goodness — My GUINNESS

195

PILOTS

THERE WERE THE LEGENDS, big names like Gentile, Bader, Townsend, Tuck and Blakeslee. But there were others, also high achievers, who were virtually unknown. Some shunned publicity and attention. Others simply died before the spotlight of fame could focus on their deeds. Either way, what did it take to be a successful fighter pilot?

Certain attributes were essential: airmanship, motivation, agressiveness, guts, good eyesight and the ability to shoot straight. One fighter pilot commented on the importance of airmanship: "It's like a cavalryman making a charge on his horse. Is it horsemanship or fighting? Well, it's no good falling off the horse, that's for sure." Derek Gilpin-Barnes, an intelligence officer, wrote: "When you are with him, you find that the 'hero' is a myth. He is armed with no callous disregard of life and death. He is not fortified with some peculiar toughness of the body or spirit. Behind the glamour of their daring and devotion lie their personalities which, to my thinking, are more fascinating still. Nor do their great deeds lose in stature if we regard them as performed, not by heroes, but by ordinary men. The fighter pilot then, is an ordinary man . . . as scared of death as the next."

As leader of the 328th Fighter Squadron, 352nd Fighter Group, at Bodney, and as the third-highest-scoring American ace in Europe, George E. Preddy was perceived as a flamboyant pilot who fought and played hard, and enjoyed the life of a fighter pilot. In this,

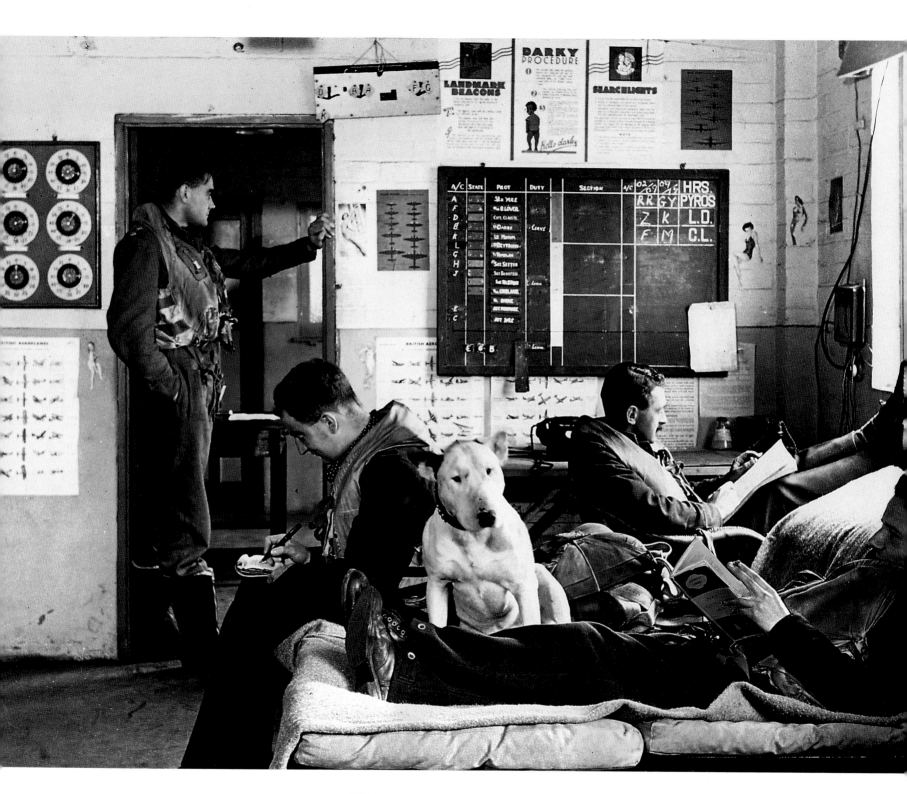

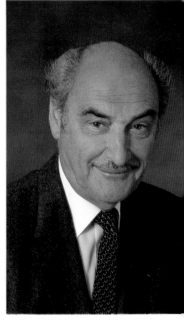

It isn't always being fast or accurate that counts, it's being willing. I found out early that most men, regardless of cause or need, aren't willing. They blink an eye or draw a breath before they pull a trigger. I won't.

John Bernard Books, in "The Shootist"

overleaf far left: Captain Allen Bunte, 4th FG, Debden. overleaf right: Pilots waiting in an RAF fighter squadron dispersal in 1942.

he conformed to the stereotypical media image. What didn't fit was the sensitive side of his nature, his penchant for writing poetry, and a deep love of family life. For such a high scorer, he is relatively unknown. In fact, the journal of the American Aviation Historical Society once described him as the "Unknown Ace." Preddy did not ultimately fall victim to the guns of the Luftwaffe. Instead, in a tragic blunder, he was shot from the sky by American flak over Koblenz on Christmas Day, 1944.

The highly successful Carroll "Red" McColpin returned to the United States at one point in the war to help train and form new fighter groups. During his stay, he was asked by General "Hap" Arnold "What is the best bomber we've got?" "Sir," replied McColpin, "I think the P-38 is the best bomber." "God, he got mad" McColpin recalls. "Why do you say that?" Arnold asked. Said McColpin, "Well, it's got two engines instead of four. It carries two thousand-pounders. Only got one guy in it instead of ten, so if you lose one, it's a lot cheaper on people . . . and also, a fighter pilot in a P-38, if you wanted to send him in to bomb something with two thousand-pounders, can probably hit the target most of the time . . . and the bombers can't."

Pilot Officer Roger Hall flew Spitfires with No. 152 Squadron at Warmwell, Dorset. "We all had to suppress fear for obvious reasons; not least was the desire to appear without it and so retain our own self-respect, for having lost this we were on the way down.

"September 17, 1942, was the day when I made my last operational flight. I had passed the point of no return. I was no longer consciously tired. I was an inanimate being actuated only by automatic reflexes. I kept very much to myself and the death wish began to dominate my mind. I was a totally irresponsible agent but I seemed to have acquired a sort of second wind. An unnatural abundance of energy flowed through me and I knew that, if once I let go, I should flounder totally and never recover again, so great would be the reaction. We had only four pilots in the flight now and we had to be at readiness in our cockpits because the German recce planes and low-level fighter-bombers were coming in low over the sea, undetected by radar and inflicting damage on the coastal districts

"Pilots in pairs spent an hour at a time at cockpit readiness and then they were relieved by the other two. We tried to read a magazine or a book or the paper at these times though it wasn't easy. Tension was about you all the time, especially when the hands of your watch crept toward the hour when you were due to be relieved. At about five minutes to the hour two reliefs would come out of the hut, carrying their helmets and taking the last few puffs of their cigarettes, and you wondered whether they would reach their machines before the alarm bell sounded for take-off. If they did not, you knew damned well that you would have to go yourself."

The Air Force Cross was authorized by Congress in July 1960. It is the USAF equivalent of the Army's Distinguished Service Cross and the Navy Cross, all three medals ranking second only to the Medal of Honor, the highest American award for gallantry in

Let us do or die!

from "Scots Wha Hae"
by Robert Burns

far left: Leo "Chief" Nomis, 71 (Eagle) Sq. top left: Walker "Bud" Mahurin, 56th FG. top center: Mahurin at Halesworth. center: James Goodson, 4th FG. bottom center: Harvey Mace and Paul Holmberg, 357th FG. above: Sgt. Pilot Peter McIntosh, 151 and 605 Sqs., RAF.

combat. There have been two retrospective awards of the Air Force Cross for acts of valor in World Was II combat that were not recognized at the time. Lieutenant Urban Drew was one of the most successful fighter pilots in the 361st Fighter Group when, on October 8, 1944, he bounced two Messerschmitt ME 262s on returning from an escort mission to Czechoslovakia. Drew spotted the two aircraft taking off from Achmer and, leaving his deputy squadron leader in charge, rolled into a near-vertical dive with his number-two and number-three aircraft, firing as he pulled out. One of the ME 262s exploded instantly and with such ferocity that Drew's Mustang was thrown about by the blast. The second 262 broke left in a steep climbing turn to escape the P-51s. Drew's official report of the action: I was still indicating about 400 MPH and I had to haul back on the stick to stay with him. I started shooting from about sixty degrees deflection, 300 yards, and my bullets were just hitting the tail section of the enemy aircraft. I kept horsing back on the stick and my bullets crept up the fuselage to the cockpit . . . I saw the canopy go flying off . . . and the plane rolled over . . . hitting the ground at about a sixty degree angle.

Drew knew, without doubt, that he had destroyed two Messerschmitt ME 262 fighters, but he couldn't prove it. His gun camera had jammed and his number two, who could have confirmed the kills, had been shot down by flak. His number three had broken away to the right and had seen only two columns of smoke and not the actual shooting down. There was insufficient evidence to support the

recommended award of the Distinguished Service Cross for Drew. Years after the event, German records confirmed that Lieutenant Drew had indeed destroyed the two ME 262s. His claim had been justified. The Air Force Board for the Correction of Military Records reviewed his case and, subsequently, recommended that Drew be awarded the Air Force Cross (which had superseded the DSC). In May 1983, Drew—now a retired major—was presented with his medal in Washington by Air Force Secretary Verne Orr.

Flying Officer E. J. "Cobber" Kain was the first Allied ace of the war. Inevitably, he was pursued by the press. Eager for a real-life hero for their readers, the war correspondents chased this twenty-one-year-old New Zealander relentlessly. Noel Monks of the London *Daily Mail* was quick to recognize the possibilities in Kain, whom he described as " . . . an officer and a gentleman." Newspaper editors believed that their readers expected their heroes to be larger than life. As ordinary men, the fighter pilots might not have captured the public imagination. They had to be dashing, romantic, good looking, extroverted . . . and far from "ordinary." Fortunately, Kain made good copy.

Kain was first rejected as an RAF recruit, which made him an even better story. That he had come from faraway New Zealand added to his appeal and that he also happened to be very good looking was even more intriguing than his ability as a pilot and brilliance as a marksman. He was the leading ace and personality during the Battle of France. By the early spring of 1940, Kain had destroyed sev-

top: Jim Goodson and his mother. above: Captain Clarence Anderson, 357th FG. far left above: P/O J. G. Pattison, 266 Sq., RAF. left: Col. Don Blakeslee, 4th FG. far left: An RAF fighter pilot.

A little curly-headed,
good-for-nothing,
And mischief-making
monkey from his birth.

from *Don Juan*
by Byron

top: P/O M. J. Herrick, 25
Sq. above: Bodney airfield.
above right: Frank Klibbe,
56th FG. below right: A
USAAF "hack" watch.

enteen German aircraft, was shot down twice and had been awarded the DFC. He appeared constantly in the newspapers until, in a change of policy, the authorities censored the use of pilots' names in order to discourage the creation of individual heroes. Overnight, "Cobber" Kain the hero became "a twenty-one-year old New Zealander." Then, recalled to England for training duties, he performed one last spirited beat-up of his French base. He misjudged a series of rolls and cartwheeled across the airfield. Kain the hero was dead, but the fighter-pilot stereotype had been born.

An "older man" who led an American fighter group into action, Hubert "Hub" Zemke was thirty when he took the 56th Fighter Group to war over Europe. Zemke was driven by a zealous and aggressive urge for combat. This tenacious man led the organization known as "Zemke's Wolfpack." He exhorted his men: "A fighter pilot must possess an inner urge for combat. The will at all times to be offensive will develop into his own tactics. I stay with an enemy until either he's destroyed, I'm out of ammunition, he evades into the clouds, I'm driven off or I'm too low on gasoline to continue the combat."

This philosophy had its effect on the Wolfpack's pilots, as shown by the kill scores of Francis Gabreski, Walker Mahurin, Dave Schilling and Bob Johnson, all of them high-scoring aces. Bob Johnson accrued twenty-eight victories, becoming the first American pilot to exceed the World War I score of twenty-six by Eddie Rickenbacker. Johnson advised new pilots: "If he comes down on you,

pull up into him and nine times out of ten, if you are nearly head-on with him, he'll roll away to his right. Then you have him. Roll onto his tail and go get him."

Similar advice was given by Don Blakeslee of the 4th Fighter Group. The pilots he led became known as the "Blakesleewaffe." He told his men that they should turn head-on into an attack and under no circumstance whatsoever should they deviate from this course of action. In a briefing, one young lieutenant timidly enquired, "But Colonel, what if the German doesn't break either?" With an icy stare, Blakeslee answered, "Then, sonny, you will have just earned your hazardous duty pay."

John McAdam, a shy young Ulsterman, was the epitome of Gilpin-Barnes' "ordinary man." Yet, as a sergeant pilot flying Spitfires with 41 Squadron during the Battle of Britain, he formed part of the backbone of the RAF's defense force. He is remembered by one who knew him as "small in stature, but a giant when it came to courage." Norman Ryder, the acting CO of 41, did his best to protect McAdam, but he had difficulty flying in formation at high altitude and was very vulnerable. Ryder sent him on leave the first time he was shot down.

During that home leave, McAdam had spent time in a local quarry firing his Browning pistol. The experience of being shot down had shaken him and he practiced firing that pistol until he could do it without flinching. He wrote home of his experiences:

Dear Pop,
Yesterday, as you know, was a big day for

the Air Force. We had been up four or five times in the morning to tame one or two recce machines, but I was not too happy because my engine was running very roughly. I still had the old "floater," EB-F.

Anyway, the raid came over and we went up. I got left behind in the main chase and so I climbed to about 20,000 feet and saw below a ME 109. From the way he went down I presume he never knew what hit him. Then I saw another of our squadron and we flew parallel about 100 yards apart and watching each others' tails. We flew over to the centre of the city above the balloons when I saw a lot of AA fire to the east of us. In a second or two I saw about five hundred bombers with a strong fighter escort above them and told my companion that I was going to investigate if he would watch my tail. Climbing up very carefully I saw that there were many separate squadrons at different levels. I chose a squadron that was about 35 or 40 strong and in line astern. I dived onto the tail of the last one. He burst into flames and I followed him down. When I was sure he was gone I zoomed up into a loop and dived down on the next in line of the squadron. By this time my machine was like a sieve with oil and glycol pouring out. However, I got the next one and as I followed him down the next of his squadron opened fire on me with a nice line in cross-fire, in addition to which I had a few other 109s and 110s chasing me. All my ammuni-

tion was gone and the plane was hardly moving. I thanked my lucky stars I had practiced my aerobatics to perfection, did a loop, rolled off the top of it and looped again until I shook them off. All this time the glycol was spewing out of the nose of the plane and the radiator temperature dropped back to zero, the oil temperature went up and finally off the clock. Then, of course, a ME 109 came to play with me so I had to do something to discourage him. I pulled the stick straight back and put full right rudder on and the plane went into a spin. I let it spin about three times and then pulled out very carefully because the machine was full of holes and not too strong. This didn't shake the 109 off and he came at me again. I trimmed the plane for a right hand gliding turn, lowered my seat, pulled my knees up and head down and took full advantage of the armour plate behind me. I heard about ten or twelve bullets hitting the plating and then miracle number one happened.

Sergeant Darling, my companion over the city, came along and with his last burst hit the 109 for six, and I continued on my way. The engine by this time was out of glycol and red hot. It seized and just stopped. The oil sprayed on the hot engine and burst into flames. I looked around for a place to land but all I could see was houses. I was going to jump for it but did not have enough height.

At last I found a field and glided towards it in a sideslip to keep the flames

below: 357th FG pilots.
bottom: 29 Sq. (RAF) pilots.
below: Sgt. Pilot George
Whipps, 602 Sq., RAF.
bottom: Major and Mrs.
Don Gentile, 4th FG.

away from the cockpit. I tried to lower the flaps and slow down but it was no use. When I thought I was about 40 feet up (I couldn't see anything because of the smoke) I pulled the stick right back, hit tail first and pancaked onto the ground. I went through a couple of walls and a few trees, cartwheeled over twice and finally came to rest upside down with me inside, unhurt. That was miracle number two.

It was getting rather hot inside and I was unable to get out. I was just going to shoot myself to get it over with when a man came along with an axe and split the side of the cockpit open and pulled me out. I was escorted into a house and of course was the centre of attention for miles around. At last a policeman came along and fixed me up with transport back to base so that was more or less that. I have a few scrapes and bruises but nothing broken and otherwise quite fit.
Yours,
John
P.S. I wangled a new uniform and flying kit out of this performance.

Walker "Bud" Mahurin was a member of Hub Zemke's Wolfpack, flying P-47 Thunderbolts from their Halesworth base in Norfolk.

"We had been grounded from operations for a week or so because of weather. When that happened we usually liked to fly the planes because they had a tendency to get sickness in the radios and what-not. I was up flying around the base and at the time my Jug had a

204

great big "bathtub" external fuel tank prior to us getting the more aerodynamic tanks. I saw a B-24 flying along at low altitude so I went alongside of it and flew formation with it. They waved and I waved and the waist gunner waved and the pilots were waving—boyish enthusiasm, I guess. We passed right over our base at probably about a thousand feet, maybe twelve hundred feet, and I had to lower flaps in order to stay with them. I got pretty close and, when it came time to leave, I dropped down below the B-24 wing and increased the throttle and started to go forward. The crew in the 24 were watching me. I tried to descend by pushing the stick forward, but the tail of my airplane kept going up and it finally was sucked into the propellers on the starboard side . . . and I suddenly felt the stick go limp, and I knew instantly what had happened and bailed out right away. The B-24 guys feathered two engines on that side and eventually made a successful landing. They thought it was a big joke . . . but, of couse, it bothered the hell out of me. I'll never forget driving back onto the base, sittin' in the back of the jeep with this huge parachute in my arms, billowing in the wind, wondering what in the hell was gonna happen to me now."

One of the first American fighter pilots in Britain in World War II was Leo Nomis, a member of No. 71 (Eagle) Squadron, who remained in the Royal Air Force for the duration of the war. He remembers a certain unauthorized trip he made to France.

"I was supposed to be doing an aircraft test. In those days you had to fly way the hell down around the estuary because they had a big balloon barrage, so I got down past Dungeness and started to cross the Channel. It seemed like I was on a rail, like a train. I just kept heading for Calais, the worst place you could head for—the worst place you could go—at sea level. I was about a hundred feet off the water to keep out of the radar. Had no idea what I was gonna do and actually had no idea why. But, the closer I got, the closer Calais was comin' so I just kept flyin' straight at it. I finally got up to the beach and it looked like it had barbed wire and God knows what . . . all kinds of obstacles, and there was a whole bunch of buildings right behind it. Not a peep out of 'em. Nothing out of them yet. Maybe they were still trying to figure out whether I had one radiator or two. A lot of guys got fooled with those 109s that way. They'd wait until they could count the radiators, and it was too late. There was a great big building . . . I didn't know what it was, and I just started firing the cannon and machine guns straight at it. If there was guys sleepin' in there, they really had a helluva surprise. I just applied all the cannon and damned near hit the building when I pulled up, and then I turned so tight I almost blacked out. This was still less than a hundred feet off the ground. Then I was heading down and there was what looked like a great big sentry box with a bunch of apparatus on top of it. So I started to fire at it and I missed it altogether. This was still with the machine guns. I'd fired all the cannon ammo at whatever in the hell that big place was . . . and they were bouncing off and ricocheting all over . . . you could see them hitting the dust.

Noise proves nothing. Often a hen who has merely laid an egg cackles as if she laid an asteroid.

—Samuel Clemens

205

below: Major Winslow M. Sobanski, 4th FG. above right: George R. Vanden Heuvel is given a ride in N51CK (44-64005) at the 1983 CAF Harlingen Airshow. The Mustang is the actual airplane *(Mary Mine)* that Vanden Heuvel flew in combat while with the 361st FG at Bottisham in 1944. right: Pilots of 19 Sq., RAF, in 1940. George Unwin is seated on the wing (third from left). above far right: George Unwin, 1990.

"I just was leisurely trying to fly out and all of a sudden I heard two muffled reports and there were two big black puffs, one under and one on the other side of the wing. They were shootin' 88mm straight trajectory and then a whole carload of Bofors stuff started to come. I was still fifty feet up, just crossing the beach . . . and it startled me so much I made a three-hundred-sixty-degree tight turn and almost blacked out again. I went back in, and all this stuff was goin' out. This is what saved me. If I'd gone straight on, they couldn't have missed. I looked behind me and it was a whole mass of black puffs plus Bofors goin' every-where . . . machine guns and whatever. I knew I had to get the hell out so I made another turn the same way only farther south. I was whip-pin' back and forth as fast as I could and had everything pushed forward and was just about out over the water and was goin' about three hundred and five miles an hour, which was pretty good for a Spitfire, and they were still gettin' pretty close. What they were doin' was shootin' ahead of me into the water and throwin' spouts up. Only thing I could do was whip it back and forth. At that speed it took me out of range, and then halfway across, they quit. They let up. They'd hit me. Only reason I knew they'd hit me was I looked down at where the rivets were on the wing over the wheel well, and there was a hole—a small hole but jagged and right where the tire was, so I knew there had to be a flat tire. I came back and when I came in—we were at Debden then—I radioed that I thought I had a flat tire. I just assumed this, in case I ground looped or went over on my back. I didn't know what the

hell was gonna happen, but I landed with the wheels down. I just swung a little bit to the right. I straightened out and no problem at all. The mechanics asked if everything was all right. I said, 'Yeah, fine . . . I got a flat tire' (they could see that). One of 'em had eyes as big as dollars and said I had a great bloody hole in that wheel well. A piece of shrapnel had come through and had missed the radia-tor by only a bit, about an inch. Needless to say, they called Petersen. Robbie Robinson, our intelligence officer, asked what happened. I said it was an aircraft test and I went and flew over Calais. It turned out to be a real problem because they were planning a raid at the time and they didn't want anybody goin' over cer-tain areas. They'd even painted the planes up different just for that . . . put that whitewash white stripes on 'em. They didn't want it to leak out. Say, you went over there and had to crash-land. The Germans would say 'What the hell are these white stripes? . . . They're not usually like that . . . . Somethin' must be up.' So, Petersen had to shut it up. He didn't report it. There was *no* flight. He raised holy hell with me. But he couldn't court-martial me. So they confiscated the cine gun film and I was confined to quarters a couple of weeks."

Obviously, not all fighter pilots could be aces. The vast majority never claimed any-thing more than a "probable"—if that. Some got no further than their first day of opera-tional duty. Pilot Officer Tommy Rose-Price joined 501 Squadron at Gravesend, fresh from training, on September 2, 1940, and was sent straight into combat with his Hurricane. Somewhere over Kent the Messerschmitts picked him off and no trace of him or his aircraft was ever found. As his commanding officer wrote a letter of condolence to the family, Rose-Price's car sat parked outside the watch office, still piled high with his unpacked gear. One squadron commander called such losses "the slaughter of the innocents."

THE A-2

"IT'S LIKE wearing your plane," said pilots about the leather flying jacket that General "Hap" Arnold had once dismissed with the remark: "get something better." But to the pilots of the U.S. Army Air Force in World War II, there *was* nothing better. The A-2 was a simple design that was improved over the years to make it more practical. Although the jacket was made from thick, tough steerhide, horsehide or goatskin, its lining was only thin cotton. There was also a lack of pockets—there were only two on the front with vertical entries and they held little more than a few small pieces of paper, a candy bar and a pack of cigarettes.

Some officers had specially added non-regulation side-entry pockets, which were located behind the official front ones. The jacket was, however, a part of the serviceman's uniform, complying to strict government specifications, and any personal alteration was forbidden, though painted embellishments were tolerated. Squadron patches and rank markings were officially acceptable.

The A-2 was a "windcheater," developed from the design of its predecessor, the A-1, which had been a favorite jacket of aviation pioneers Charles Lindbergh and Jimmy Doolittle. Though not perfect, the A-2 was a good, all-purpose garment. Airmen felt comfortable in it. With a full-length front zipper that fastened up to the collar, knitted wool cuffs and waistband, it kept the wind out and the edge off cold temperatures. It was, after all, designated as an intermediate summer-weight jacket and if it had had a warmer lining it would not have been so versatile. When temperatures were so low that the A-2 no longer offered reasonable protection, airmen wore a shearling-lined jacket, the B-3.

The A-2 design was finally standardized on May 9, 1931, and the army went shopping for suitable manufacturers to produce the garment. It was thought that sportswear makers would be appropriate as they would have the know-how and the necessary machinery to do the job. Manufacturers of shoes, raincoats and outerwear were used as well. They were contracted to produce a given number of garments and then were sent the approved government specs so that patterns could be drawn up. Although the manufacturers had to strictly adhere to the design, each had their own house style. For example, there were differences in the curvature of pocket flaps and in collar points, and in the shade of brown used to dye the leather. Even the sizes varied from maker to maker. An Aero Leather size 40 was considerably larger than a Perry Sportswear size 40.

The original specifications required that the A-2 be made from three-ounce horsehide in the color of Seal Brown, quite a dark brown with a reddish tint. By the beginning of World War II, demand for the garment was such that not enough horsehide could be obtained, and an updated spec was expedited that permitted the use of steerhide and goatskin. At the end of the jackets' production in 1943, the majority had been made of steerhide, the most readily available leather of the time.

The A-2 was not merely a functional garment. It was a status symbol that marked its owner as part of an élite band and was worn with macho pride. American fighter pilots were not the only ones to wear the jacket during the war. Bomber crews also had them. And, although superseded by another design in 1943, the A-2 remained the most popular flying jacket with American airmen throughout the war, in all theaters of operation.

Flamboyant artwork often decorated the fronts and backs of A-2 jackets. It frequently replicated the nose art painted on the wearer's aircraft. Pinup girls of the Vargas variety were popular subjects, and the name of a wife or girlfriend, hometown or state was often displayed. Some designs were suggestive, some lewd. Some carried threats directed at the enemy and a tally of missions already flown. Such decoration, while against army regulations, proliferated and helped to boost aircrew morale.

The jacket art seemed harmless enough until, on November 26, 1943, a B-17 of the 351st Bomb Group was shot down over Germany, its captured crew all wearing A-2s bearing the name MURDER INC. With the Nazi propaganda machine anxious to denigrate the Allied *Terror-Flieger*, such a gift for the Germans was a considerable embarrassment to the Army Air Force. From then on a degree of censorship was imposed on A-2 decoration.

For airmen of the Royal Air Force there was no equivalent to the A-2. The nearest approximation was the sheepskin-lined Irvin flying jacket. The Irvin was a wonderful design, but its bulky form meant that it was never as practical as the A-2. Also, King's Regulations forbade the defacing of Air Ministry property by painting on slogans or emblems. Thus, decoration on Irvins does not feature as one of the art forms of World War II and such personalizing was rare. It was common practice among RAF fighter pilots to signify their membership in that élite band by simply leaving the top button of their tunic undone. The practice probably derived from the need for greater comfort and freedom of movement in the cramped fighter cockpit, and to allow scarves to be tucked into the tunic at a time when service dress was still worn for flying duties. A cartoon character of the time, Pilot Officer Prune, provided still another explanation, nonchalantly pointing out that his top button had been shot off during a dogfight. But the top-button routine and the Irvin were no match for the A-2, and more than one RAF pilot managed to acquire one for his personal use.

Today, original and even reproduction A-2 jackets are highly sought after. Some purchasers feel that the jacket must be painted, or have a well-worn, distressed look—a used appearance implying the experience of combat.

Walter Konantz of the 338th Fighter Squadron, 55th Fighter Group, recalls the story of his own battle-damaged A-2.

"On January 13, 1945, I was circling Geibelstadt airdrome, getting ready to strafe it for the second time in a week. I noticed a couple of German planes taxiing, then saw one take off. I watched him while he made a climbing one-hundred-eighty-degree turn to the left, passing under me in the opposite direction. I did a

1. No smoking at any time or under any circumstances.
2. Drink intelligently and sparingly.
3. Eat sensibly.
4. Exercise regularly and diligently.
5. Learn all possible about flying or any other job at hand.
6. Always be willing to go out of way to learn something new.
7. Always try to give the other man a boost.
8. Fight hardest when down and never give up.
9. Don't make excuses but make up with deeds of action.
10. Learn from experience.
11. Listen to others and profit by criticism.
12. Live a clean life.
13. Trust in God and never lose faith in Him.

"The Rules to Live By" of Major George E. Preddy, Jr. 352nd FG

The mean of true valor lies between the extremes/of cowardice and rashness.

—Cervantes

left: William O'Brien, 357th FG.

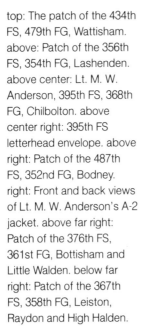

top: The patch of the 434th FS, 479th FG, Wattisham. above: Patch of the 356th FS, 354th FG, Lashenden. above center: Lt. M. W. Anderson, 395th FS, 368th FG, Chilbolton. above center right: 395th FS letterhead envelope. above right: Patch of the 487th FS, 352nd FG, Bodney. right: Front and back views of Lt. M. W. Anderson's A-2 jacket. above far right: Patch of the 376th FS, 361st FG, Bottisham and Little Walden. below far right: Patch of the 367th FS, 358th FG, Leiston, Raydon and High Halden.

tight one eighty and got in behind him. It was an ME 262 jet and he had not yet accelerated to high speed. We had had the new K-14 gunsight installed a week previously and I had never fired the guns using the new sight. It worked perfectly and I clobbered him with over forty strikes, setting his left engine on fire. He took no evasive action, even after the first hit. He then spiraled into the ground and exploded. Since I still had some ammo left I picked out a parked plane on the ground and started a strafing pass. Just as I got in range of the parked JU 88, I saw that it was a burned-out hulk from our strafing of a week past, so I didn't fire. However, the hornet's nest was stirred up and light flak was coming from everywhere. A single .30 caliber bullet entered my cockpit from the left side, cut a groove in the sleeve of my jacket and hit the radio control box on the right side of the cockpit. This, of course, disabled my radio and when I climbed up out of there not another P-51 was in sight.

"The weather was lousy and without a radio I hesitated to try going back to England without the help of a DF steer, so I found a single P-47, joined up with him and signaled that my radio was out and that I wanted to land with him. He took me to St. Trond, Belgium, where I spent the night and returned to England the next day. Meanwhile, back at the base, my barracks mates had assumed the fiery crash at Geibelstadt was me since they had heard nothing from me on the radio, and were in the process of dividing up my personal belongings as I walked in the door.

"Wish I had that jacket now for a souvenir, but I foolishly turned it in for a new one."

In 1987 the U.S. Air Force decided to reintroduce the A-2 jacket in conjunction with the fortieth anniversary of the service. In a climate of severely restricted budgeting the Air Force requested $7.4 million for the procurement of the new jackets for its pilots. Early in the 1987–88 budget cycle the appropriations committee of the U. S. Senate deleted the proposed funding, some members declaring the purchasing of millions of dollars worth of jackets "expensive and frivolous." The Air Force, however, wanted the jackets in order to help improve the morale of aircrew and perhaps to improve retention in the service. It considered the jacket an excellent means to rekindle the esprit de corps of its front-line flying crews. It lobbied long and hard to retain the jacket-procurement program in the budget and, for a while, it prevailed. Air Force pilots were soon wearing the new A-2s. In 1989, however, the House Armed Services Committee deleted funding for the jackets for fiscal 1989 and informed the Air Force that, from then on, each pilot would have to buy his own.

In the end a $5.2 million contract for 53,000 A-2 jackets was awarded to the Cooper Sportswear Manufacturing Co., Newark, New Jersey. It was the largest military contract ever for flight jackets. The Cooper jacket was specified to be in accordance with the Willis & Geiger Style Number A-2, the Avirex Style Number 2107G, or equivalent. The first Cooper jackets were delivered to the Air Force in May 1988.

The A-2 was worn with pride, and never more so than when battle-scarred.

Airman, down to earth,/Painting the town red,/Swingbands merely enlarge the hollow/Singing in your head.

from "Song"
by Gordon Symes

Reason and judgement are the qualities of a leader.

—Tacitus

211

LITTLE FRIENDS: SUCCESS AT LAST

WITH THE ADVENT of long-range daylight escort missions in midsummer 1943, the American fighter pilot was severely tested both physically and mentally. Until then, the duration of his time in the air on any one European mission had seldom been more than two hours. Now, with the new long-range fuel tanks, the missions would be extended considerably. Robert C. Strobell was one of the pilots who regularly flew these demanding missions with the Metfield-based 351st Squadron of the 353rd Fighter Group. He still remembers the unpleasant occasion over Germany when pressure from hours of sitting on a hard parachute and dinghy pack dislocated his hip joint. Even the mildest head colds could cause excruciating sinus pain, and the simple need to relieve oneself could bring unbearable discomfort. On another trip, Strobell landed the fighter back in England with his bladder fit to burst. He leaped from the Thunderbolt the moment it rolled to a stop in its revetment and "let go at the back of the airplane." Looking up, he was face to face with a startled farmer, his wife and their children. They could not have known or imagined the four and a half hours of discomfort Strobell had just endured.

For Strobell, and all fighter pilots in the ETO, flak was what worried them most. If the harmless-looking little puffs got you, you were gone. Robert Strobell finally accepted what his commanding officer, Major Glenn Duncan, was telling his pilots. "Pay no attention to it. Once it starts, there is nothing you can do about it." Enemy fighters, however, were a different matter. Although, unlike the flak, something could be done about them,

merely sighting them would "immediately crank up your tension by about five notches," says Strobell. "They could be sighted at a great distance as 'bogeys' or 'bandits,' bogeys being unidentified aircraft and bandits enemy aircraft. Seeing them meant that you would close on them to kill or be killed. Believe me, it pumps up your senses in a second." Over Germany there were other fears too. Strobell recalls: "When you first start flying fighters in combat you have a tendency to listen to the engine. You watch all the engine gauges—temperature, oil pressure, manifold pressure and RPMs—rather closely. And you listen. It probably comes from the sobering thought that it might quit over enemy territory. After a few missions, you finally get the message. And that is [that] there is nothing that this watching and listening will do to prevent it if it's going to happen. Suddenly, you are free of this self-imposed tension."

One instrument, though, was watched intently by all pilots during these long-range escorts—the fuel gauge. Strobell: "Time and distance became a matter of grave concern. Deep penetrations into Germany extended the P-47 to its maximum range. When you were in enemy territory and you knew that you had reached the halfway point of the flight, you started to pray that you would not see or engage enemy fighters. To do so meant opening up the throttle and burning off large amounts of gasoline rapidly in a dogfight, leaving you with not enough fuel to make it back to England. When this occurred, it became a most stressful situation . . . like the time I just made it back to Woodbridge emer-

We would rather die on our feet than live on our knees.

—Franklin Delano Roosevelt

below and far right: The control tower at Kings Cliffe, former base of the 20th Fighter Group. right: A pillbox at Kings Cliffe, 1990.

gency airbase and touched down as the engine quit, out of gasoline. At that moment, my wing man went barreling past me on the runway. He'd landed from the opposite direction.

214

We have met the enemy and they are ours.

—Oliver Hazard Perry

That was cutting it too close."

The new lengthy missions were tough on the American fighter pilots, but they were beginning to pay off. On July 28, 1943, P-47s of the 4th Fighter Group, Debden, routed the Luftwaffe. Equipped with the new long-range fuel tanks, the Americans were protecting the returning B-17s. The Germans were amazed to encounter them over Emmerich on the Dutch-German border, far beyond the P-47's normal range. The Thunderbolts shot down nine ME 109s and FW 190s, claimed one probable and six damaged, with only one American loss. The 56th Fighter Group, rivals of the 4th, had similar success over the Frankfurt area in early October. As forty twin-engined Messerschmitt ME 110 *Zerstorer* swept in to attack the American bombers, they were surprised by a mass of Thunderbolts bearing down on them. The American fighters were more than three hundred miles from their English base. The heavy, unwieldy Messerschmitts had no chance to lob rockets into the bomber formation, nor were they any match for the P-47s. The German force was decimated, with twenty-one of the ME 110s and eight other fighters being destroyed. Admittedly, there were substantial American bomber losses, but, without their little friends, these would surely have been greater. It was a major blow to the Luftwaffe.

In the latter part of 1943, Thunderbolts provided most of the fighter cover, being capable of a 350-mile radius of action with their extra tanks. It was hoped, however, that the P-38 Lightning would be even more effective with its 450-mile radius. Unfortunately, that

216

left: The ops room state board at the 65th Fighter Wing ops block, Saffron Walden. above: Major Willard Millikan and other 4th FG pilots speculate on the fate of their fellow pilots after a major air battle in Germany.

was not to be. Despite a fine performance in other theaters of the war, the P-38 was not good enough to turn the tide for the U.S. fighter forces in the European air war. Engine problems and a poorer-than-anticipated performance against the Luftwaffe limited its effectiveness. Nevertheless, it did have some successes.

Jack Ilfrey flew the P-38 with the 79th Fighter Squadron of the 20th Fighter Group at Kings Cliffe. He became one of the few aces in Europe on this type of aircraft. In *Happy Jack's Go-Buggy*, Ilfrey scored eight confirmed aerial victories, most of them during escort missions. Over Germany on May 24, 1944, he downed two ME 109s, one in conventional fashion. The second Messerschmitt collided with Ilfrey's starboard wing, ripping off a five-foot section. He faced the nightmare of a long journey back to base in a crippled airplane over Nazi-occupied territory. He made it back to Kings Cliffe, but his belief that he was "too damned good to get shot down" was badly shaken.

The *real* success story of the American escort-fighter force was emerging by early 1944. Extending the range of the escorts even further, the P-51 Mustang surpassed the 450-mile radius of the P-38. With a greater internal fuel capacity, plus external tanks, the Mustang was capable of reaching the Polish border from its East Anglian bases. It was more than a match for any interceptor the Germans could send against the bomber formations and even took on their new jets.

The early Mustangs of the USAAF were assigned to the 9th Air Force as tactical fight-

Rumors had been flying hot and heavy that we were being transferred from P-47s to P-51s. We had heard a lot of talk about this amazing plane. By cutting the fire power to four machine guns and using a new type of carburetor, it was capable of 1,800-mile flights with its two belly tanks. Our P-47s had only one belly tank which was slung underneath the fuselage. The 51s had them slung under each wing, with two more permanent tanks in the wing and another tank just to the rear of the cockpit. On February 22 the rumors became a fact; one P-51 landed and we were all (sixty pilots) ordered to fly it in preparation for the change-over. It was a beautiful airplane; it reminded me of the Spitfire with its huge in-line engine. And, like the Spitfire, it was glycol-cooled. We queued up on the plane like housewives at a bargain sale. The time in the air was spread very thin, forty minutes was all the time I had in the air in a 51 when

"Hawker Typhoon, Normandy 1944." A painting by Frank Wootton representing an operation by 121 Wing, 83 Group, RAF, attacking German tank concentrations in France.

ers to support the impending invasion of Europe. But the 8th Air Force, in its strategic role, was struggling with the escort problem, often sustaining unacceptable attrition in its bomber force. It was quickly realized that these new fighters had been miscast. The 354th Fighter Group (the first Mustang unit) was then reassigned from the 9th to the 8th Air Force for escort work. By December 1943 they were fully operational. General William Kepner, commander of 8th AF Fighter Command, said of the P-51: "It is distinctly the best fighter we can get over here. They are going to be the only satisfactory answer." The Mustang was now arriving in large numbers, making possible the success of the 8th Air Force in Europe. Kepner had been right.

As the strength of the Eighth increased dramatically towards the end of 1943, General Arnold signaled a New Year's message to his commanders: "This is a MUST. Destroy the enemy air force wherever you find them, in the air, on the ground and in the factories." The result was "Big Week." In February, a massive, unprecedented and sustained assault was unleashed on the German aircraft industry by the 8th Air Force. More than a thousand bombers took part in a day-by-day pounding of the Reich, escorted now by the new Mustangs, as well as by Thunderbolts and Lightnings. Nearly a thousand fighters protected the bomber force all the way from England to the targets and back again. In their planning, the commanders had projected possible losses of as many as two hundred bombers on the first day alone. The actual figure was twenty one, thanks largely to the bombers' "little friends." Success at last—overwhelming

on the morning of the 28th the group flew to Steeple Morden base in their P-47s and traded them for P-51s. The planes didn't have their auxiliary tanks on, but they were full of fuel and the machine guns were loaded. Our briefing was held on the ground among our 51s. No flying back to Debden for us, but off on a fighter sweep to France. We were familiarizing ourselves with this plane the hard way.

from *The Look of Eagles*
by John T. Godfrey

below right: Martlesham Heath and the control tower/watch office, 1990.
right: 8th AF poker chips.
below: cigarette pack collectible cards showing RAF squadron crests.

numbers, improved organization and tactics, coupled with high morale and an outstanding new fighter were, at last, giving Allied air power the edge over the Luftwaffe.

Stepped up in boxes and strung out for hundreds of miles, the thousand or so B-17s and B-24s were protected by a similar number of fighters weaving back and forth to keep station with their slower charges. The fighters flew in the Luftwaffe-style "finger-four," the position of each fighter corresponding to the fingertips of an outstretched hand. Other formations of fighters would be sweeping the sky ahead of the main bomber force. Such a massive aerial assembly looked invincible and, by this stage in the war, it nearly was. In "Big Week" alone, the Luftwaffe lost 225 fighter pilots, dead or missing, and 141 wounded—and hundreds of new aircraft. Fully one tenth of their defending fighter force had been destroyed.

PLAYER'S CIGARETTES

AUDAX OMNIA PERPETI

No. 54 (FIGHTER) SQUADRON.
R.A.F.

PLAYER'S CIGARETTES

QUID SI COELUM RUAT

No. 56 (FIGHTER) SQUADRON.
R.A.F.

The 8th Air Force now vigorously pursued the assault on Germany. With growing Allied air superiority, the escorts were encouraged to seek out German interceptors aggressively. As one Luftwaffe fighter pilot put it: "No longer was it a case of their bombers having to run the gauntlet of our fighters, but of our having to run the gauntlet of both their bombers and fighters." By March–April 1944, the Luftwaffe had essentially been defeated—outfought over its home territory. But for the encouragement of the beleaguered German nation, its propaganda machine churned out stories of crippling American losses and glorious Luftwaffe victories. Believing them, one German farmer leveled his old shotgun at a downed Luftwaffe flier, hanging by his parachute from a tree. The rustic was unimpressed by the airman's profanity. "So, the pig of an American *Terror-Flieger* speaks German, eh?"

Berlin was the next obvious target after "Big Week." The Mustang had demonstrated its range and combat capability and on March 4, 1944, a small force of B-17s, accompanied by twenty Mustangs of the 4th Fighter Group, hit the city. Reichsmarshall Göring had once boasted that "no enemy plane would ever fly over Reich territory." At the end of the war, during his brief captivity, he admitted that when he saw those fighters over Belin, he "knew the game was up."

Sometimes strafing railway engines produced spectacular results. On August 2, 1944, a flight of Mustangs from the 364th Fighter Group shot up a train whose wagons happened to contain V-1 flying-bomb warheads. The attack occurred near Rémy, France. As the P-51s strafed, the fourth and last aircraft was suddenly enveloped in a huge explosion. The train had vanished, leaving a long row of craters where the wagons had stood. Such was the force of the blast that the other three Mustangs were flung upside down. Above, the re-

He drew a circle that shut me out—/Heretic, rebel, a thing to flout. But Love and I had the wit to win./We drew a circle and took him in.

from "Outwitted" by Edwin Markham

Cowards die many times before their deaths;/The valiant never taste of death but once.

from *Julius Caesar*, act 2, scene 2 by Shakespeare

Don't cheer, boys, the poor devils are dying.

—Captain John W. Philip, at the Battle of Santiago, 1898

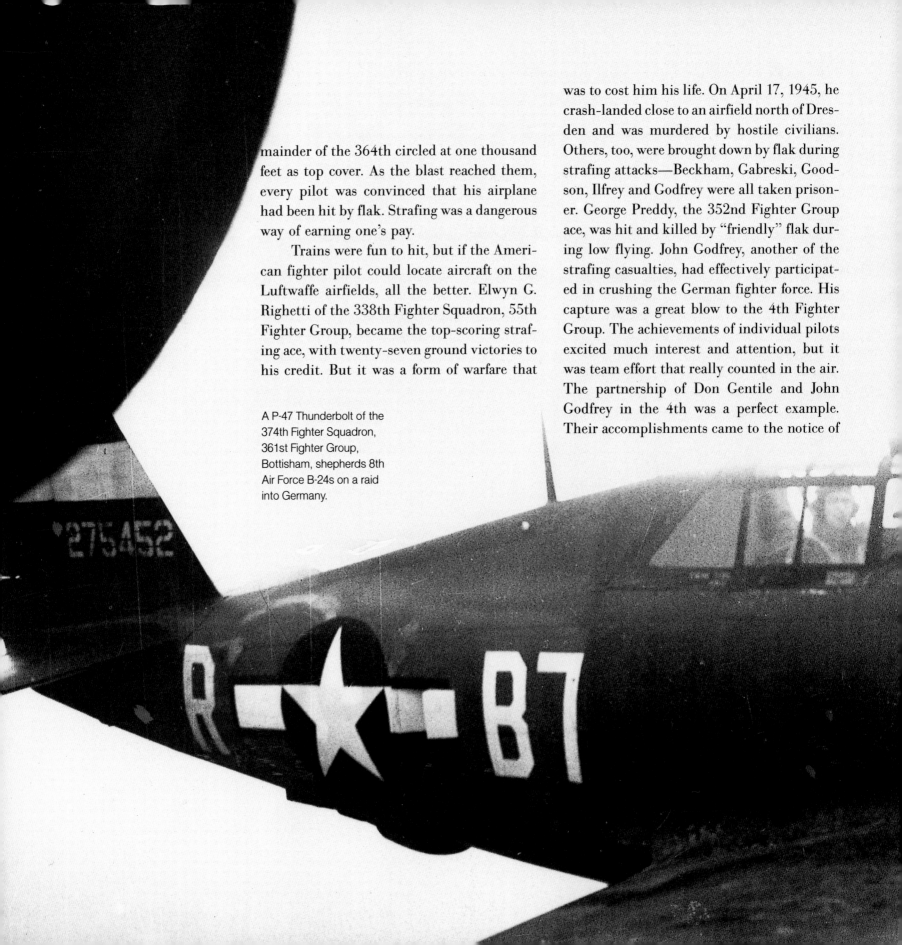

mainder of the 364th circled at one thousand feet as top cover. As the blast reached them, every pilot was convinced that his airplane had been hit by flak. Strafing was a dangerous way of earning one's pay.

Trains were fun to hit, but if the American fighter pilot could locate aircraft on the Luftwaffe airfields, all the better. Elwyn G. Righetti of the 338th Fighter Squadron, 55th Fighter Group, became the top-scoring strafing ace, with twenty-seven ground victories to his credit. But it was a form of warfare that

A P-47 Thunderbolt of the 374th Fighter Squadron, 361st Fighter Group, Bottisham, shepherds 8th Air Force B-24s on a raid into Germany.

was to cost him his life. On April 17, 1945, he crash-landed close to an airfield north of Dresden and was murdered by hostile civilians. Others, too, were brought down by flak during strafing attacks—Beckham, Gabreski, Goodson, Ilfrey and Godfrey were all taken prisoner. George Preddy, the 352nd Fighter Group ace, was hit and killed by "friendly" flak during low flying. John Godfrey, another of the strafing casualties, had effectively participated in crushing the German fighter force. His capture was a great blow to the 4th Fighter Group. The achievements of individual pilots excited much interest and attention, but it was team effort that really counted in the air. The partnership of Don Gentile and John Godfrey in the 4th was a perfect example. Their accomplishments came to the notice of

Winston Churchill, who referred to the pair as a latter-day Damon and Pythias. Göring is alleged to have said of these particular "Debden Gangsters" that he would gladly give two of his best squadrons for their capture. A deadly team, they alternated roles as wing man and leader, amassing an impressive score.

RAF fighter pilots had frequently provided withdrawal cover, escorted bombers part of the way out and shepherded stragglers on the way back, but they were never fully integrated into the fighter force of the mass daylight raids by the 8th. For Johnny Johnson, one of RAF Fighter Command's leading aces, it was a constant frustration: "How we longed for more drop tanks so that some of the many hundreds of Spitfires based in Britain could play their part in the great air battle over Germany instead of being confined to unprofitable sweeps over the familiar but now barren hunting grounds where a man could complete a tour of operations and never fire his guns in anger. We regretted this lack of vision about long-range fighting, for the Spitfire was the best close-in fighter of the lot. With a little foresight the Spitfires could have fought very well in Germany and could have helped the Eighth in its great venture, but it was not to be." This was the American fighter pilot's moment of glory; the RAF fighter pilot had had his during 1940.

It is, perhaps, appropriate that the last word should go to a B-17 tail gunner: "Every time I see a P-51 pilot, I want to go up and shake his hand."

High above us at about 35,000 feet we can see some small specks in groups of four. Each of these tiny dots has a white tail feather. This is the most beautiful sight in the world, because we realize that they are Thunderbolts, our fighter escort. The white plumes are vapor trails. We truck drivers really love these boys. They do a swell job. Their rendezvous with us is right on time. In their groups of four, they skate across the sky, weaving back and forth . . .

from *Letters From England* by J. M. Bennett, Jr.

above left: A bad end for a Mustang of the 357th FG at Leiston, above center: Major General William E. Kepner, Commander, VIII Fighter Command, USAAF, from August 1943 to August 1944. left and below left: P-38 crashes in England. below: Major James Howard, 354th FG Medal of Honor recipient.

Lt. Robert H. Richards, 4th FG, flew as wingman with Maj. John T. Godfrey, the 4th's highest scoring ace. They were old friends and shared many good and bad times, including Richards's final trip from Debden, March 4, 1944.

Bob was flying on my wing over the Channel. He called me, "Hello Shirt Blue Red Leader, this is Red Two. My motor's acting up, am returning to base." "Roger, Red Two." I didn't know it then, but those were the last words I was to hear from Bob. Motor difficulty was common in those days, and over the radio I could hear other boys reporting trouble. On approaching the Dutch coast my own engine started coughing and spitting. It was my turn now. Of the sixteen planes that took off that morning, only three from our squadron were able to meet the bombers over Berlin. Those three returned safely to base. The three missing boys were from the other two squadrons. Weather was very bad over England. I started to let down through the clouds, but when ice formed on my wings, I turned back toward the Channel. Emerging from the clouds I flew south, letting down gradually until 500 feet above the Channel, then I turned back to England and flew at six hundred feet just below the cloud base. Bob was not at Debden when I landed, but I didn't worry, and in fact gave no thought to it even an hour later when I still had no word. Probably he had landed at Martlesham Heath to see J.J. and just forgot to call the base. I was still sitting in the dispersal hut when the phone in the intelligence room rang. I heard low talking but the words were indistinct. Mac, the intelligence officer, approached me with a bottle and a glass. At the end of every mission a glass of whiskey was always given to the pilot, if he wished it, to settle his nerves. "Here, Johnny, this is a bonus day. Have another drink." I gladly accepted the offer of the free drink, but was suspicious of Mac, who didn't look into my eyes as he usually did when he handed a drink to me. His presence suddenly made me uncomfortable. "Somebody's got to tell you, Johnny, and I guess I'm the one. A call just came through from the RAF. Bob's plane crashed at Framlingham. He was still in the cockpit. He's dead, Johnny." His words hit me like a lightning bolt. It just didn't seem possible— not Bob, my war buddy. After living together for two years, our comradeship had strengthened into a love which for me was even greater than the feeling I had for my own brothers. We had shared everything, clothes, money, and yes, even girls. I knew his faults and merits just as he knew mine. I cried inwardly, but I

didn't break down. Our base chaplain made all the arrangements for Bob's funeral. The bus that was to take us to the cemetery was waiting in front of the officer's mess at 10:30. Mrs.C, J.J., Jimmy Goodson, Bob's C.O., Larry, Bob's crew chief, the boys from the orchestra, Lieutenant Charlotte Fredericks and three other nurses from the nearby hospital all climbed in for the ride to the cemetery twenty miles away, near the city of Cambridge. It was a quiet and sad journey. J.J. and I sat together, but we were each preoccupied with our own thoughts and very few words were spoken. The chapel was surrounded by a carefully cut lawn on which were hundreds of white crosses in neat little rows. There were no other stone markers or tombs, only the bleak little crosses on which name, rank and serial number were painted in black letters, showing the final resting place of American airmen. When we entered the chapel a pine box completely covered by the American flag was resting near the altar. This held the remains of Bob's mangled body. As a house of God it lacked the spiritual feeling of churches I had been accustomed to. It was not a church of life, where marriages and baptisms were

EAST SUFFOLK POLICE.

FRAMLINGHAM _____ Station,

5th _day of_ March, _____ 19 44.

The Chief Constable,

     I beg to report that at 1130 hours Saturday, 4th March, 1944, an American P.51 Mustang Fighte 'plane, marked V.F.1 (36786) Home Station - Debden, crashed in a field about 800 yards S.W. of Durban's Farm, Framlingham.

     The 'plane was completely smashed but did not catch fire, wreckage was scattered over a wide area.

     It was piloted by Lt. R. H. Richards, age 23, who was killed, his body was found near the wreckage. The U.S.A.A.F. Station, Parham, was informed and the body removed to that station.

     The fields concerned are in the occupation of Mr. Cecil Randall, Red House Farm, Kettleburgh. There was no damgge to civilian property.

P.H.Q. & D.H.Q. informed by telephone.

William A. [signature]

T/Sergeant.

Lt Robert H. Richards 336 f/Sqn 4 f/Group

P51-B 43-6786

A/C Arrived at 4th on 28 Feb '44

RCAF

blessed when people started out on their new lives; here only the end of life was blessed—and the atmosphere seemed haunted by the young souls whose lives were taken away from them in the bloom of youth. The prayers were not too long, for we had been a little late in arriving, and the schedule of burial services was timed in a cold and impersonal manner. No sooner was Bob's coffin carried out, than another one took its place in this church of the dead. "Ashes to ashes and dust to dust," the chaplain said, and with the faint sounds of the bugle beginning The Last Call, Bob's body was lowered into the ground. We stood there, all of us clinging to the memory of Bob as we last remembered him.

from *The Look of Eagles*
by John T. Godfrey

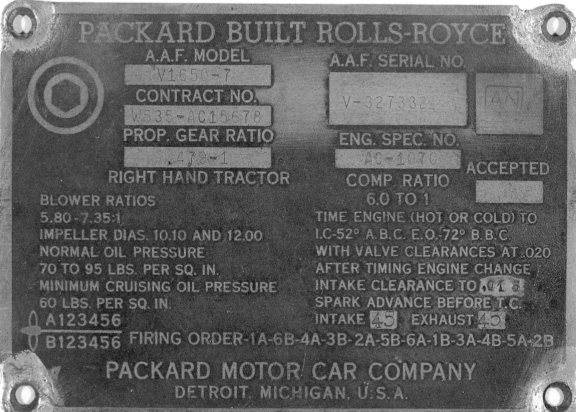

PACKARD BUILT ROLLS-ROYCE

A.A.F. MODEL
V1650-7
A.A.F. SERIAL NO.
V-327332
AN

CONTRACT NO.
W535-AC15678
PROP. GEAR RATIO
.479-1
ENG. SPEC. NO.
AC-1070
ACCEPTED

RIGHT HAND TRACTOR
COMP. RATIO
6.0 TO 1

BLOWER RATIOS
5.80 - 7.35:1
IMPELLER DIAS. 10.10 AND 12.00
NORMAL OIL PRESSURE
70 TO 95 LBS. PER SQ. IN.
MINIMUM CRUISING OIL PRESSURE
60 LBS. PER SQ. IN.
A123456
B123456   FIRING ORDER-1A-6B-4A-3B-2A-5B-6A-1B-3A-4B-5A-2B

TIME ENGINE (HOT OR COLD) TO
I.C-52° A.B.C. E.O.-72° B.B.C.
WITH VALVE CLEARANCES AT .020
AFTER TIMING ENGINE CHANGE
INTAKE CLEARANCE TO .075
SPARK ADVANCE BEFORE T.C.
INTAKE 45   EXHAUST 45

PACKARD MOTOR CAR COMPANY
DETROIT, MICHIGAN, U.S.A.

far left: The East Suffolk Constabulary report on the crash of Bob Richards's aircraft near Framlingham. above left: John Godfrey. above right: RCAF cadet Richards. left: A Merlin engine manufacturer's plate from a P-51 Mustang.

GOING BACK

OF THE HALF-MILLION American airmen stationed in England, there must have been many who were thankful to shake its damp soil from their feet at the end of the war. Staff Sergeant Henry D. Wertz of the Steeple Morden–based 355th Fighter Group expressed their feelings:

Someday to America we'll return,
And behind us some bridges we will burn,
But as sure as there is sadness, joy and bliss,
There are some things of England we will miss.

The *Daily Mirror* and its sweetheart "Jane,"
Walks in the meadow, through the lane,
But when we are back in America once more,
To enjoy the things for us there in store,
We will soon forget the English way,
And settle at home, e'er more to stay!

Not all the Yanks, though, turned their backs on Britain for good. Some are now eager to come back. American fighter-group veterans return frequently for one last look. It is said that as men grow older they find more strongly in their hearts the memory of their youth. It is an inexplicable but powerful emotion that draws them back. But coming back can be painful as well as happy. There is sadness at the sight of the cemeteries and wayside memorials. Even those who were not part of the war cannot fail to be moved by the thousands of white memorial markers that stand row upon row beside the Wall of Missing at the Madingley Cemetery, near Cambridge. Today

232

The parents of Pilot Officer Roy Marchand watch as his widow, Jean, places a wreath on Marchand's grave at Bromley after the war. P/O Marchand was killed in action with 73 (Hurricane) Squadron on September 15, 1940.

A few of The Few. Sixty-five Battle of Britain pilots gather for a photograph commemorating the fiftieth anniversary of the Battle. The location is Bentley Priory (1990), north of London, wartime headquarters of RAF Fighter Command. For a listing of those pictured here, please see page 244

I remember my youth and the feeling that will never/come back any more—the feeling that I could last forever, outlast the sea, the earth, and all men.

from *Youth*
by Joseph Conrad

He was only a lad, but then he would go,/I'm heartsick, dear Lord, but proud of him tho, Our country needed him, he heard the call, Light's gone from life, for he is my all.

Who knows the thots of mothers who wait, Whether in grandeur, or lowly state,/Who knows the sacrifice of those who give/Their all, their sons, that we might live?

"Those Who Wait" from *Rhymes of a Lost Battalion Doughboy*

When you are old and gray and full of sleep, And nodding by the fire, take down this book.

from "When You Are Old" by W. B. Yeats

His speech was a fine example, on the whole,/Of rhetoric, which the learn'd call "rigmarole."

from *Don Juan* by Byron

right: The 353rd Fighter Group briefing room at Raydon.

it is a place of pilgrimage for returning veterans. Most commemorated here were airmen with the U.S. 8th and 9th Air Forces, who died before their time. Those vets who come back have, for the most part, led long and fulfilling lives, and one returning airman confessed recently to a feeling of guilt as he scanned name after name. "Each one of them," he said, "should and could have been me."

At Steeple Morden the veterans keep coming back, not all of them having "settled at home, e'er more to stay." Their focus is the imposing 355th FG memorial at the edge of the abandoned base. It is well kept, in stark contrast to the old airfield around it. Here, weed-choked roadways and perimeter tracks meander aimlessly among cultivated farmlands and the soil is fertile with the scattered debris of war: a fuel filler cap, a crushed Zippo lighter, a press-stud fastener marked CHICAGO, spent .50 caliber shell casings and mounds of brick rubble. All are echoes of the past. Casual visitors with just the slightest sense of history can tell there is something special about these places. Each crumbling roadway to nowhere is a memory lane, each dilapidated hut a reminder of lost youth. One historian said of these places: "If there are ghosts, then they are here."

Decades on and still they come. Sometimes alone, sometimes in happy, noisy organized tour groups. Veterans associations are the enthusiastic planners of these parties. The visits are arranged with military precision and follow established patterns: the airfield and its environs, the local pubs, the "liberty" towns

like Cambridge and Ely, the memorials and, inevitably, the American Cemetery at Madingley. Such was the form of the 361st Fighter Group Association's 1990 UK reunion, culminating in a "48" to London . . . but advancing years and the presence of wives made this last a more restrained affair than it was in 1944. At Bottisham, as at Steeple Morden, there are memorials to those who flew from the base. At other airfields there are memorials too, but not always in carved stone. Some are much less obvious. At Little Walden, for example, the state board is still carefully preserved in the old Ops block, now a garage. The owners have thoughtfully ensured its preservation. Nearby, the original control tower has been restored to usable condition and is now an architect's office. These airfields where so much happened will not be forgotten even though man and nature continue to erase most traces of their existence.

It is not only the veterans themselves who cross the Atlantic to return to the former bases. Families and friends of those who once served here are also drawn to these places—people like Gerard Duffy who, as a New York schoolboy, was fascinated by the tales of his older cousin John Dyer, who had been a P-38 Lightning pilot with the 20th Fighter Group. Gerard was determined to locate and visit Kings Cliffe, where it had all happened.

During the 1980s, Duffy took time out from a study visit to Oxford to find the airfield. Being a private pilot, he rented a Cessna 150 and overflew the site. It was all just as he had imagined it. The tower still stood and, viewed from the air, the remains of the Kings

right: Huts at Steeple Morden. below: The destiny of a Little Walden Nissen.

Those only deserve a monument who do not need one.

—Hazlitt

left: The 355th Fighter Group memorial at Steeple Morden. below left: The memorial in Tangmere village. below: A Raydon hut, 1990.

The Bird of Time has but a little way/To flutter—and the Bird is on the Wing.

from *The Rubaiyat of Omar Khayyam*

Cliffe air base were clearly visible. He set up an approach for a landing, just as his cousin had done so many times. He passed over the track of the disused runway and decided to return later to view the place from ground level. By coincidence, Duffy had chosen the very day that Kings Cliffe village was holding a garden party to raise funds for a 20th Fighter Group memorial. The villagers welcomed him warmly. Some remembered his cousin and pointed out Dyer's name and photograph in their records of the 55th Fighter Squadron. Duffy was surprised and deeply touched at the affection shown by these strangers. They still

'Ah, sad and strange as in dark summer dawns The earliest pipe of half-awakened birds To dying ears, when unto dying eyes/The casement slowly grows a glimmering square; So sad, so strange, the days that are no more.

"Tears, Idle Tears" by Alfred, Lord Tennyson

above: The bicycle repair facility of the 353rd Fighter Group at Raydon in March 1945.

remembered with gratitude the contribution and sacrifices made by young Americans so long ago.

For both American and British airmen, revisiting their old haunts is not always pleasant. There can be sadness at the dereliction, vandalism and change. Some prefer not to go back.

For all who do return, it is a moving experience. Eudora Seyfer, wife of a 353rd Fighter Group armorer George A. Seyfer, accompanied her husband on his return to Raydon.

"I am sitting in a bus traveling narrow country roads bordered by green hedgerows. My husband sits beside me. We are in the part of England known as East Anglia, mid-morn-ing on a bright Saturday. I am one of fourteen wives on the bus, watching both the scenery and the unfolding drama inside.

"Our husbands, some with thinning gray hair, some with slightly arthritic limbs, several with vials of heart medicine tucked handily in their pockets, lean forward in their seats, peering out the bus windows through the tops of their bifocals—excited and anxious as little boys. Each wears a specially ordered cap with 353RD FIGHTER GROUP, EIGHTH AIR FORCE printed on the front. They are looking for what's left of Raydon Airfield where they lived for two long, lonesome years during World War II.

" 'I say, it must be near here,' says our travel agent in dignified British English. (His maps of England do not show old World War II airfields.)

" 'Look!' Suddenly, one of the men points across a flat field toward a bulky black shadow looming against a blue horizon. 'That's a hangar!'

" 'That has to be Raydon,' says another voice with a funny catch.

Our visit had been carefully planned, even written up in the village newspaper. First we are to stop at the Peabody farm. Mr. Peabody now owns most of the land that was once Raydon Airfield.

" 'Welcome back to Raydon,' Peabody says as he boards the bus. 'As you can see, there is no longer an airfield here, but more of Raydon survives than most World War II airfields. I'd like to show you about.'

"The big bus pulls onto blacktop road and stops amid a cluster of metal Quonset-type buildings. These are the remaining

240

buildings, now used by the government. And here, too, is the big black hangar.

"The men fan out among the buildings. The three who were pilots head toward the hangar, those who were mechanics, armorers and radiomen head toward other buildings. I follow my husband, who walks with his friend Charley Graham on the remains of the runway. Weeds are growing through the cracks in the old cement.

" 'Remember when we were standing right here when Colonel Ben's plane crashed?' Charley says.

"Slowly the men drift back toward the bus. I sense a sort of sadness, a letdown. Is this really Raydon? Are these few old buildings in the middle of a farm field all that's left to show for the years spent here? So long ago, the memories faint. Was it real—that war? Reluctantly, they board the bus.

"Then, from a farm beyond the lane, a woman calls to us. 'Wait! Wait!' She runs toward the bus holding something in her hand.

"She reaches the group breathless and laughing. 'Forty years ago when you were here, I was a little girl living on my father's farm. One of you hit a baseball over the fence into our farmyard. I found it, but I didn't throw it back. I kept it all these years.' She smiles sheepishly. 'When I read you were coming, I thought you'd want to see it.'

"The men gather around her, laughing, each holding the old baseball for a moment, then passing it on. Somehow it proves that Raydon was real, that the 353rd Fighter Group was here—and that the men were young and vital and strong enough to hit a baseball way over into that farmyard. We thank her and climb back onto the bus. There is a spirit of joy now.

"On to town. Two hundred people live in Raydon. Most of them are here to celebrate the day with us. There are races and games in the schoolyard. Inside, a pot-luck supper is waiting: chicken pies, Cornish pasties, potted shrimp. 'You are the first group to come,' they tell us.

"The next morning, we dress in our best clothes. The bus takes us to the tiny Anglican church built in the year 1200 and packed to capacity this Sunday morning. The Americans sit together in the front. When the service ends, Charley Graham stands and asks to say a word.

" 'We have a gift for you.' He holds *the* check, our collective gift. 'We have one thousand American dollars to be spent in any way you choose. We ask only one thing: that a little of it be spent for a plaque in this church remembering the men of the 353rd Fighter Group who served at Raydon so that our children and our grandchildren, when they come to visit, will know that we were here.'

"There is silence in the ancient church; the organ begins to play 'The Star-Spangled Banner.' I look down the rows and see tears on every cheek. How strange life is, I think. An old baseball brought those long-ago days back to life, and a little plaque will keep them living.

"We walk from the cool stone church into the bright morning. We say good-bye and board the bus."

One day Ed Hauser, Jack Rich and I were riding our bicycles around the perimeter track at Raydon. I had set a rabbit snare behind a brush pile a few days earlier. When we came even with the brush pile, I told them that I wanted to go behind it. When I walked around it, I chased up a rabbit that ran directly into the snare. I stabbed it with my trench knife. I told them that the rabbit ran in front of me and that I threw my knife at it. I never told them differently.

—Dale Snoke,
former Station
Quartermaster,
353rd FG, Raydon

Those wartime years have gone, and left no traces,/Fresh tides of youth have swept them all away;/New buildings have arisen by the river,/And there are few who think of yesterday;/Yet sometimes, in the middle of September Though Spitfires scream no more across the sky,/As dusk comes down, you cannot see the pavement/Where ghosts in blue are walking down the High.

from "Oxford in Wartime"
by Mary Wilson

Grass is the forgiveness of nature—/her constant benediction . . ./Forests decay, harvests perish, flowers vanish,/but grass is immortal.

—Ingalls, speech, 1874

England's sun was slowly setting o'er the hilltops far away, Filling all the land with beauty at the close of one sad day.

from "Curfew Must Not Ring To-night" by Rosa H. Thorpe

Every man must get to heaven his own way.

—Frederick the Great

above: The "Early Treatment" center at Goxhill. right: A memorial at Martlesham Heath. right center: The 11 Group Battle of Britain memorial at Uxbridge. below right: A hardstand tie-down. far right: Three images of Raydon after a gentle early evening rain in April 1990.

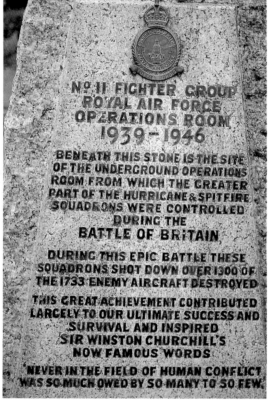

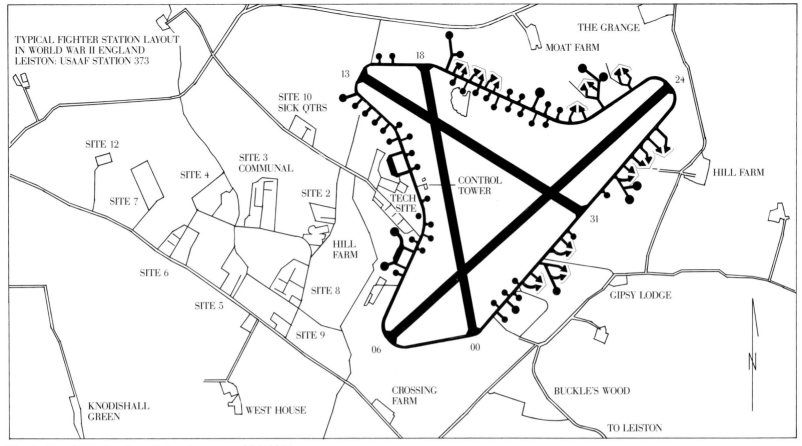

TYPICAL FIGHTER STATION LAYOUT
IN WORLD WAR II ENGLAND
LEISTON: USAAF STATION 373

THE GRANGE
MOAT FARM
SITE 10
SICK QTRS
SITE 12
SITE 3
COMMUNAL
SITE 4
SITE 2
HILL FARM
SITE 7
CONTROL
TOWER
TECH
SITE
HILL
FARM
SITE 6
SITE 8
SITE 5
GIPSY LODGE
SITE 9
KNODISHALL
GREEN
WEST HOUSE
CROSSING
FARM
BUCKLE'S WOOD
TO LEISTON

The Battle of Britain pilots pictured on pages 234–235 are:

1. Fl.Lt.John Lauder
2. Grp.Cpt.Brian Kingcome
3. Sq.Ldr.Arthur Riseley
4. Wing Comm.Ivor Cosby
5. Fl.Lt.Gerald Holder
6. Wing Comm.Wilfred Sizer
7. Wing Comm.Vivian Snell
8. Fl.Lt.Robert Plenderleith
9. Sq.Ldr.Kenneth Carver
10. Sq.Ldr.Bob McGugan
11. Fl.Lt.Leslie Harvey
12. Wing Comm.James Thomson
13. Wing Comm.Michael Ingle-Finch
14. Wing Comm.Ralph Havercroft
15. Sgt.Norman Barron
16. W/O Geoffrey Garside
17. Fl.Lt.Freddie Gash
18. Sq.Ldr.Boleslaw Drobinski
19. Wing Comm.Hugh Beazley
20. Fl.Off.Eric Poole
21. Grp.Cpt.James Cunningham
22. Wing Comm.John Barnes
23. Fl.Lt.Ludwik Martel
24. Wing Comm.Peter Parrott
25. Fl.Lt.Owen Burns
26. Wing Comm.Terence Kane
27. Sq.Ldr.Jocelyn Millard
28. Air Comm.John Ellacombe
29. Wing Comm.Patrick Barthropp
30. Sq.Ldr.Henryk Szczesny
31. Wing Comm.William Gregory
32. Grp.Cpt.Peter Matthews
33. Wing Comm.Derek Dowding
34. Fl.Lt.Stefan Kleczkowski
35. Sq.Ldr.Ronald Stillwell
36. Air Chief Marshal Sir
    Christopher Foxley-Norris
37. Wing Comm.Pat Hancock
38. Air Marshal Sir Harry Maguire

39. Sq.Ldr.Frank Usmar
40. Fl.Lt.William Walker
41. Air Comm.Christopher Mount
42. Air Chief Marshal Sir
    Frederick Rosier
43. Grp.Cpt.William David
44. Grp.Cpt.Alan Murray
45. Fl.Off.Len Bowman
46. Fl.Lt.Maurice Pocock
47. Lt.Comm.Adam MacKinnon
48. Fl.Lt.James Culmer
49. Fl.Lt.Donald Anderson
50. Fl.Lt.William Corbin
51. Fl.Lt.John Ditzel
52. Air Vice Marshal Harold
    Bird-Wilson
53. Fl.Lt.Roger Hall
54. Fl.Lt.Basil Quelch
55. Fl.Lt.John Toombs
56. Wing Comm.Douglas Grice
57. Sq.Ldr.Miroslav Mansfeld
58. Sq.Ldr.Kenneth Lusty
59. Air Vice Marshal George
    Chamberlain

60. Air Comm.Clive Baker
61. Grp.Cpt.Desmond Sheen
62. W/O Bob Cook
63. Wing Comm.Hugh Kennard
64. Wing Comm.Ronald Kellett
65. Wing Comm.Geoffrey Page

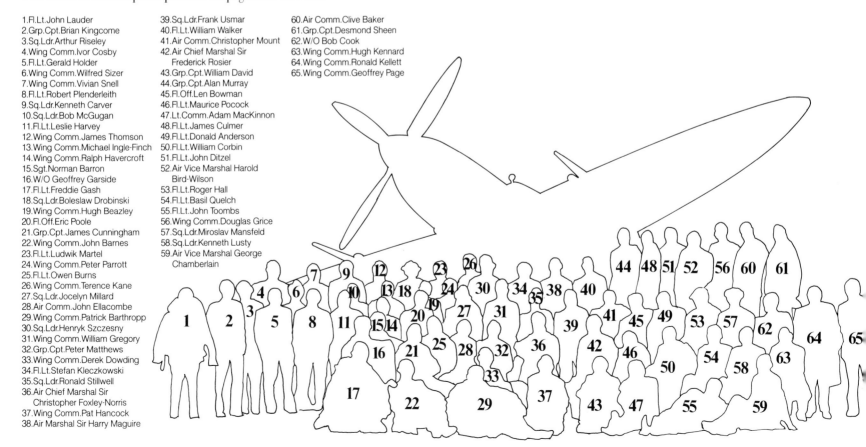

LITTLE FRIENDS

CONCEPT, DEVELOPMENT, EDITING,
PRINCIPAL RESEARCH, COLOR PHOTOGRAPHY
AND DESIGN: PHILIP KAPLAN

TEXT: ANDY SAUNDERS

PICTURE CREDITS

Photographs by Philip Kaplan are credited: PK. Photographs from the author's collection are credited: AC.
Jacket front: AF Museum; back: PK. P2-3: PK, P7: AF Museum.
OVER HERE P8-9: AC, P10-11: Imperial War Museum, P12: Popperfoto, P13: all USAF, P14: top left-R. Hofton, top center-PK, top right-PK, bottom-AC, P15: PK, P16: Portsmouth Publishing, P17: both: AC, P18: top-M. Sheldrick, center-Popperfoto, P19: top-PK.
FLYING THE MISSION P20-21: DeGolyer Library, Southern Methodist University, Dallas, Texas, P22-23: PK, P25: AC, P26: all-PK, P28-29: AC, P30-31: PK, P32: AF Museum, P33: top-Walter Konantz, bottom-AF Museum.
THE IRON P34: courtesy Michael O'Leary, P36-37: courtesy William Hess, P38-39: all PK, P40: USAF, P42-43: AC, P43: top-PK, P44: all AC, P46: courtesy Merle Olmsted, P47: PK, P48-49: AC, P50: top-PK, bottom: Jim Rush, P51: PK, P52-53: AC, P54-55: all PK, P56: bottom-courtesy Nick Berryman, P57: AC, P58: left (both)-PK, center (both)-B.R. Jethwa, P59: center-AC, right-PK P60: AC, P60-61: AC, P62-63: PK.
TAKING CARE OF BUSINESS P64-65: courtesy Andy Saunders collection, P67: top (both)-PK, bottom (both)-Jim Rush, P68 and 69: courtesy Denis Robinson, P70-71: courtesy Frank Wootton, right-PK, P72: courtesy Andy Saunders collection, P73: AC, P74-75: all PK.
GROUND BOUND P76: USAF, P78: top-PK, bottom-AC, P79: PK, P80: top-courtesy Merle Olmsted, bottom-courtesy Quentin Bland, P81: AC, P82-83: Jim Rush, P83: top-AF Museum, bottom-PK, P84: AC.
ON THE NOSE P86-87: courtesy Phillips Fine Art Auctioneers, P87: PK, P88: top left-courtesy Kristall Productions Ltd., top-Kristall Productions Ltd., bottom-DeGolyer Library, Southern Methodist University, Dallas, Texas, P89: USAF, P90: PK, P91: top left and bottom: PK, top-courtesy Andy Saunders collection, P92: top left-courtesy Andy Saunders collection, bottom left-courtesy Merle Olmsted, right, DeGolyer Library, Southern Methodist University, Dallas, Texas, P93: top left-courtesy Air Chief Marshal Sir Christopher Foxley-Norris, top and bottom-courtesy Merle Olmsted.
ON BECOMING AN EAGLE P94: courtesy Malcolm Bates, P95: all PK, P97: all courtesy Arthur Roscoe, P98: all PK, P99: courtesy Diana Barnato-Walker, P101: all courtesy Arthur Roscoe, P102-103: AC, P104: Popperfoto, P105: courtesy Arthur Roscoe.
SPECIAL OPERATIONS P106: both PK, P107: AC, P108: DeGolyer Library, Southern Methodist University, Dallas, Texas, P110-111: courtesy Malcolm Bates, P111: AC, P112:
courtesy Beryl Green, P114: top-Jim Rush, bottom-PK, P115: PK, P116-117: courtesy Beryl Green, left-courtesy Andy Saunders collection.
THE VILLAGERS P118: both PK, P119: PK, P120-121: Popperfoto, P122: top left and right-PK, bottom left-PK, bottom right-courtesy Lou Fleming, P123: top and bottom left and top center-courtesy Lou Fleming, other photos-PK, P124: courtesy Merle Olmsted, P125: Imperial War Museum, P126: both PK, P127: all PK.
LITTLE FRIENDS: THE BEGINNING P128: AC, P130: top left and right and bottom left-PK, bottom right-Jim Rush, P131: all PK, P132-133: Bundesarchiv-Koblenz, P134-135: Jim Rush, P136-137: AC, P138: PK-courtesy David Wade, P139: PK.
THOSE GIRLS P140-141: Popperfoto, P142: courtesy Chrystabel Leighton-Porter, P143: top-Daily Mirror Newspapers, P143: top left and bottom-courtesy Chrystabel Leighton-Porter, top right-PK, P144: both courtesy Chrystabel Leighton-Porter, P145: USAF, P146: courtesy Margaret Mayhew, P147: top left-courtesy Kristall Productions Ltd, top center-courtesy Kath Preston, top right-PK, bottom-courtesy Dave Kramer and Merle Olmsted, P149: DeGolyer Library, Southern Methodist University, Dallas, Texas, P150: Portsmouth Publishing, P152: top left-courtesy Kristall Productions Ltd, left-courtesy Evelyn Clarke, right-AC, P153: DeGolyer Library, Southern Methodist University, Dallas, Texas.
VERY SPECIAL DELIVERY P154-155: all PK, P156: courtesy Diana Barnato-Walker, P157: The Hulton-Deutsch Collection, P158: top and bottom left-PK, top-The Hulton-Deutsch Collection, P159: both PK, P160: top-courtesy Diana Barnato-Walker, bottom-The Hulton-Deutsch Collection, P162: all PK, P164: AF Museum, P165: AF Museum.
OTHER FRIENDS P166: PK, P167: top-Jim Rush, bottom-PK, P168: top-courtesy Andy Saunders collection, bottom-courtesy R.C. Harris, Jr., P168-169: courtesy Kristall Productions Ltd., P170: top-courtesy Andy Saunders collection, bottom-PK, P171: top-courtesy Kaz Budzik, bottom-PK, P172: courtesy Andy Saunders collection, P173: courtesy Andy Saunders collection.
A GERMAN ESCORT PILOT P174: both courtesy Peter Osborne and Ulrich Steinhilper, P175: courtesy Andy Saunders collection, P177: courtesy Andy Saunders collection, P178: courtesy Peter Osborne and Ulrich Steinhilper, P180: courtesy Andy Saunders collection, P183: courtesy Andy Saunders collection, P184: left-courtesy Peter Osborne and Ulrich Steinhilper, right-courtesy Andy Saunders collection, P185: Popperfoto.
AT LIBERTY P187: top-DeGolyer Library, Southern Methodist University, Dallas, Texas, bottom (both)-PK, P189: top and bottom left-courtesy Merle Olmsted, bottom right-USAF, P190: top (both) and bottom right-PK, bottom left-courtesy R.C. Harris, Jr., P192: Imperial War Museum, P193: courtesy Merle Olmsted, P194: PK, P195: courtesy Andy Saunders collection.
PILOTS P196: DeGolyer Library, Southern Methodist University, Dallas, Texas, P197: Popperfoto, P198: top left and center-PK, top right-AF Museum, center-courtesy James Goodson, bottom-courtesy Merle Olmsted, P199: courtesy Andy Saunders collection, P200: top-courtesy Andy Saunders collection, bottom: Popperfoto, center-USAF, P201: top-courtesy James Goodson, bottom-courtesy Merle Olmsted, P202: top-courtesy Andy Saunders collection, bottom-PK,

The windshield in front of the gun sight looked like a cobweb with a small hole in the center. I felt a sharp tug on my left temple as the bullet creased me before it splat into the armor plate by my head. For a second the concussion of the bullet knocked me senseless, but I came to with my plane climbing. I could feel blood dripping down my forehead. Quickly I adjusted my goggles. They were close-fitting and I hoped they would keep the blood from running into my eyes. Then the cracking of a voice over the RT sent me numb with fright, "Johnny, you're streaming glycol." I looked at my instruments and saw that my engine temperature registered in the dangerous red area. One of two things would happen very shortly—either my engine would freeze or it would blow up. All reasoning left me and I panicked. Still keeping the plane in a climbing position, I worked frantically to pull the emergency release which would send my canopy free from its sliding racks. My hand fumbled desperately but shook so much I had to use the other hand to steady it. A blast of air rushed into the cockpit as the canopy tore free. Now all I had to do was unbuckle my harness straps and step over the side. Ten minutes ago I had watched a man bail out of a plane, and his parachute hadn't opened; I tried to erase the picture of the plummeting man from my mind. I wanted to say something calm to the boys before I bailed out, but when I did speak it was in a high-pitched voice, screaming with despair. "I'm bailing out, boys. Tell Charlotte I'll see her when I get back!" Reaching up to yank the helmet and earphones off my head, I hesitated as I heard the calm voice of Freddie Glover: "Don't jump, Johnny. There's still a chance. Now sit back and relax for a second. You're still flying and the plane won't blow up. Look at your instruments and tell me how your oil pressure is." "Normal, Freddie." "Good, that's a good sign. Now unscrew your wobble pump and start priming your engine. That'll force raw gas into your cylinders and have the same effect as glycol. No bull, Johnny—I've heard of somebody else doing it, and it works." The wobble pump was on my dashboard; it had a small handle similar to an outboard motor's starting handle, and when pulled out would spring back. With my right hand I pulled out the handle and then thrust it back in to feed the gas into the cylinders. It didn't

P203: top-courtesy William Hess, bottom-PK, P204: top-courtesy Merle Olmsted, bottom-courtesy Andy Saunders collection, P205: top-courtesy Andy Saunders collection, bottom-USAF, P206: AC, P207: top-Richard Paver, top right-PK, bottom-courtesy Andy Saunders collection.
THE A-2 P208: top-AC, bottom-courtesy Merle Olmsted, P210: bottom left and right-PK, other photos-PK courtesy Dave Hill, P211: PK courtesy Dave Hill.
LITTLE FRIENDS: SUCCESS AT LAST P213: USAF, P214-215: all PK, P216: AC, P217: USAF, P218-219: courtesy Frank Wootton, P220: courtesy Merle Olmsted, P221: AC, P222: PK, P223: Jim Rush, P224-225: AF Museum, P226: top left and bottom-courtesy Merle Olmsted, top right-Popperfoto, P227: courtesy William Hess, P228-229: all courtesy Robert Best, P230: AC, P231: top left and center-courtesy Robert Best, top right-PK, bottom Jim Rush courtesy Michael O'Leary.
GOING BACK P232-233: courtesy Andy Saunders collection, P234-235: courtesy You magazine, P237: courtesy Robert Strobell, P238-239: all PK, P240: AC, P242-243: all PK.

ACKNOWLEDGMENTS

We thank Margaret Mayhew and Julie Saunders. Without their encouragement, concern and most magnificent contributions this book would literally not have been possible.

We are particularly indebted to the following people whose enthusiastic assistance has contributed enormously to the development and preparation of this book for publication: Malcolm Bates, Diana Barnato-Walker, Robert Best, Kazimierz Budzik, Gary Eastman, Lou Christian Wilson Fleming, Beryl Green, Stephen Grey, R.C. Harris, Jr., Bill Hess, Dave Hill, Jack Ilfrey, Walter J. Konantz, Edith Kup, Chrystabel Leighton-Porter, Walker M. Mahurin, Eric Marsden, Carroll McColpin, Merle Olmsted, Geoffrey Page, Alan Reeves, Eudora Seyfer, Yanks Air Museum, Chino, Ca.

Special thanks to all of the following, whose kind help in providing additional photographs, book and article reference materials, the loans and gifts of personal memorabilia, interviews, research information and other forms of assistance, have aided greatly in the development of this work: Scarlett and Michael Amspaugh, Bailey Bros. & Swinfen Ltd., Paddy Barthropp, Nick Berryman, Tony Bianchi, Len Biggs, Guy Black, Quentin Bland, Keith Braybrooke, Stephen Brooks, Harley L. Brown, Anthony C. Chardella, Evelyn Clarke, Barbara Darkes, Alan Deere, Peter Dimond, Neville Duke, Chris Ellis, Major Eddie Ellis-Jones, David Fairbairn, Seymour B. Feldman, Gilly Fielder, Sir Christopher Foxley-Norris, Royal Frey, James Goodson, James A. Gray, Roger Hall, Wing Commander Pat Hancock, George Hazel, Jack Heath, G.C. Heighington, Mrs. J.L. Henshaw, Robin Higham, Dave Hill, Robert Hofton, Ralph Hull, Pauline and Ben Jupp, Neal Kaplan, Richard King, Jimmy Kyle, Bob Loomis, Mike Mathews, Ella Mayhew, Bert McDowell, Jr., Tilly McMaster, Len Morgan, Leo Nomis, Michael O'Leary, Peter Osborne, W. Bruce Overstreet, Charles Neville Overton, Richard Paver, Kath Preston, David Price, Jeffrey Quill, Gordon and Winston Ramsey, Jack Raphael, Denis Robinson, Arthur Roscoe, Dilip Sarkar, C.R. Savage, Martin Sheldrick, Anne and Richard Stamp, Ulrich Steinhilper, Robert C. Strobell, Terry Thompson, Denis Todd, Anne and Dickey Turley-George, George Unwin, David Wade, Jock Wells, Tim Wells, Frank Wootton, Hub Zemke.

The German Escort Pilot: Adapted from *Spitfire on My Tail*, by Ulrich Steinhilper and Peter Osborne. Copyright ©1990 Peter Osborne and Ulrich Steinhilper. ISBN 1-872836-00. Available from Independent Books, 3, Leaves Green Crescent, Keston, Bromley, BR2 6DN, England.

The "48 To London" portion of *At Liberty*, by permission of Anthony Chardella, 369th FS Association.

The "Remembering Raydon" portion of *Going Back*, by permission of Eudora Seyfer and *Mature Outlook* magazine.

BIBLIOGRAPHY

Appleby, John T., *Suffolk Summer*, East Anglian Magazine Ltd., 1948.
Barclay, George, *Fighter Pilot*, William Kimber, 1976.
Bekker, Cajus, *The Luftwaffe War Diaries*, Doubleday & Co., 1964.
Bergel, Hugh, *Flying Wartime Aircraft, ATA Ferry Pilot*, David and Charles, 1972
Birch, David, *Rolls Royce and The Mustang*, Rolls Royce Heritage Trust, 1987.
Bishop, Edward, *The Guinea Pig Club*, Macmillan & Co. Ltd., 1963.
Black, Adam and Charles, *The WAAF in Action*, London: 1944.
Blake, *Readiness at Dawn*, Victor Gollancz Ltd., 1941.
Brickhill, Paul, *Reach for the Sky: Douglas Bader, His Life Story*, Collins, 1954.
Brookes, A.J., *Fighter Squadron at War*, Ian Allen Ltd., 1980.
Calder, Angus, *The People's War: Britain 1939–45*, Granada, 1969.
Cassin-Scott, Jack, *Women At War 1939–45*, Osprey, 1980.
Cheesman, E.C., *Brief Glory*, Harborough Pub. Co. Ltd., 1946.
Collier, Richard, *Eagle Day: The Battle of Britain*, E.P. Dutton Co., 1966.
Costello, John, *Love, Sex and War 1939–45*, Pan Books, 1985.
Crook, D.M., *Spitfire Pilot*, Faber & Faber Ltd.

Curtis, Lettice, *The Forgotten Pilots (The ATA)*, Nelson & Saunders, 1971.

Duke, Neville and Wingate, Alan, *Test Pilot*.

Duxford Aviation Society, *Duxford Diary 1942–1945*, 1989.

Fiedler, Arkady, *Squadron 303 (Polish)*, Letchworth Printers Ltd.

Forrester, Larry, *Fly for Your Life: Robert Stanford-Tuck*, Bantam Books, 1973.

Foxley-Norris, Sir Christopher, *A Lighter Shade of Blue*, Ian Allen, 1978.

Francillon, Rene J., *USAAF Fighter Units Europe 1942–45*, Sky Books Press, 1970.

Freeman, Roger A., *Mighty Eighth War Manual*, Jane's, 1984.

Godfrey, John, *The Look of Eagles*, Random House, 1958.

Goodson, James A., *Tumult in the Clouds*, St. Martin's Press, 1983.

Hall, Grover C., Jr., *1000 Destroyed (4th Fighter Group)*, Aero Publishers Inc., 1978.

Hall, Roger, *Clouds of Fear*, Coronet Books, 1975.

Haugland, Vern, *The Eagle Squadrons*, Ziff Davis Flying Books, 1979.

Haugland, Vern, *The Eagle's War*, Jason Aronson, 1982.

Hawkins, Ian, *The Münster Raid, Bloody Skies over Germany*, Aero/Tab Books, 1990.

Hess, William N., *P-47 Thunderbolt at War*, Doubleday & Company, 1976.

Higham, Robin, and Williams, Carol, *Flying Combat Aircraft of the USAAF*, Volumes 1 and 2, Iowa State University Press, 1978.

HMSO, *Air Sea Rescue*, London, 1942.

Ilfrey, Jack, *Happy Jack's Go-Buggy*, Exposition Press.

Johnson, Group Captain J. E., *Wing Leader*, New York: Ballantine Books, 1957.

Kent, Group Captain J.A., *One of The Few*, William Kimber, 1971.

Kyle, James, *Typhoon Tale*, Biggar & Co., 1989.

Lloyd, Ian, *Rolls Royce, The Merlin at War*, Macmillan Press Ltd., 1978.

Loomis, Robert D., *Great American Fighter Pilots of World War II*, Random House, 1961.

Mason, Francis K., *The Hawker Hurricane*, Aston Publications, 1987.

Maurer, Maurer, *Air Force Combat Units of World War II*, Franklin Watts Inc.

Miller, Kent D., *Escort: The 356th Fighter Group On Operations Over Europe 1943–1945*, Academy Publishing Corp., 1985.

Morris, Danny, *Aces and Wingmen II*, Aviation USK, 1989.

Murrow, Edward R., *This Is London*, Simon & Schuster, 1941.

Neil, Wing Commander T. F., *Spitfire: From the Cockpit*, Ian Allen, 1990.

Nelson, Derek and Parsons, Dave, *Hell-Bent for Leather: The Saga of the A2 and G1 Flight Jackets*, Motorbooks, 1990.

Nesbitt-Dufort, John, *Scramble: Flying the Aircraft of WW2*, Speed and Sports Publications, 1970.

Ogley, Bob, *Biggin on the Bump*, Froglets Publications, 1990.

Page, Geoffrey, *Tale of a Guinea Pig*, Corgi Books, 1981.

Peaslee, Budd J., *Heritage of Valor*, J.B. Lippincott Company, 1964.

Polish Air Force Association, *Destiny Can Wait (History of the Polish Air Force in Great Britain)*, William Heinemann Ltd., 1949.

Pratt Boorman, H.R., *Hell's Corner, 1940*, Kent Messenger.

Price, Alfred, *The Spitfire Story*, Jane's, 1982.

Quill, Jeffrey, *Birth of a Legend: The Spitfire*, London: Quiller Press Ltd., 1986.

Reynolds, Quentin, *A London Diary*, Random House, 1941.

Richards, Denis, *Royal Air Force 1939–1945, Vol. I, The Fight at Odds*, Crown Copyright, 1953.

Robertson, Bruce, *US Army and Air Force Fighters 1916-61*, Harleyford Pub. Ltd., 1961.

Scott, Desmond, *Typhoon Pilot*, Arrow Books, Century Hutchinson.

Scutts, Jerry, *Lion in the Sky*, Patrick Stephens, 1987.

Shores, Christopher, *Duel for the Sky*, Grum Street, 1985.

Steiner, Edward, *King's Cliffe*.

Steinhoff, Johannes, *The Final Hours*, The N.A. Pub. Co., 1985.

Sutton, Barry, *Way of a Pilot*, Macmillan, 1942.

Taylor, Eric, *Women Who Went to War 1938–46*, Grafton Books (Collins), 1989.

Taylor, Telford, *The Breaking Wave, WWII in the Summer of 1940*, Simon & Schuster, 1967.

352nd Fighter Group Association, *The Bluenosed Bastards of Bodney*, 1990.

Townsend, Peter, *The Odds Against Us*, William Morrow & Co., 1987.

Trevor, Elleston, *Squadron Airborne*, Ballantine Books, 1962.

Turner, John Frayn, *The Bader Tapes*, The Kensal Press, 1986.

USAF Hist. Studies: No. 156, *Development of The Long-Range Escort Fighter*, MA/AH Publishing.

Valant, Gary M., *Vintage Aircraft Nose Art*, Motorbooks International.

Varian, Horace L., *The Bloody Hundredth: Missions and Memories of a World War II Bomb Group*.

Wagner, Ray, *Mustang Designer*, Orion Books, 1990.

Washington Infantry Journal Press, *The 56th Fighter Group in World War II*, Infantry Journal Press, 1948.

Weir, Flying Officer A.N.C., *Verses of a Fighter Pilot*, Faber and Faber.

Williams, P., and Harrison T., *McIndoe's Army*, Pelham Books, 1979.

Willis, John, *Churchill's Few*, Michael Joseph, 1985.

Wood, Derek, and Dempster, Derek, *The Narrow Margin*, McGraw-Hill Book Company Inc., 1961.

Woolnough, John H., *Stories of The Eighth*, The 8th Air Force News, 1983.

Wynn, Kenneth G., *Men of the Battle of Britain*, Glidden Books, 1989.

work easily. Freddie was flying close to me now and continued his encouragement as I worked the pump in and out. "Freddie, it's working. My engine temperature is away from the danger zone." "Good, Johnny—now throttle back and don't push your engine. Try to keep climbing; the higher we go the cooler the air will be—every little bit helps." I throttled back and began climbing at only fifty feet a minute, continually pushing my wobble pump in and out, in and out. Freddie and his wingman left me when I reached 18,000 feet. He had done his job well, and now my safe return would rest on the strength of my arm and the fuel supply.

Patteau, my wingman, was flying in a zigzag manner, first on one side, then on the other—protecting my tail. My plane had been hit near Berlin, 675 miles from Debden. The chances of getting back seemed very remote, but desperately I pumped and pumped, injecting life into my dying engine. Gone were the thoughts of the two enemy aircraft I had destroyed. Flak and enemy fighters no longer seemed threats to me. By the second hand of my plane's clock I counted one, two, three, four . . . sixteen times a minute I worked the plunger.

Three hours more to Debden equaled almost three thousand injections; and if I subtracted the time I had started, it would make . . . but I couldn't think. This type of calculation was too much for me at the moment. The wind whistling through the cockpit was cold and penetrating. Regrettably I lost height in an attempt to find a warmer layer of air. The agonies of the flesh were forgotten when my engine spit and died. A frantic search of my instrument panel made me hastily switch on the reserve gas tank. The motor caught, but the instruments had made me aware of a greater threat. Thirty-nine gallons of gas left, and I had no idea of my exact position. Then I saw it. Thank God, just ahead of me was the Channel. I had lost the battle for height as my cold body demanded warmer and warmer air. I was at four thousand feet when the plane left the shores of Holland. The glove on my right hand had frayed open from the continual friction of the hot handle of the plunger. What had been blisters under the glove were now red welts bleeding, slippery flesh, and the plunger kept slipping from my grasp. Blasts of air continued to blow into the cockpit with

SELECTED FIGHTER INFORMATION SUMMARY

UNITED STATES OPERATIONAL FIGHTER AIRCRAFT/ETO (PRINCIPAL)

LOCKHEED P-38J LIGHTNING. SPAN: 52', LENGTH: 37'10", HEIGHT: 9'10". PERFORMANCE: 414 MPH AT 25,000 FEET, CRUISE: 250-320 MPH, RATE OF CLIMB: 30,000 FEET IN 13½ MINUTES. BOMB LOAD: 4,000 LBS OR TEN-5" ROCKETS. POWER: TWO ALLISON V1710-89/91 1,425 HP IN-LINES. ARMAMENT: ONE 20MM CANNON AND FOUR .50 CALIBER MACHINE GUNS. RANGE: 450 MILES OR 850 MILES WITH DROP TANKS.

REPUBLIC P-47D THUNDERBOLT. SPAN: 40' 9½", LENGTH: 36'1", HEIGHT: 14'8". PERFORMANCE: 433 MPH AT 30,000 FEET, CRUISE: 210-275 MPH, RATE OF CLIMB: 30,000 FEET IN 20 MINUTES. BOMB LOAD: THREE 1,000 LB OR TEN-5" ROCK-ETS. POWER: ONE PRATT & WHITNEY R-2800-59, 2,000 HP RADIAL. ARMAMENT: EIGHT .50 CALIBER WING MACHINE GUNS. RANGE: 590 MILES AT 25,000 FEET OR 950 MILES WITH DROP TANKS.

NORTH AMERICAN P-51B MUSTANG. SPAN: 37', LENGTH: 32' 3", HEIGHT: 13'8". PERFORMANCE: 440 MPH AT 30,000 FEET, CRUISE: 210-320 MPH, RATE OF CLIMB: 30,000 FEET IN 12½ MINUTES. BOMB LOAD: TWO 500 LB. POWER: ONE PACKARD MERLIN V-1650-3 OR-7, 1,380 HP INLINE. ARMA-MENT: FOUR .50 CALIBER WING MACHINE GUNS. RANGE: 700 MILES OR 1,500 MILES WITH DROP TANKS.

NORTH AMERICAN P-51D MUSTANG. SPAN: 37', LENGTH: 32'3", HEIGHT: 13'8". PERFORMANCE: 437 MPH AT 25,000 FEET, CRUISE: 210-320 MPH, RATE OF CLIMB: 30,000 FEET IN 13 MINUTES. BOMB LOAD: TWO 500 LB OR TEN-5" ROCKETS. POWER: ONE PACKARD V-1650-7, 1,490 HP INLINE. ARMAMENT: SIX .50 CALIBER WING MACHINE GUNS. RANGE: 700 MILES OR 1,500 MILES WITH DROP TANKS.

UNITED STATES OPERATIONAL FIGHTER

AIRCRAFT/ETO (ADDITIONAL)

VICKERS-SUPERMARINE SPITFIRE VB. SPAN: 36'10", LENGTH: 29'11", 12'7". PERFORMANCE: 369 MPH AT 19,500 FEET, CRUISE: 270 MPH AT 5,000 FEET, RATE OF CLIMB: 4,750 FEET PER MINUTE. POWER: ONE ROLLS-ROYCE MERLIN 45, 1,470 HP INLINE. ARMAMENT: TWO 20MM CANNON AND FOUR .303 WING MACHINE GUNS. RANGE: 395 MILES.

VICKERS-SUPERMARINE SPITFIRE IX. SPAN: 36'10", LENGTH: 31'4", HEIGHT: 12'7¼". PERFOR-MANCE: 408 MPH AT 25,000 FEET, CRUISE: 325 MPH AT 20,000 FEET, RATE OF CLIMB: 4,100 FEET PER MINUTE. BOMB LOAD: 750 LBS. POWER: ONE ROLLS-ROYCE MERLIN 61, 1,565 HP INLINE. AR-MAMENT: TWO 20MM CANNON AND TWO .50 CAL-IBER WING MACHINE GUNS. RANGE: 235 MILES.

VICKERS-SUPERMARINE SPITFIRE XI (PR). SPAN: 36'10", LENGTH: 31'4½". PERFORMANCE: 422 MPH AT 27,500 FEET, CRUISE: 340 MPH AT 20,000 FEET, RATE OF CLIMB: 4,350 FEET PER MINUTE. POWER: ONE ROLLS-ROYCE MERLIN 63 OR 70, 1,640 HP INLINE. RANGE: 1,360 MILES.

BRITISH OPERATIONAL FIGHTER AIRCRAFT/ ETO (PRINCIPAL)

HAWKER HURRICANE IIB. SPAN: 40', LENGTH: 32'3", HEIGHT: 13'1½". PERFORMANCE: 340 MPH AT 21,000 FEET, CRUISE: 307 MPH, RATE OF CLIMB: 20,000 FEET IN 7½ MINUTES. BOMB LOAD: 1,000 LBS OR EIGHT ROCKETS. POWER: ONE ROLLS-ROYCE MERLIN XX, 1,280 HP INLINE. ARMAMENT: TWELVE .303 WING MACHINE GUNS. RANGE: 985 MILES WITH EXTERNAL TANKS OR 480 MILES WITHOUT TANKS.

VICKERS-SUPERMARINE SPITFIRE 1A. SPAN: 36'10", LENGTH: 29'11", HEIGHT: 8'10". PERFOR-MANCE: 362 MPH AT 19,000 FEET, CRUISE: 315 MPH AT 20,000 FEET, RATE OF CLIMB: 20,000 FEET IN 9½ MINUTES. POWER: ONE ROLLS-ROYCE MER-LIN III, 1,030 HP INLINE. ARMAMENT: EIGHT .303 WING MACHINE GUNS. RANGE: 395 MILES.

VICKERS-SUPERMARINE SPITFIRE IX. SPAN: 36'10", LENGTH: 31'4", HEIGHT: 12'7¼", PERFOR-MANCE: 408 MPH AT 25,000 FEET, CRUISE: 325 MPH AT 20,000 FEET, RATE OF CLIMB: 4,100 FEET PER MINUTE. BOMB LOAD: 750 LBS. POWER: ONE ROLLS-ROYCE MERLIN 61, 1,565 HP INLINE. AR-MAMENT: TWO 20MM CANNON AND TWO .50 CAL-IBER WING MACHINE GUNS. RANGE: 235 MILES.

VICKERS-SUPERMARINE SPITFIRE IXE. SPAN: 36'10", LENGTH : 31'4", HEIGHT: 12'7¼". PERFORMANCE: 416 MPH AT 27,500 FEET, CRUISE: 322 MPH, RATE OF CLIMB: 20,000 FEET IN 6.4 MINUTES. BOMB LOAD: 750 LBS. POWER: ONE ROLLS-ROYCE MERLIN 70, 1,710 HP INLINE. ARMAMENT: TWO 20MM CANNON AND TWO .50 CALIBER WING MACHINE GUNS. RANGE: 980 MILES WITH EXTERNAL TANKS OR 430 MILES WITHOUT TANKS.

VICKERS-SUPERMARINE SPITFIRE XIVE. SPAN: 36'10", LENGTH: 32'8", HEIGHT: 12'8½". PERFORMANCE: 448 MPH AT 26,000 FEET, CRUISE: 362 MPH AT 20,000 FEET, RATE OF CLIMB: 20,000 FEET IN 7 MINUTES. BOMB LOAD: 1,000 LBS. POWER: ONE ROLLS-ROYCE GRIFFON 65, 2,050 HP INLINE. ARMAMENT: TWO 20MM CANNON AND TWO .50 CALIBER WING MACHINE GUNS. RANGE: 460 MILES OR 850 MILES WITH DROP TANKS.

HAWKER HURRICANE I. SPAN: 40', LENGTH 31'4", HEIGHT: 13'1½". PERFORMANCE: 328 MPH AT 20,000 FEET, CRUISE: UNKNOWN, RATE OF CLIMB: 20,000 FEET IN 8½ MINUTES. POWER: ONE ROLLS-ROYCE MERLIN III, 1,030 HP INLINE. ARMAMENT: EIGHT .303 WING MACHINE GUNS. RANGE: 425 MILES.

HAWKER TYPHOON IB. SPAN: 41'7", LENGTH: 31'11½", HEIGHT: 15'4". PERFORMANCE: 414 MPH AT 11,500 FEET, CRUISE: 330 MPH, RATE OF CLIMB: 15,000 FEET IN 5 MINUTES 50 SECONDS. BOMB LOAD: 2,000 LBS OR EIGHT 60 LB ROCKETS. POWER: ONE NAPIER SABRE IIC, 2,200 HP INLINE. ARMAMENT: FOUR 20MM CANNON. RANGE: 510 MILES OR 980 MILES WITH DROP TANKS.

HAWKER TEMPEST V. SPAN: 41', LENGTH: 33'8", HEIGHT: 16'1". PERFORMANCE: 436 MPH AT 15,000 FEET, CRUISE: 391 MPH AT 18,800 FEET, RATE OF CLIMB: 15,000 FEET IN 5 MINUTES. BOMB LOAD: 2,000 LBS. POWER: ONE NAPIER SABRE IIC, B OR C, 2,180 HP, 2,200 HP OR 2,260 HP INLINE. ARMAMENT: FOUR 20MM CANNON. RANGE: 740 MILES OR 1,530 MILES WITH DROP TANKS.

BRITISH OPERATIONAL FIGHTER AIRCRAFT/ ETO (ADDITIONAL)

BRISTOL BEAUFIGHTER TF X. SPAN: 57'10", LENGTH: 41'8", HEIGHT: 15'10". PERFORMANCE: 303 MPH AT 1,300 FEET, CRUISE: 249 MPH AT 5,000 FEET, RATE OF CLIMB: 5,000 FEET IN 3½ MINUTES. BOMB LOAD: 2,127 LBS. POWER: TWO BRISTOL HERCULES XVII, 1,770 HP RADIALS. ARMAMENT: FOUR 20MM CANNON, RANGE: 1,470 MILES.

DE HAVILLAND MOSQUITO FB VI 2. SPAN: 54'2", LENGTH: 40'10¾", HEIGHT: 15'3½". PERFORMANCE: 362 MPH AT 6,200 FEET, CRUISE: 325 MPH AT 15,000 FEET, RATE OF CLIMB: 15,000 FEET IN 9½ MINUTES. BOMB LOAD: 2,000 LBS. POWER: TWO ROLLS-ROYCE MERLIN 25, 1,635 HP EACH, INLINE. ARMAMENT: FOUR 20MM CANNON AND FOUR .303 MACHINE GUNS. RANGE: 1,270-1,650 MILES.

GERMAN OPERATIONAL FIGHTER AIRCRAFT/ ETO (PRINCIPAL)

FOCKE WULF FW 190. SPAN: 34'6", LENGTH: 29'7", HEIGHT: 13'. PERFORMANCE: 408 MPH AT 15,750 FEET, CRUISE: 296 MPH, RATE OF CLIMB: 20,000 FEET IN 9.1 MINUTES: BOMB LOAD: 1,100 LBS. POWER: ONE BMW 801, 1,700 HP RADIAL. ARMAMENT: FOUR 20MM AND TWO 13MM CANNON. RANGE: 525 MILES.

MESSERSCHMITT ME 109. SPAN: 32'6½", LENGTH: 29'4", HEIGHT: 8'6". PERFORMANCE: 452 MPH AT 19,685 FEET, CRUISE: 310 MPH, RATE OF CLIMB: 16,400 FEET IN 3 MINUTES. BOMB LOAD: 1,200 LBS. POWER: ONE DAIMLER BENZ 605, 1,500 HP INLINE. ARMAMENT: ONE 30MM AND TWO 15MM CANNON. RANGE: 440 MILES.

MESSERSCHMITT ME 110. SPAN: 53'5", LENGTH: 41'7", HEIGHT: 13'1". PERFORMANCE: 342 MPH AT 22,900 FEET, CRUISE: 200 MPH, RATE OF CLIMB: 18,000 FEET IN 7.9 MINUTES. BOMB LOAD: 2,000 LBS. POWER: TWO DAIMLER BENZ, 1,475 HP EACH, INLINE. ARMAMENT: TWO 30MM AND TWO 20MM CANNON, AND TWO 7.92MM MACHINE GUNS. RANGE: 1,305 MILES.

GERMAN OPERATIONAL FIGHTER AIRCRAFT/ ETO (ADDITIONAL)

MESSERSCHMITT ME 262 SCHWALBE. SPAN: 40'11½", LENGTH: 34'9½", HEIGHT: 12'7". PERFORMANCE: 540 MPH AT 19,700 FEET, CRUISE: UNKNOWN, RATE OF CLIMB: 3,937 FPM (INITIAL). BOMB LOAD: 1,100 LBS. POWER: TWO JUNKERS JUMO, 1,980 LBS THRUST EACH. ARMAMENT: FOUR 30MM CANNON AND TWENTY-FOUR 50MM ROCKETS. RANGE: 652 MILES AT 30,000 FEET.

MESSERSCHMITT ME 163B-1A KOMET. SPAN: 30'7.3", LENGTH: 19'2.3", HEIGHT: 9'.66". PERFORMANCE: 596 MPH BETWEEN 9,850 FEET AND 29,530 FEET, RATE OF CLIMB: 29,530 FEET IN 2 MINUTES 36 SECONDS. POWER: ONE WALTER

tornado force. I didn't think I could stand it much longer. I called my wingman. "Patty, I don't think I have enough gas to make it. Call Air Sea Rescue for a fix. I'm switching over now." My left hand flicked the button which would set my radio on the Air Sea Rescue frequency. I listened in a daze as Patty informed them of my plight, and they gave him a vector onto the nearest field. If I could last twenty-one more minutes I could make it. The ground control officer seemed calm and confident, as if there were nothing to worry about. They knew my exact position at all times, and if I did bail out, a seaplane would be sent in minutes. How long is twenty-one minutes? To me it was measured by the times my weary arm worked the plunger in and out. If my gas holds out, I can make it. If I can press the plunger several hundred more times, England will be under my wing. My wheels touched down at Beccles. No circling of the field for me; I landed on the nearest runway—with no regard for wind or traffic. I didn't even taxi to the control tower; I pulled off on a grassy plot near the end of the runway and shut off the engine. I climbed out of the cockpit and lit a much needed cigarette. There was a dance that night at Debden. Freddie Glover was standing at his usual place, supporting the far end of the bar. I walked over to him; I pushed his money, which was lying on the bar top, back to him and in its place I put a five-pound note.

from *The Look of Eagles* by John T. Godfrey

In the fall of 1944 I was on a weekend pass to London and while window shopping, I happened by a pet shop that had a Scottie puppy in the window. I had left an aging Scottie at home when I joined the Army Air Force in 1943. I went in to look at the puppy and pet it. When the pet shop owner removed the pup and set it on the floor, it wagged its tail and ran over to me in a frenzy of excited greeting. I had no intention of buying the dog but with such a display of "love at first sight," I left the pet shop with the pup under my trench coat and headed for the train back to Colchester and the 55th Fighter Group. We lived in twelve-man Nissen huts and housebreaking the puppy, now named Lassie II, did have some problems. She eventually learned and

HWK 509A-2 ROCKET, 3,748 LBS THRUST. ARMAMENT: TWO 30MM CANNON. MAXIMUM ENDURANCE: 7½ MINUTES.

EIGHTH USAAF FIGHTER OPERATIONS (COMBAT GROUPS)
AUGUST 1942 THROUGH MAY 1945

NUMBER OF DAYS WITH OPERATIONS	368.00
AV. NUMBER OF SORTIES PER OP DAY	628.85
TOTAL SORTIES FLOWN	261039
TOTAL SORTIES LESS SPARES & ABORTS	257443
CREDIT SORTIES	242931
EFFECTIVE SORTIES	234393

AIRCRAFT SORTIES BY TYPE OF MISSION
HEAVY BOMBER SUPPORT	207857
STRAFING & BOMBING SWEEPS	49586

NUMBER OF AIRCRAFT DROPPING BOMBS	14990
BOMB TONNAGE DROPPED ON TARGETS	4980.7
AIRCRAFT MISSING IN ACTION	2048

ENEMY AIRCRAFT CLAIMS IN THE AIR
DESTROYED	5222
PROBABLY DESTROYED	348
DAMAGED	1568

ENEMY AIRCRAFT CLAIMS ON THE GROUND
DESTROYED	4250
PROBABLY DESTROYED	23
DAMAGED	2886

EIGHTH USAAF FIGHTER GROUND CLAIMS/ETO
FEBRUARY 1944 THROUGH APRIL 1945

TARGET	DESTROYED	DAMAGED	TOTAL
LOCOMOTIVES	4660	2791	7451
OIL TANK CARS	1500	1422	2922
TRAINS	20	226	246
GOODS RR WAGONS	6069	23929	29998
ARM'D VEHICLES AND TANKS	178	253	431
FLAK TOWERS AND GUN POSITIONS	270	557	827
MOTOR TRUCKS	3858	3091	6949
OTHER VEHICLES	1021	720	1741
TUGS, BARGES AND FREIGHTERS	129	853	982
RR STATIONS AND FACILITIES	51	234	285
RADIO AND POWER STATIONS	102	294	396
OIL STORAGE TANKS	73	127	200
HANGARS AND MISC BUILDINGS	234	600	834

EIGHTH USAAF PHOTO AND MAPPING OPERATIONS
7TH PHOTO GROUP
MARCH 1943 THROUGH APRIL 1945

TOTAL SORTIES FLOWN	4593
TOTAL CREDIT SORTIES	4247
EFFECTIVE SORTIES	3354
AIRCRAFT LOST/MIA	53
AIRCRAFT CATEGORY E	15
AIRCRAFT MISSING	0
PILOTS KILLED IN ACTION	9
PILOTS MISSING IN ACTION	46

PRU ESCORT
7TH PHOTO GROUP
JANUARY 1945 THROUGH APRIL 1945

TOTAL SORTIES FLOWN	937
TOTAL CREDIT SORTIES	880
EFFECTIVE SORTIES	853
AIRCRAFT LOST/MIA	5
AIRCRAFT CATEGORY E	5
AIRCRAFT MISSING	0
E/A CLAIMS/DESTROYED	0
E/A CLAIMS/PROBABLY DESTROYED	1
E/A CLAIMS/DAMAGED	1
PILOTS KILLED IN ACTION	0
PILOTS MISSING IN ACTION	4

EIGHTH USAAF FIGHTER AIRCRAFT ATTRITION

P-47 THUNDERBOLT
APRIL 1943 THROUGH MAY 1945

MISSING IN ACTION	529
CATEGORY E	176
MISSING	44
WAR WEARY	176
NON-OPERATIONAL SALVAGE	131
GAINS FROM PREVIOUS LOSSES	13
NET INVENTORY LOSS	1043

P-38 LIGHTNING
OCTOBER 1943 THROUGH MAY 1945

MISSING IN ACTION	266
CATEGORY E	84
MISSING	2

WAR WEARY	29
NON-OPERATIONAL SALVAGE	74
GAINS FROM PREVIOUS LOSSES	4
NET INVENTORY LOSS	451

P-51 MUSTANG
JANUARY 1944 THROUGH MAY 1945

MISSING IN ACTION	1235
CATEGORY E	514
MISSING	132
WAR WEARY	168
NON-OPERATIONAL SALVAGE	190
GAINS FROM PREVIOUS LOSSES	38
NET INVENTORY LOSS	2201

AERIAL VICTORIES
HIGHEST SCORING USAAF FIGHTER GROUPS/ETO

GROUP	SCORE
56FG/8AF	665.50
354FG/9AF	599.24
357FG/8AF	595.50
31FG/12AF-15AF	570.50
4FG/8AF	548.95
82FG/12AF-15AF	548.00
325FG/12AF-15AF	520.00

AERIAL VICTORIES
HIGHEST SCORING USAAF FIGHTER SQUADRONS/ETO

GROUP	SCORE
353FS/354FG/9AF	289.50
487FS/352FG/8AF	235.50
61FS/56FG/8AF	232.00
62FS/56FG/8AF	219.50
364FS/357FG/8AF	212.00
317FS/325FG/12AF-15AF	209.00

EIGHTH USAAF OPERATIONAL DEFINITIONS

SORTIE: A "sortie" is an aircraft airborne on a mission against the enemy (synonymous with terms: aircraft dispatched, aircraft airborne and aircraft taking off).

A/C CREDIT SORTIE: An "aircraft credit sortie" is deemed to have taken place when an airplane, ordered on an operational mission and in the performance of that mission, has entered an area where enemy anti-aircraft fire may be effective or where usual enemy fighter patrols occur; or when the airplane in any way is subjected to enemy attack.

EFFECTIVE SORTIE: An "effective sortie" is a sortie that carries out the purpose of the mission. An aircraft, when loaded with bombs or markers, is considered an effective sortie when it has released one or more armed bombs or markers, either by individually sighting or upon that of the formation leader, such sighting being made with the use of sighting or radar equipment, in a deliberate attempt to destroy or mark a target. Aircraft not loaded with bombs or markers are considered effective sorties if they carry out the purpose of the mission, e.g., drop leaflets, drop chaff, carry out weather flights, take photos, provide escort, carry out diversion as ordered, etc. Lost aircraft, unless definitely known to have been lost before reaching the target, are to be considered as effective sorties.

NON-EFFECTIVE SORTIE: A "non-effective sortie" is a sortie that for any reason fails to carry out the purpose of the mission.

MISSING: If personnel have not returned.

WOUNDED: (i.e., due to enemy action) qualified by such words as "slightly" or "seriously."

KILLED: (or FATALITIES when pertaining to aircraft accident deaths).

INJURED: (i.e., not due to enemy action) qualified by such words as "slightly" or "seriously."

ENEMY AIRPLANE LOSSES

DESTROYED: An enemy aircraft in flight shall be considered destroyed when (1) it is seen to crash, (2) it is seen to disintegrate in the air or to be enveloped in flames, (3) it is seen to descend on friendly territory and be captured, (4) the pilot and entire crew are seen to bail out.

An enemy aircraft not in flight shall be considered destroyed when: (1) it is seen by photograph to have been blown apart or burnt out, (2) it is seen by strike photo to have been within unobstructed lethal radius of a fragmentation bomb, (3) it is seen to sink in deep water, (4) it is known to have been aboard a carrier or other ship at the time of a confirmed sinking.

PROBABLY DESTROYED: An aircraft shall be considered "probably destroyed" when: (1) while in flight the enemy airplane is seen to break off combat under circumstances which lead to the conclusion that it must be a loss, although it is not seen to crash, (2) the enemy airplane is so damaged by bombing or strafing as to have less than an even chance of being repaired.

OUR AIRCRAFT LOSSES

OPERATIONAL LOSSES

MISSING IN ACTION: Airplanes which are known to be lost in enemy territory or at sea.

CATEGORY E (salvage): An airplane damaged beyond economical repair while engaged in or in performance of an operational mission.

MISSING (unknown): Airplanes reported as believed to have landed in friendly territory on the Continent, unlocated and/or unheard of during the month of loss or 30 days thereafter. (Applies only to operations after D-Day.)

NON-OPERATIONAL LOSSES

WAR WEARY: Tactical aircraft that because of age, obsoles-

became the beloved pet of the whole barracks and was the official mascot of the 338th Fighter Squadron. One afternoon I was scheduled for a local test hop in a P-51 and decided to take Lassie for her first airplane ride. There was no place to carry her in the cramped cockpit so I spread my heavy jacket over the flat surface of the radio just behind the armor plate and set her on the jacket. After take-off I looked back at her several times and she seemed to be enjoying the flight. When the time came to land, I temporarily forgot about the dog and entered the standard fighter traffic pattern which was to fly toward the approach end of the runway at tree top level and when reaching the end of the runway, breaking upward in a steep left-hand climbing turn to slow up for lowering the landing gear and flaps. Normally, the fighter would pull three or four Gs in the initial hard climbing turn. Immediately after the "break" I remembered the dog and turned around to look at her. The G forces had her pinned down like a bear skin rug. I eased off on the turn so she could raise her head and completed the landing. She rode with me in the P-51 on two or three other local flights but she never made a combat mission as we had no canine oxygen masks.

One day while I was on a mission over Germany, someone let her out of the barracks and she headed for my parking area down on the flight line. While crossing a road she was hit by a GI ambulance and badly injured. The ambulance driver, knowing the dog, picked her up and took her to the base hospital. When I landed from the mission and got to the hospital, the Group Flight Surgeon, Capt. Randolph Garnett, had me hold her while he took X-rays on the "people" machine. She had a broken left hind leg near the hip joint. I held her again while he manipulated and set the broken leg. He then wrapped a plaster cast around the leg and middle of her body. We attached an aileron pulley to the end of the leg cast so she could roll the stiff leg on smooth surfaces. After four weeks, we removed the cast and she was as good as new.

After finishing my combat tour in February 1945, Lassie and I rode in a B-17 to the staging camp in northern England to begin our journey home. Not knowing what the troop ship captain would think about a dog on board, I gave her two sleeping pills a few hours prior to boarding and smuggled her up the

cence, excessive repair requirements or other reasons are classified as permanently unfit for combat.

NON-OPERATIONAL SALVAGE: An aircraft damaged beyond economical repair while not in performance of an operational mission (accidents not due to enemy action, training flights, etc.).

OTHER DEFINITIONS

MISSION: Any ordered flight. There are three types of missions:

SERVICE MISSION: A mission such as ferrying personnel, material or aircraft within or between theaters of operations when no enemy opposition is expected.

TRAINING MISSION: A mission for training purposes.

OPERATIONAL MISSION: (Combat operational mission or combat mission). An ordered flight with the designed purpose of operating against the enemy.

ENCOUNTER: An encounter is deemed to have taken place whenever unfriendly airplanes meet, whether a combat ensues or not.

COMBAT: Combat is deemed to have taken place whenever contact is made with opposing forces and fire is exchanged or developed by one side or the other

ROYAL AIR FORCE

FIGHTER COMMAND
ORDER OF BATTLE, AUGUST 8, 1940

No. 10 Group		
Pembrey	No. 92	Spitfire I
Exeter	No. 87	Hurricane I
	No. 213	Hurricane I
St. Eval	No. 234	Spitfire I
Roborough	No. 247	Gladiator II
Middle Wallop	No. 238	Hurricane I
	No. 604	Blenheim IF
	No. 609	Spitfire I
Warmwell	No. 152	Spitfire I
No. 11 Group		
Debden	No. 17	Hurricane I
Martlesham Heath	No. 25	Blenheim IF
	No. 85	Hurricane I
North Weald	No. 151	Hurricane I
Rochford	No. 56	Hurricane I
Hornchurch	No. 41	Spitfire I
	No. 54	Spitfire I
	No. 65	Spitfire I
	No. 74	Spitfire I
Tangmere	No. 43	Hurricane I
	No. 601	Hurricane I
Westhampnett	No. 145	Hurricane I
Northolt	No. 1	Hurricane I
	No. 257	Hurricane I
Kenley	No. 64	Spitfire I
	No. 615	Hurricane I
Croydon	No. 111	Hurricane I

Biggin Hill	No. 32	Hurricane I
	No. 610	Spitfire I
Gravesend	No. 501	Hurricane I
Manston	No. 600	Blenheim IF
No. 12 Group		
Church Fenton	No. 73	Hurricane I
	No. 249	Hurricane I
Leconfield	No. 616	Spitfire I
Kirton-in-Lindsey	No. 222	Spitfire I
	No. 264	Defiant I
Ringway	No. 264	Defiant I
Digby	No. 29	Blenheim IF
	No. 46	Hurricane I
	No. 611	Spitfire I
Coltishall	No. 66	Spitfire I
	No. 242	Hurricane I
Wittering	No. 229	Hurricane I
	No. 266	Spitfire I
Colly Weston	No. 23	Blenheim IF
Duxford	No. 19	Spitfire I
No. 13 Group		
Acklington	No. 72	Spitfire I
	No. 79	Hurricane I
Usworth	No. 607	Hurricane I
Drem	No. 605	Hurricane I
Turnhouse	No. 232	Hurricane I
	No. 253	Hurricane I
Prestwick	No. 141	Defiant I
Catterick	No. 219	Blenheim IF
Aldergrove	No. 245	Hurricane I
Wick	No. 3	Hurricane I
Castletown	No. 504	Hurricane I
Sumburgh	No. 232	Hurricane I
Dyce	No. 603	Spitfire I
Montrose	No. 603	Spitfire I

ORDER OF BATTLE FIGHTER COMMAND, JUNE 3, 1943

No. 9 Group		
Woodvale	No. 198	Typhoon Ib
Valley	No. 406	Beaufighter VIF
Honiley	No. 96	Beaufighter VIF
No. 10 Group		
Fairwood Common	No. 307	Mosquito II
Colerne	No. 151	Mosquito II
	No. 183	Typhoon Ib
Predannack	No. 264	Mosquito II
St. Mary's	No. 1449 Flt.	Hurricane IIb
Perranporth	Nos. 132, 412, 610	Spitfire Vb
Harrowbeer	No. 193	Typhoon Ib
	*No. 414	Mustang I

Exeter	No. 125	Beaufighter VIf		No. 118	Spitfire Vb
	No. 266	Typhoon Ib	Ludham	No. 195	Typhoon Ib
	No. 310	Spitfire Vb	Matlaske	No. 56	Typhoon Ib
Church Stanton	Nos. 312 and 313	Spitfire Vb	Wittering	No. 141	Beaufighter If
			Digby	Nos. 19 and 402	Spitfire Vb
Middle Wallop	No. 164	Hurricane IV	Wellingore	No. 416	Spitfire Vb
	No. 456	Mosquito II	Coleby Grange	No. 410	Mosquito II
	*No. 16	Mustang I	Hutton Cranswick	No. 315	Spitfire Vb
Ibsley	Nos. 129 and 504	Spitfire Vb	Church Fenton	No. 25	Mosquito II
	No. 616	Spitfire VI			
Warmwell	No. 257	Typhoon Ib		No. 308	Spitfire Vb
	No. 263	Whirlwind I	York	*No. 231	Tomahawk II
Andover	*No. 169	Mustang I		*No. 613	Mustang I
Old Sarum	*No. 658	Auster III	Sawbridgeworth	*No. 2	Mustang I
No. 11 Group					
Tangmere	Nos. 197 and 486	Typhoon Ib	Bottisham	*No. 4	Mustang I
Merston	No. 485	Spitfire Vb	Snailwell	*Nos. 170 and 309	Mustang I
Westhampnett	No 167	Spitfire Vb	Firbeck	*No. 659	Auster III
Ford	No. 256	Mosquito XII	Stapleford	*No. 656	Auster III
	No. 418	Boston III	No. 13 Group		
	Fighter Interception Unit	Beaufighter	Catterick	No. 306	Spitfire Vb
Odiham	*Nos. 168 and 268	Mustang I	Scorton	No. 604	Beaufighter VIf
Kenley	Nos. 403 and 421	Spitfire IX	Acklington	No. 350	Spitfire Vb
Redhill	Nos. 401 and 411	Spitfire Vb		No. 409	Beaufighter VIf
Dunsfold	*Nos. 400 and 430	Mustang I	Drem	No. 340	Spitfire Vb
Biggin Hill	Nos. 341 and 611	Spitfire IX	Ayr	No. 64	Spitfire Vb
				No. 488	Beaufighter VIf
Friston	No. 41	Spitfire XII	Macmerry	*No. 63	Mustang I
Lympne	No. 1	Typhoon Ib	Perth	*No. 652	Auster III
Hawkinge	No. 91	Spitfire XII	No. 14 Group		
Gravesend	No. 174	Typhoon Ib	Skeabrae	Nos. 66 and 234	Spitfire Vb
West Malling	No. 3	Typhoon Ib	Castletown	No. 131	Spitfire Vb
	No. 85	Mosquito XII	Peterhead	No. 165	Spitfire Vb
Detling	*No. 318	Hurricane I			
	*No. 655	Auster III			
	*No. 1 C.A.C.U.	Spitfire IIb			
Hornchurch	Nos. 222 and 453	Spitfire IX			
Manston	No. 137	Whirlwind I			
	No. 609	Typhoon Ib			
Bradwell Bay	No. 29	Beaufighter If			
	No. 247	Typhoon Ib			
North Weald	No. 124	Spitfire VI			
	Nos. 331 and 332	Spitfire IX			
Hunsdon	No. 157	Mosquito II			
	No. 515	Defiant II			
Northolt	Nos. 303 and 316	Spitfire IX			
Heston	Nos. 302 and 317	Spitfire Vb			
Castle Camps	No. 605	Mosquito II			
Martlesham Heath	No. 501	Spitfire Vb			
Penshurst	*No. 653	Auster III			
R.A.F., Northern Ireland					
Ballyhalbert	No. 130	Spitfire Vb			
No. 12 Group					
Coltishall	No. 68	Beaufighter VIf			

*Tac/R and A.O.P. Squadrons temporarily allocated to Fighter Command prior to the forming of 2nd T.A.F.

THE MERLIN

The Rolls-Royce Merlin aero engine may be the most important aircraft powerplant of World War II. It is certainly among the most significant aircraft engines of all time. Its contribution to Allied victory in WWII was exemplified by its fighter applications in the Mustang, Spitfire and Hurricane.

In 1915 Sir Henry Royce developed and demonstrated a new 12-cylinder in-line Vee powerplant of 225 horsepower. This engine became the basis for that powering the Supermarine S6B Schneider Cup racing seaplane which set a winning world speed record for Britain in September 1931 of 407 mph. While not intended for

gang plank inside a laundry bag.

I kept her hidden under my bunk until we left port in case she was discovered and possibly put ashore. Safely at sea, I brought her up on deck and happily discovered there were three other dogs on board. One belonged to the ship's crew and the other two were "stowaways." Lassie spent most of her time on a big hatch cover just aft of the galley. Consequently, the dogs ate real well on steak scraps from the galley. When we docked in New York, I repeated the sleeping pill routine and smuggled her off the ship to avoid any possible hassle over customs or quarantine.

After Lassie's successful immigration to the U.S. I was released from the Air Force, got married, and started working as a flight instructor at the Nevada, Missouri, Municipal Airport. Lassie went with me every day to the airport and I assumed she would lie around the office waiting for me while I was flying. I soon found this not to be true. I had just taken off with a student and happened to look back behind me and there was Lassie pounding

down the runway as hard as she could go in pursuit of the departing Cub. When I made a left turn, she made a left turn and was running parallel with

253

the airplane. We circled around for a quick landing and picked up the panting dog and put her in the Cubs open baggage compartment. From then on she always rode in the plane with me while instructing students and seemed to enjoy the stalls, spins, occasional loops, and hundreds of landings. She "logged" at least two hundred flying hours there in addition to her military flying time. At this same time I was also in an Air Force Reserve unit at Kansas City flying AT-6s, C-45s and C-47s. She rode in all those planes several times, once making a flight to Peoria, Ill, and back on the lap of the AT-6 rear seat passenger. Lassie accompanied me and my wife when I was recalled to active duty again in 1951. When we were stationed at George AFB at Victorville, California, in 1953, Lassie's years began to catch up to her and she was in failing health. She got worse and it became necessary to have her put to sleep. Her final flight was aboard a Flying Tiger Air Freight DC-4, her body sealed in a metal box. My parents drove to the Kansas City Airport to return her to Lamar to be buried near the other Scottie I had left in 1943.

—Walter J. Konantz, Pilot, 55th Fighter Group

military use, this engine design was quickly developed by Rolls-Royce to meet a high-performance military requirement and was designated PV (private venture) 12. It was specified to deliver 1,000 horsepower and provide up to 100 hours of maintenance-free operation. In 1933 the new engine was named "Merlin" after the Arthurian magician of legendary powers. It underwent months of trials and experienced major mishaps and failures including cracked cylinders, broken rods and failed bearings. In July 1934 though, the Merlin was successfully tested in a 100-hour run made at a rating of 750 hp. The directors of Hawker Aircraft Ltd, Kingston-upon-Thames, then selected the engine to power their Hawker Hart and Hawker Fury aircraft.

Every Hurricane and Spitfire flying in the Battle of Britain during the summer and autumn of 1940 was fitted with a Merlin. Now designated Merlin III, it was rated at 1,030 hp at 6,250 feet. The aircraft it powered were more than effective against the Messerschmitt ME 109E adversary.

Soon the demands of high-altitude aerial combat stimulated the development of later Merlin variants incorporating a two-stage, two-speed supercharger and an injection-type carburetor. The supercharger literally breathed new life into the motor at altitudes above 19,000 feet where it cut in automatically. It could, if necessary, be manually overridden, however.

In combat the Merlin, like all liquid-cooled in-line engines, was more susceptible to damage by enemy fire than was its radial counterpart, but this drawback was easily outweighed by its many advantages over the other aero engines of the day.

In six years of wartime, the Rolls-Royce Merlin evolved through 88 separate Marks and was fitted in nearly 70,000 Allied aircraft. In that period a total of 150,000 Merlin aero engines were produced by Rolls' factories in Derby, Crewe and Glasgow, and by the Ford Motor Company in Britain, as well as the Packard Motor Company in Michigan. This total does not include the Packard-built Merlins produced to power USAAF aircraft.

The first Merlin was capable of just over 800 horsepower. Wartime refinement wrought an ultimate variant of more than 2,500 hp. In the 1990s the Merlin endures. Its toughness and adaptability is impressively demonstrated in competition at the Reno Air Races each September when contemporary versions of the engine generate nearly 4,000 hp.

MERLIN-ENGINED MILITARY AIRCRAFT

SINGLE-STAGE, SINGLE-SPEED SUPERCHARGED
MERLIN I: BATTLE
MERLIN II: SPITFIRE I, HURRICANE, BATTLE
MERLIN XII/30: SPITFIRE II, BARRACUDA
MERLIN 45/46: SPITFIRE V

SINGLE-STAGE, TWO-SPEED
MERLIN X: WHITLEY, WLLINGTON, HALIFAX
MERLIN XX: HURRICANE, LANCASTER, BEAU-FIGHTER, MOSQUITO, HALIFAX, DEFIANT, LANCASTRIAN

TWO-STAGE, TWO-SPEED INTERCOOLED
MERLIN 61/64: SPITFIRE IX
MERLIN 66/70/76/85: SPITFIRE IX, MOSQUITO, LINCOLN
MERLIN 100: MOSQUITO
MERLIN 130: HORNET
MERLIN 140: STURGEON
PACKARD MERLIN: MUSTANG

ADDITIONAL MERLIN-POWERED TYPES
HORSLEY (TESTBED), YORK, TUDOR, HENLEY, CANADAIR DC4M, P40, HOTSPUR, WINDSOR, WELKIN, AMIOT 356, HA112, CASA 2111

In this glimpse of the fighter pilot experience in World War II England, we offer only a representative selection of the people, places and events that made up that experience. It was not our intention to provide a comprehensive coverage of personnel, squadrons, groups, stations or commanders. We hope that *Little Friends* conveys a sense of what it was like to be a combat fighter pilot in that time and place.

INDEX

Air Fighting Development Unit, 109
Air Transport Auxiliary, 154, 155, 157, 158, 159, 161, 163, 164
Albert, Eddie, 100
American Eagle Club, 191
American Melody Club, 191
Anderson, Clarence, 201
Anderson, Donald, 235
Anderson, M.W., 210
Arnold, Henry H., 96, 199, 208, 220
Audley End, 187
Ayre, John Butler, 104, 105

Bader, Douglas, 86, 87, 90, 134, 136, 137, 138, 196
Baker, Clive, 235
Barclay, George, 65, 72
Barnato, Barney, 154
Barnato, Woolfe, 154
Barnato-Walker, Diana, 154, 155, 156, 157, 158, 160, 161, 163, 164
Barnes, John, 234
Barrow, Norman, 234
Barrymore, Diana, 100
Barthropp, Patrick, 6, 234
Beamish, Victor, 134
Beaumont, Walter, 71, 72
Beaverbrook, Lord, 154
Beazley, Hugh, 234
Beckham, Walter, 224
Berck-sur-Mer, 129, 133
Berlin, 21, 27
Berryman, Nick, 50, 52, 54, 56
Biggin Hill, 10, 100, 152, 195
Biggs, Len, 159, 161
Bird-Wilson, Harold, 235
"Big Week," 220, 222, 223
Blakeslee, Donald, 96, 196, 200, 202
Blaymires, Peggie, 148, 150, 153
Bodney, 196, 202
Bognor Regis, 164
Bolt Head, 103, 104
Bottisham, 119, 122, 123, 125, 126, 127, 236
Bottisham Hall, 122
Bovingdon, 138
Bowman, Len, 235
Boyd, Adrian, 85
Brandon, 188, 191
Brasted, 152, 195
Brettell, Gordon, 103
British Refresher Training Course, 94
Brooklands Flying Club, 154

Brown, Harley, 148, 150
Bruce, Nigel, 100
Brussels, 163
Budzik, Kazimierz, 166, 167, 168, 169, 170, 171, 173
Bunte, Allen, 196
Buono, Vic, 96, 97
Burns, Owen, 234

Calais, 134, 205, 206
Cambridge, 151, 188, 191, 236
Camm, Sydney, memorial, 58
Canbury Park, 58
Carpenter's Arms, The, 120
Carver, Kenneth, 234
Casablanca, 166
Casson, Buck, 136, 137, 138
Chamberlain, George, 235
Chapin, Emily, 157, 158
Chequers, The, 18, 19, 195
Chesil Beach, 74
Chesters, Peter, 184
Christian, Thomas, 123, 126
Church Fenton, 139
Churchill, Walter, 96
Churchill, Winston, 96, 154, 225
Circus, 106, 129, 133, 134
Civil Pilot Training Program, 94
Clayton Knight Committee, 94, 96
Cochran, Jacqueline, 157, 158
Coltishall, 96
Coningham, AVM, 161, 163
Coningsby, 49, 50
Cook, Bob, 235
Coombe House, 190, 191, 192, 193
Coquelles, 174
Corbin, William, 235
Cosby, Ivor, 234
Crosby, Bing, 189
Crown, The, 195
Croydon, 80
Culmer, James, 235
Cunningham, James, 234

Dahne, Manfred, 180
David, William, 235
Day, Paul, 49
Daymond, Gus, 100
Debden, 13, 18, 20, 32, 99, 100, 104, 105, 106, 109, 151, 152, 153, 206, 216, 217, 225
Deere, Alan, 47
Dieppe, 10, 11, 138
Digby, 18
Ditzel, John, 235
Doolittle, Jimmy, 208
Dover, 134, 164
Dowding, Derek, 234
Dowling, Forrest, 101

Drobinski, Boleslaw, 234
Duke, Neville, 130, 134
Duncan, Glenn, 213
Dungeness, 129, 133, 163, 205
Dunkirk, 16, 19, 96, 174
Dunlop, Maureen, 157
Düsseldorf, 96
Duxford, 35, 93, 189
Dye, James, 7

Eagle Squadron, 10, 17, 91, 94, 96, 99, 100, 102, 104, 205
Eagle Squadron, 100
Eaker, Ira, 119
Earhart, Amelia, 155
East Grinstead hospital, 109
Eastleigh, 156
East Wretham, 93, 186
8th USAAF, 10, 35, 96, 100, 104, 105, 119, 138, 192, 220, 222, 225, 236
Ellacombe, John, 234
Emmerich, 216
Erikson, Leif, 100

55th Fighter Group, 21, 33, 209
55th Fighter Squadron, 240
56th Fighter Group, 35, 139, 202, 216
56 Operational Training Unit, 96
58 Operational Training Unit, 173
Fighter Collection, The, 35, 91
Filton, 80
Finucane, Brendan, 134
Fiske, Billy, 96
501 Squadron, 206
Fleming, Lou Christian Wilson, 123, 126
Ford, 164
4th Fighter Group, 17, 20, 35, 99, 104, 105, 106, 148, 216, 217, 224
14th Fighter Group, 139
41 Squadron, 202
43 Squadron, 90, 91
48th Fighter Squadron, 139
401 Squadron, 103
412 Squadron, 103
434th Fighter Squadron, 210
487th Fighter Squadron, 210
Forrest, Dave, 123
Fowler flap, 59
Fowlmere, 14, 18, 19, 195
Foxley-Norris, Sir Christopher, 93, 232, 235
Frankfurt, 216

Gabreski, Francis, 202, 224
Galland, Adolf, 45, 90, 136, 137
Garden House Hotel, The, 151

Garside, Geoffrey, 234
Gash, Freddie, 234
Geibelstadt, 209, 211
Gentile, Don, 93, 96, 196, 205, 224
Gilpin-Barnes, Derek, 196, 202
Godfrey, John, 32, 224, 231
Golden Lion, The, 194
Good Intent, The, 195
Goodson, James, 148, 198, 201, 224
Gore, Margot, 157, 164
Göring, Hermann, 136, 223, 225
Goxhill, 15, 22, 31, 106, 148, 238, 242
Grable, Betty, 140
Graham, Charlie, 241
Grangemouth, 173
Gravesend, 206
Gray, James A., 94, 95, 96, 100
Great Sampford, 100, 103
Green George, 106, 107, 109, 111
Gregory, William, 234
Grey, Stephen, 35, 39, 54, 55, 87, 91
Greyhound, The, 120
Grice, Douglas, 235

Halesworth, 193, 204
Hall, Roger, 65, 67, 71, 199, 235
Hall, Jon, 100
Hamble, 155, 156, 162, 163, 164
Hamilton, J.S., 173
Hancock, Pat, 235
Harker, Ronnie, 43
Harvey, Leslie, 234
Havercroft, Ralph, 234
Hawkinge, 75
Hazebrouck, 134
Heap, Edith, 150, 151, 153
Heath, Jack, 119, 120, 121, 124, 125, 126, 127
Heighington, George, 11, 16
Hendon, 36
Herrick, M.J., 202
Hitler, Adolf, 90
Hiveley, Howard, 92, 96, 99
Hofer, Ralph, 88
Hofton, Robert, 14
Holder, Gerald, 234
Hole in the Wall, The, 120
Holmberg, Paul, 198
Hornchurch, 195
Horse and Jockey, The, 74
Hopkins, Wallace, 89
Howard, James, 227
Hull, 148
Hunter, "Monk," 100, 138
Hurricane, 35

Ilfrey, Jack, 130, 131, 219, 224
Ingle-Finch, Michael, 234

JG 26, 136
JG 52, 174
Johnson, Amy, 155, 158
Johnson, Bob, 202
Johnson, Johnny, 225
Jorgensen, Hans Jorgen, 173
Junkin, Samuel, 10

Kain, E. J., 201, 202
Kane, Terence, 234
Kellett, Ronald, 235
Kennard, Hugh, 235
Kenley, 10, 80
Kepner, William, 220, 226, 227
Kingcome, Brian, 234
Kings Cliffe, 56, 148, 214, 215, 219, 236, 239
King's Cross, 187
King's Head, The, 120
Kirton-in-Lindsey, 94, 98
Kleczkowski, Stefan, 235
Klibbe, Frank, 203
Knettishall, 186
Koblenz, 199
Konantz, Harold, 33
Konantz, Walter, 21, 33, 209
Kruzel, Joseph, 126
Kuhle, Helmet, 174
Kyle, Jimmy, 36, 41, 43

Lakenheath, 191
Lang, Dora, 158
Lauder, John, 234
Leigh-Mallory, Trafford, 96, 99
Leighton-Porter, Arthur, 144
Leighton-Porter, Chrystabel, 140, 142, 143, 144
Leiston, 17, 77, 83, 146, 147, 189, 226
Lightning, P-38, 35
Lindbergh, Charles, 208
Litlington, 124
Little Walden, 26, 236, 238
Little Wilbraham, 119
Loder, John, 100
London, 33, 94, 100, 138, 163, 173, 186, 188, 191, 236
Lowe, Evelyn "Tiggy," 152
Lusty, Kenneth, 235
Lympne, 114
Lynn, Vera, 140

Mace, Harvey, 198
MacKinnon, Adam, 235
MacLachlan, James, 109, 112, 113, 114, 115, 116, 117
Madingley, 231, 236
Mae West, 23, 85, 109

Maguire, Sir Harry, 235
Mahurin, Walker M., 139, 198, 202
Mamedoff, Andy, 96
Manton, "Minnie," 129
Manston, 16, 182
Marchand, Roy, 85, 232, 233
Marsden, Eric, 47, 80, 81, 84, 85
Martel, Ludwik, 234
Martlesham Heath, 18, 93, 96, 130, 151, 222, 242
Mauriello, Sam, 97
Matching Green, 173
Matthews, Peter, 234
McAdam, John, 202
McColpin, Carroll, 17, 94, 95, 99, 100, 102, 103, 199
McEvoy, Theodore, 133
McGerty, Thomas, 101
McGugan, Bob, 234
McKennon, Pierce, 106, 107, 108, 109, 110, 111
McIntosh, Peter, 199
Merston, 130
Metfield, 212
Middleditch, Tom, 121
Mierzwa, Boguslaw, 129
Millard, Jocelyn, 234
Millikan, Willard, 217
Mills, Hank, 213
Mines Field, 45
Mitchell, Reginald Joseph, 45, 50
Mölders, Werner, 93, 129
Monks, Noel, 201
Morlaix, 100, 102, 103, 104
Mount, Christopher, 235
Mount Farm, 221
Murray, Alan, 235
Mustang, P-51, 35
Museum of Flying, Santa Monica, 62

N.A.A.F.I., 150
National Fire Service, 148
Nelson, Jimmy, 100
Nesbitt-Dufort, John, 45
Nicholson, Mary, 158
9th USAAF, 10, 35, 219, 220, 236
92 Squadron, 134, 195
95th Bomb Group (H), 139
Nomis, Leo, 100, 198, 205
Northolt, 133, 163, 167
Norwegian Airmen's Memorial, 170
Number 15 Ferry Pool, 155, 157, 158, 161
Nuthampstead, 8
Nuthouse, The, 191

O'Bannon, T.B., 221

O'Brien, William, 208
Olds, Robin, 43
Olmsted, Merle, 77, 78, 85
100th Bomb Group (H), 139
111 Squadron, 11
121 Squadron, 94, 99, 100
133 Squadron, 17, 94, 99, 100, 103
145 Squadron, 80, 84, 85
151 Squadron, 90
152 Squadron, 65, 71, 199
197 Squadron, 36
O'Neill, John, 133
Orr, Verne, 201

Page, Geoffrey, 52, 109, 115, 235
Pankratz, Wilhelm, 85
Parker, Pat, 158
Parrott, Peter, 234
Pattison, John, 200
Pegwell Bay, 182
Penshurst, 184
Peterson, Chesley, 100
Peterson, Richard, 96
Pett, Norman, 140, 144
Plenderleith, Robert, 234
Pocock, Maurice, 235
Poole, Eric, 234
Preddy, George, 196, 199, 224
Prenzlau, 106
Preston, Kath, 146, 147, 152, 153
Proctor, F/Sgt., 194

Quelch, Basil, 235

RAF Air-Sea Rescue Squadron, 73
RAF Bomber Command, 129
RAF Fighter Command, 94, 96, 100, 105, 109, 129, 134, 138, 139, 195, 225
RAF Museum, 36
Rainbow Corner, 191
Raydon, 2, 186, 236, 237, 239, 240, 241, 243, 244
Red Cross Voluntary Aid Detachment, 154
Red Lion, The, 151
Rémy, 223
Reynolds, Quentin, 100
Richards, Robert, 228, 229, 230, 231
Rickenbacker, Eddie, 202
Righetti, Elwyn, 224
Riseley, Arthur, 234
Robinson, Denis, 68, 69, 71, 75
Robinson, "Robbie," 206
Rodeo, 106
Romsey, 191
Roosevelt, Eleanor, 152

Roscoe, Arthur, 94, 95, 97, 100, 101
Rose-Price, Tommy, 206, 207
Rosier, Frederick, 235
Russell, Hack, 96
Rüttger, Karl, 176, 177, 178

Sadlowska, Slawa, 171
Saffron Walden, 151, 216
St. Omer, 137, 163
St. Trond, 211
Salmon, Honor, 158
Samuelsen, Emil, 170, 171, 173
Savage, Cecil, 119, 124, 125
Schieverhofer, Lothar, 181, 182, 184
Schilling, Dave, 202
Sealand, 161
2nd Tactical Air Force (RAF), 41, 161, 168
17 Squadron, 151
71 Squadron, 11, 94, 96, 99, 100, 104, 205
73 Squadron, 85
74 Squadron, 184
78th Fighter Group, 93
79th Fighter Squadron, 219
Seyfer, Eudora, 240
Seyfer, George, 240
Shaftesbury, 191
Ship, The, 195
Shipman, Mark, 88
Sheen, Desmond, 235
Sholto Douglas, 96, 104
601 Squadron, 129, 133
607 Squadron, 99
616 Squadron, 136
Sizer, Wilfred, 234
Sobanski, Winslow, 206
Solak, Jeorge, 168
Southampton Water, 68, 155
Spaatz, Carl, 104
Spitfire, 35
Sprague, Bob, 96, 101
Stack, Robert, 100
Stanford-Tuck, Robert, 93, 184, 196
Steeple Morden, 118, 119, 124, 125, 232, 236, 238, 239
Steinhilper, Ulrich, 174, 178, 180, 183, 184
Stevens, Richard, 90
Stillwell, Ronald, 235
Strobell, Robert, 212, 213
Stoney Cross, 191
Straight, Whitney, 133
Sutton Bridge, 96
Swaffam Bulbeck, 119
Swan, The, 120
Sweeny, Charles, 94, 96
Szczesny, Henryk, 234

Tangmere, 18, 68, 80, 85, 136, 163, 164, 195, 239
Tangmere Military Aviation Museum, 79, 90, 91
Thetford, 186, 191
Thomson, James, 234
31st Fighter Group, 10, 19
303 Squadron, 129, 133
307th Fighter Squadron, 10
308th Fighter Squadron, 10, 11
308 Squadron, 167, 168
309th Fighter Squadron, 10
328th Fighter Squadron, 196
332 Squadron, 173
335th Fighter Squadron, 106
338th Fighter Squadron, 21, 209, 224
350 Squadron, 11, 16
351st Bomb Group (H), 209
351st Fighter Squadron, 212
352nd Fighter Group, 196, 224
353rd Fighter Group, 186, 212, 241
354th Fighter Group, 220
355th Fighter Group, 124, 232, 236
356th Fighter Group, 93
357th Fighter Group, 77
359th Fighter Group, 93, 186
361st Fighter Group, 119, 126, 201, 236
362nd Fighter Squadron, 77
364th Fighter Group, 223
364th Fighter Squadron, 189
367th Fighter Squadron, 211
376th Fighter Squadron, 211
390th Bomb Group (H), 139
Thunderbolt, 35
Tobin, Eugene, 96, 97
Todd, Dennis, 194
Toombs, John, 235
Townsend, Peter, 196
12 Group, 96, 99
20th Fighter Group, 56, 60, 148, 219, 236, 239
21 Squadron, 129
242 Squadron, 90
263 Squadron, 194
Typhoon, 35

Unicorn, The, 195
Unwin, George, 207
U.S.A.F. Museum, 56
Usmar, Frank, 235
Uxbridge, 242

V-1 Buzz Bomb, 33, 188, 223
V-2 rocket, 188
Vanden Huevel, George, 207
Vargas, Alberto, 209
Virtuti Militari, 171

Voss, Sigi, 176, 177, 178

Waddington, 74
Walker, Derek, 161, 163, 164
Walker, William, 235
Wareham, 75
Warmwell, 65, 67, 71, 72, 194, 199
Washington Club, The, 191, 194
Waskiewicz, Jan, 167, 168
Westhampnett, 10, 85
Whipps, George, 205
Willow Run, 191
Windmill Girls, The, 148, 149
Wissler, Denis, 151
Wittering, 56, 109
Wolf, Kurt, 176, 177, 178, 179, 184
Women's Air Service Pilots (WASPs), 158, 164, 165
Women's Auxiliary Air Force, 150
Woodbridge, 213
Wootton, Frank, 70, 218
Wormingford, 21, 202
Wright, David, 192

Yeadon, 151

Zemke, Hubert, 78, 139, 202, 204
Zima, Rudolph, 168